POETICS AND PRAXIS
'AFTER' OBJECTIVISM

CONTEMPORARY

NORTH AMERICAN

POETRY SERIES

editors Alan Golding,

Lynn Keller, and

Adalaide Morris

POETICS AND PRAXIS
'AFTER' OBJECTIVISM

edited by W. SCOTT HOWARD

and BROC ROSSELL

UNIVERSITY OF IOWA PRESS, IOWA CITY

University of Iowa Press, Iowa City 52242
Copyright © 2018 by the University of Iowa Press
www.uipress.uiowa.edu
Printed in the United States of America

Design by Richard Hendel

The University of Iowa Press is a member of Green Press Initiative
and is committed to preserving natural resources.

Printed on acid-free paper

Library of Congress Cataloging-in-Publication Data
Names: Howard, W. Scott, editor. | Rossell, Broc, editor.
Title: Poetics and praxis 'after' objectivism / edited by W. Scott Howard and Broc Rossell.
Description: Iowa City : University of Iowa Press, 2018. | Series: Contemporary
North American poetry series | Includes bibliographical references and index. |
Identifiers: LCCN 2018005479 (print) | LCCN 2018018617 (ebook) |
ISBN 978-1-60938-593-4 | ISBN 978-1-60938-592-7 (pbk. : alk. paper)
Subjects: LCSH: American poetry—20th century—History and criticism—Theory, etc. |
American poetry—21st century—History and criticism—Theory, etc. | Object (Aesthetics)
in literature. | Poetics—History—20th century. | Poetics—History—21st century.
Classification: LCC PS323.5 (ebook) | LCC PS323.5 P64 2018 (print) |
DDC 821/.60911—dc23
LC record available at https://lccn.loc.gov/2018005479

CONTENTS

ACKNOWLEDGMENTS

Thanks to the editors of *Blackbox Manifold* 16 (2016)
for permission to reprint Alan Golding's essay, "Macro, Micro,
Material: Rachel Blau DuPlessis's *Drafts* and the Post-Objectivist Serial
Poem." Thanks also to the following artists for permission to include
images of their work in Julie Carr's chapter: fig. 1 and fig. 2,
Linda Norton, untitled collages from the series "Dark White,"
2014; fig. 3, Maria Damon, "Poetry 1" (linen and cotton).

We wish to thank our editors at the University of Iowa Press,
Dee Morris, Lynn Keller, and Elizabeth Chretien, for their support
of this project. Their guidance has been central. We are also grateful
to our teachers, students, peers, families, and friends;
this book is for them.

INTRODUCTION

'AFTER' OBJECTIVISM:

SINCERITY, OBJECTIFICATION, CONTINGENCY

W. SCOTT HOWARD & BROC ROSSELL

A monster owl
out on the fence
flew away. What   For the beginning is assuredly
is it the sign   the end—since we know nothing, pure
of? The sign of   and simple, beyond
an owl.[1]   our own complexities[2]

The entire matter involves the process of active literary omission
and a discussion of method finding its way in the acceptance of
two criteria: sincerity and objectification.[3]

Among the many literary and poetic schools, movements, and epochs, Objectivism is perhaps the most inchoate and influential because of its indeterminate and intersectional ethos, in the midst of multiple new directions for contemporary poetics and praxis in the United States, Canada, and the United Kingdom from the 1930s onward. By 'poetics' we mean discourses of writing; by 'praxis,' forms of making, or, more fundamentally, action—two interconnected artistic principles central to literary production generally, and to the tradition at the heart of this book, which we underscore in our volume's title and elaborate in the pages that follow.

Whereas Romantic poets were concerned with ego and imagination, Symbolists with symbols, Imagists with images, Surrealists with the surreal, Projectivists with projected breath and voice, and postmodernists with varieties of repetition within inescapable structures, the Objectivist poets weren't exclusively concerned with objects per se. They were concerned with the *objective*, in all the senses of that word: with writing that occurs from disinvested *seeing and thinking with things as they exist*.[4]

The legacy of Objectivism central to this book begins with the February 1931 volume of *Poetry* magazine[5] edited by Louis Zukofsky, follows and resists channels of modernist and postmodernist poetics and praxis, and includes the works of twentieth- and twenty-first-century writers who engage distinctive practices that are direct expressions of key Objectivist methods and priorities that we and our authors investigate. Despite the eclectic, international, and robust gathering of artists, writers, and traditions assembled for Zukofsky's "Objectivists" volume, this complex legacy has often been mistakenly reduced (in the field of criticism) to the works of four American poets (Zukofsky, Charles Reznikoff, Carl Rakosi, George Oppen) plus one British poet (Basil Bunting) and just one (American) woman poet (Lorine Niedecker).

Our collection examines late twentieth- and early twenty-first-century poetics and praxis through the diversified legacy of Objectivism and the Objectivists from 1931 to the present. This Objectivist tradition is emphatically not associated with the mid-twentieth-century philosophical system also known as Objectivism popularized by Ayn Rand and Leonard Peikoff (c. 1943). Our volume concerns that part of second-generation literary modernism that opposed Romanticism, Symbolism, Imagism, and Surrealism as well as other contemporary high and low modernisms. In fact, one of the enduring characteristics of Objectivism is a resilient resistance to closure and containment vis-à-vis existing literary practices or schools. As a result, *Objectivism* makes straightforward definition difficult because it emerged and developed within a context of energetic and generative disagreements, rather than as a 'movement' per se. Ruth Jennison argues that the Objectivist poets inherited from first-generation modernists (Joyce, Woolf, Pound, H. D., Yeats, Moore, Eliot, etc.) experimental breaks "with prior systems of representation" and strove to link those disjunctions with "a futurally pointed content of revolutionary politics"—expropriating their predecessors' formal tools "to announce a rupture not with the past but into the future."[6] "'*No myths* might be the Objectivist motto,'" writes Mark Scroggins (after Hugh Kenner).[7]

So, how to make sense of this jumble of (dis)interests and values for this so-called poetics without a movement? If Objectivism may be defined generally as a poetics and praxis that prioritizes disinterested "seeing, of thinking with the things as they exist,"[8] to quote Zukofsky's classic line, that short answer doesn't give away what follows in this introduction. The Objectivists suggested we establish those priorities ourselves, that we not look to their statements as explanations, and that we even challenge the idea of a specific 'Objectivist' school to which they were aligned or which they countered. As a way of embodying the Marxist and communist politics they generally espoused, they shared ownership of and responsibility for literary production with their peers and rejected the notion of genealogical literary influence.

One of the interesting results of the rejection of literary sequentialism is that such disjunctive and oppositional practices became highly influential in their own right. This introductory essay thus examines Objectivism both as a discrete phenomenon in poetics and as a coalescence of methods that have, in many ways, always existed. Objectivism, we shall try and show, both exists and doesn't.

We write in the spirit of the epigraphs for this introduction, of the abiding concerns of Niedecker and William Carlos Williams for a poetics of particulars that spark and subvert interpretation, and of Zukofsky's praxis of sincerity, objectification, and (we argue) *contingency*. For this volume's investigation of poetics and praxis *'after'* Objectivism and the Objectivists, we begin with renewed skepticism, questioning foundational assertions in the field of scholarship, such as "theirs was an amorphous movement, for they had neither programme nor agenda";[9] and "there are objectivists but no Objectivism";[10] and "Objectivism would remain undelineated as a theory [because] its metaphysical and aesthetic commitments are in contradiction with each other."[11] We would ask again, what was Objectivism?[12] Was there ever a coherent collective of writers, or a common language to unravel?[13] Who were (and who were not) the foundational "Objectivists"?[14] Which of their particular methods and values have contributed most significantly to "contemporary transformations of Objectivism,"[15] and how do writers, readers, and teachers in today's Anglophone world relate to this conflicted, yet vital legacy?

One practical way of answering these questions is to acknowledge Objectivism as a transhistorical and transnational poetics that we'll refer to as lowercase objectivism—that is, as a modality of discrete avant-garde practices born in the milieu and political climate of the 1930s, identified and elaborated by kindred artists and writers across centuries and oceans. In his esteem for Charles Reznikoff's poems, Louis Zukofsky suggests as much: "Yet the objectification which is a poem, or a unit of structural prose, may exist in a very few lines. [. . .] The good poems of today are not far from the good poems of yesterday."[16] With this in mind, the chapters and conversations in this collection celebrate Objectivism in the open, capacious spirit of the February 1931 volume of *Poetry*, as an inclusively local, international, and interdisciplinary ethos and reclaim Objectivist poetics and praxis for contemporary writers who are concerned with radical integrations of lyric subjectivities, contingent disruption, historical materialism, and forms of activism within and beyond academia. We collectively argue for a reconfiguration of Objectivism in terms of *sincerity, objectification, and contingency*, which we address in more specific terms below.[17]

Poetics and Praxis 'After' Objectivism includes ten essays and a round-table coda, all written for this volume. This collection of new materials from emerging and established poets and scholars engages a network of communities in the United States, Canada, and the United Kingdom and examines late twentieth- and early twenty-first-century poetic praxis within and against the dynamic, disparate legacy of Objectivism and the Objectivists. What were they *after*, and—perhaps most important—what else has come and gone 'after' Objectivism? Our title invokes the complexity of these many meanings for "after"—against, behind, following, post-, resistant, and so forth—as the essays and conversations gathered here deliver critiques of aesthetics and politics; of race, class, and gender; and of the literary and cultural history of the movement's development and disjunctions from 1931 to the present.

The February 1931 "Objectivists" issue of *Poetry* (which is the most cited single volume in the journal's history) challenged the literary field in a spirit of international and interdisciplinary disruptive innovation[18] situated within and against a kaleidoscope of Symbolist, Surrealist, Imagist, and assorted modernist practices. This diversity and hybridity are defining characteristics of Objectivism, yet those core complexities resist synthesis. One month after the volume's publication, for instance, publisher Harriet Monroe excoriated Zukofsky's "barbed-wired entanglements."[19] His various assertions and eclectic methods there clarify and amplify the difficulty of summarizing Objectivism and Objectivist principles. Zukofsky contributed poetry—from *A*, the "Seventh Movement: 'There Are Different Techniques'" (which draws deeply from Bach's score for his sacred oratorio, *St. Matthew Passion*, c. 1727)—two essays, commentary in the *Symposium* paratexts, and a collaborative translation and discussion of André Salmon's poetry—all of which, taken together, form a collage of materials more than a focused argument.

As an example, Zukofsky's first essay, "Program: 'Objectivists' 1931," examined the work of several contemporaries — Pound, Williams, Marianne Moore, Eliot, e. e. cummings, Wallace Stevens, Robert McAlmon, and Reznikoff — who, along with *all* of the "contributors to this [issue of *Poetry*]" have "written in accordance with the principles heading this note."[20] By "this note" Zukofsky was referring to his essay's epigraph: "An Objective: (Optics) — The lens bringing the rays from an object to a focus. (Military use) — That which is aimed at. (Use extended to poetry) — Desire for what is objectively perfect, inextricably the direction of historic and contemporary particulars" (268).[21] Charles Bernstein elucidates: "The lens focuses the rays coming from an object, making the image ready for projection or microscopic examination. [. . .] Poetry is not the realization of such a utopia but, in contrast, what is *aimed at*: an aspiration grounded in the historical practice of the art of configuring words."[22] And Monique Vescia argues that the "visual and optical terms Zukofsky often uses to characterize Williams' work" informed his "decision to frame a new poetic theory in photographic terms" attuned to "an American culture preoccupied with new visual technologies and their ability to make a record of 'the real.'"[23]

One aspiration of Objectivism, then, was documentation. Zukofsky elaborated upon "Program: 'Objectivists' 1931" in a revised essay, "An Objective" (first published in 1967),[24] widely recognized as a key statement on Objectivist poetics, and from which we assemble these lines concerning the emergent notions of sincerity, objectification, and contingency:

> It is understood that historic and contemporary particulars may mean a thing or things as well as an event or a chain of events. [. . .] Writing occurs which is the detail, not mirage, of seeing, of thinking with the things as they exist, and of directing them along a line of melody. [. . .] Presented with sincerity, the mind even tends to supply [. . .] the totality not always found in sincerity and necessary only for perfect rest, complete appreciation. This rested totality may be called objectification — the apprehension satisfied completely as to the appearance of the art form as an object. That is: distinct from print [. . .] there exists, though it may not be harbored as solidity in the crook of an elbow, writing [. . .] which is an object or affects the mind as such. [. . .] A poem as object [. . .] experienced as an object. [. . .] The desire for what is objectively perfect, inextricably the direction of historic and contemporary particulars — A desire to place everything — everything aptly, perfectly, belonging within, one with, a context — [. . .] A poem. The context based on a world —. (*Prepositions*, 12–15)

To paraphrase, the desire embodied by sincerity—that is, a sincerity not to be understood as a personal or individual characteristic but something even more social than Lionel Trilling's highly influential definition of sincerity as "a moral life in the process of revising itself,"[25] sincere *relations*—as enacted within and fulfilled by a "rested totality," thereby producing a poem as the "context" of its making. Zukofsky's essay articulates a kind of desire in the poet, for and in the world, that is dependent on her relation *to* that world, an ever-shifting relationship that the central twentieth-century Marxist theorist Étienne Balibar characterizes as "an absolute precariousness or 'contingency' of the conditions of existence, just as ownership (of oneself, of objects) amounts to a generalized dispossession."[26]

The "absolute precariousness" Balibar asserts as the distinctive quality of contingency is central to our argument, both within context of the 1931 "Objectivists" volume of *Poetry* and '*after*.' This precarity extends spatially, across the physical and geographical world; socially, in the relations that condition all sites of literary production; and temporally, in the imperfections of recorded history and the uncertainty of future events. A sincerity that is relational and contextual rather than immanent and projected relinquishes ownership of the poem-as-object, via what Zukofsky first described in "Sincerity and Objectification" (1931) as "the process of active literary omission" (273), or, as we read it, the poet's intervention *against literariness*. As a result, our idea of sincerity has less to do with solitary, essentialized lyricism or the "*over*heard" poet[27] (to cite John Stuart Mill's infamous metaphor, which more easily invokes the image of a prison cell than a poet at work) than the faithful record of conditions in which parties gather. As Lyn Hejinian remarks, this "sense of contingency is intrinsic to [an] experience of the self as a relationship rather than an essence" to be contained and released.[28] To omit 'literary' qualities from (objective) textual production is to make room for the nonliterary, and even the antipoetical—what we will see Zukofsky refer to below as "entire aspects of thought" (273).

Zukofsky demonstrates a similar understanding of relational sincerity in the 1931 "Objectivists" volume. We know that Zukofsky's prose works should be read as intertextual assemblages and not as explanations per se, but we think an honest argument can be made for recovering these values of *contingency* for Objectivist poetics. Such precarity was key for Zukofsky, Parker Tyler, Charles Henri Ford, and René Taupin in their contributions to the Symposium section of the "Objectivists" volume of *Poetry*, as we shall demonstrate.

For instance, "An Objective" (1967) blends together Zukofsky's two essays from the February 1931 issue of *Poetry* and in doing so omits most of the content[29] from "Program: 'Objectivists' 1931" in favor of "the constant theme first expressed as 'Sincerity and Objectification.'"[30] Our ellipses in the block quote above (from "An Objective") enact a similar kind of relational and active literary omission in order to illustrate one possible alignment of principles: *Objectivism* concerns attention to material, sonic, and visual details within their contingent contexts; emphasizes literal signification more than figurative, mimesis more than metaphor; and presents concrete things not as vehicles for either abstract concepts or interpretations but as compositions resulting from structural relationships.

To simplify,[31] we offer Zukofsky's statement that the "entire matter involves the process of active literary omission and a discussion of method finding its way in the acceptance of two criteria: sincerity and objectification" (273). And we also observe, following Zukofsky's 1931 text, that "the process of active literary omission" in "Reznikoff's shorter poems" exemplifies the precarious contingency embodied in a poetics concerning "entire aspects of thought: economics, beliefs, literary analytics, etc" (273). And so to the abiding importance of sincerity and objectification, in the understanding of this subject, we would add the principle of contingency, which has not yet received the critical attention warranted by a key component of Objectivist praxis.[32]

This is tricky, uneven ground to cover. Because Zukofsky and some of his colleagues challenged even the provisional identity given to the Objectivists and Objectivism by the February 1931 volume of *Poetry*, we're also concerned with Oppen's hindsight corrections—"*will* / played out against the poem / relates, could relate to the / Objectivist Sincerity and Objectification! Stronger / I think more useful *now* than that objectivist formulation" (c. 1974)[33]—and with Rexroth's admonition (c. 1971) that "almost all the people that Zukofsky picked as Objectivists didn't agree with him, didn't write like him or like one another, and didn't want to be called Objectivists"[34]—as well as with Rakosi's early critique (c. 1932):

I know from my talks with Zukofsky at the time that Reznikoff was his model for an Objectivist, but if Reznikoff was an Objectivist, Zukofsky is not and never was one. [. . .] I see that [Zukofsky's] definition was tailor-made for *his work* and that his frame of reference was already the tour-de-force. I see too why it struck me as curious and wrong. He had omitted all reference to the poet's relation to the real world, except for his insistence on particulars, and that was at odds with his argument.[35]

Such ambivalence engendered Zukofsky's typical attitude when discussing Objectivism, as he said in conversations from 1968 and 1969 (thereafter variously published) when looking back to the fraught context that shaped the February 1931 issue of *Poetry*:

> When I was a kid I started the Objectivist movement in poetry. There were a few poets who felt sympathetic towards each other and Harriet Monroe at the time insisted, we'd better have a title for it, call it something. I said, I don't want to. She insisted; so, I said, alright, if I can define it in an essay, and I used two words, *sincerity* and *objectification*, and I was sorry immediately. But it's gone down into the history books; they forgot the founder, thank heaven, and kept the terms, and, of course, I said *objectivist*, and they said *objectivism* and that makes all the difference.[36]

All the difference between an "-ist" and an "-ism"? All the difference, that is, between an act or actor on the one hand and the characterization of that act on the other; between a quality and an identity, or praxis and ideology, between the poem-as-object and the literariness it resists.

Because of such generative, contentious diversity since the inception of the Objectivist legacy, the editors of the foundational study, *The Objectivist Nexus*, argue that the "resistance *to* nexus [has always been] part of the construction *of* nexus"[37] and that their sequentialist, genealogical methodology for the collection would attend to "difference and disparity, [. . .] [to] rupture as well as continuity, [. . .] dispersion as well as origin" consistent with "a relationship among writers based on their shared meditations, but not necessarily shared conclusions or even practices, about the particulars of their writing life and their historical position" (22). Rachel Blau DuPlessis and Peter Quartermain employ the 'nexus' heuristic to invoke "ligatures joining items serially, or a set of crossings that may proceed outward in a variety of directions from a nodule of importance" (7), and structure their volume around six poets—Bunting, Niedecker, Oppen, Rakosi, Reznikoff, and Zukofsky—"treating them as a nexus for poetic production and for critical and poetic reception" (2) within a robust field of modernist poetics that also informs the work (c. 1999) of "several contemporary investigative poets—Lyn Hejinian, Charles Bernstein, and Jean Day" among many others, including Nathaniel Mackey, Susan Howe, and Gary Snyder—who "follow quite different compositional practices" and yet participate in "a continuous and continuing construction" of an Objectivist canon (18).

Nexus remains to date the most comprehensive single volume of scholarship and criticism on this subject, and our work here celebrates that collection's resilience. Our argument concerning sincerity, objectification, and contingency answers Charles Altieri's call in that volume for precise definitions of such key concepts (32–33). It also elaborates on claims by DuPlessis and Quartermain that "Objectivist writing [is] aware of its own historical contingency and situatedness," and that "Objectivist poetics [is] a site of complexity, contestation, interrogation, and disagreement" (6). Whereas the second of those assertions receives attention throughout their volume's chapters, the first receives no further treatment beyond this single mention. Furthermore, no contributor to *Nexus* examines the significance of contingency as a key component to Zukofsky's protean discourse (1931–1967).[38]

While the methodology in *Nexus* works well for the editors' selection of six foundational poets vis-à-vis "the actual material, social, psychological, and aesthetic circumstances of literary production and transmission" (22), their historiographic "three-dimensional model of participation, production, and reception over time" (22) and their formulation for cultural poetics (20–22)[39] altogether emphasize a genealogical project concerned with a common origin of, meditation upon, and singular concern with "their writing life and their historical position" (22) that, in our reading, contradicts the methodological heterogeneity and contingent disruption set in motion by Zukofsky and his colleagues within the context of the February 1931 volume of *Poetry*.

We seek to complement the literary-historical narratives[40] that shaped the methodology of *Nexus* and have, in turn, decisively informed the field since 1999. We aim in three directions: to acknowledge and question narratives of genealogical development; to investigate the complex relationships of contemporary poets toward Objectivist poetics and praxis; and to ask to what extent values afforded by this movement remain relevant to poets working today—what future, or futures, such lines of flight might have in store.

We therefore want to emphasize the irreducible pluralities and paradoxes in such predications—of origins, meditations, concerns, positions, people—as a way of shifting the conversation from genealogical historicisms to discrete avant-garde practices. As Gerald Bruns usefully notes, Objectivists (like the Surrealists and Language poets) traded in practices rather than theories and shared the idea that "poetry is not simply another species of discourse, a particular way of using language that can be contrasted with other discursive genres (philosophy, for example)"; rather, poetry is "an exploration and experience of language in all of its formal, material, and semantic dimensions, including its historical conditions of existence within an array of [disruptively contingent] social and cultural contexts."[41]

We recognize the essential realities of history and materialism, but we propose a subtle (yet critical) shift slightly away from such narratives into the midst of things, to "the opposite of a history."[42] In fact, these core values of sincerity, objectification, and contingency invoke a wide range of historical and material practices, including observations of social disorder from Blake and Shelley to Amiri Baraka; attunements to the 'word as such' from Russian Formalism to concrete poetry, from Projective Verse to the L=A=N=G=U=A=G=E school; and from paratactic to prose-based and broadly assemblist modalities (e.g., collage, installation, remediation). These examples also provide potentially useful methods for contemporary poetries of witness, documentation, translation, pastiche, performance, and so on.

These core values also raise the question as to whether the rejection of the subject (if that is to be a corollary of 'objective' or 'objectivist' writing) is an assertion of privilege. The 'birth of the subject' *is* the historically lyric form. There is no such thing as the death of the author, if we author each other; "the death of the author is the murder of me,"[43] argues Ruth Ellen Kocher, and any de facto equivalence of all human subjective experience, even in the name of solidarity, at the very least minimizes forces of subjection and subjugation and, at worst, reifies them. These ethical questions are fundamental to notions of history, inheritance, and legacy—that is, the degree to which any particular poetic tradition, but especially one composed almost exclusively of a single demographic, can be said to inform another. This question lies at the core of the canonicity that is genealogical criticism's project.

In the ever-widening context of Objectivism's emergence, we remember Williams's reflection (c. 1930) that "the poem, like every other form of art, is an object, an object that in itself formally presents its case and its meaning by the very form it assumes."[44] Although he would locate the beginning of Objectivism "in [Zukofsky's] apartment on Columbia Heights, Brooklyn" (in his conversations there with Zukofsky, Reznikoff, and Oppen), Williams was equally emphatic to acknowledge Gertrude Stein "for her formal insistence on words in their literal, structural quality of being words, who had strongly influenced us" (264, 265). We also find relevance to Objectivist practices in Stein's "continuous present"; in Moore's "straight writing";[45] in Olson's declarations that "form is never more than an extension of content" and that "Objectism is the getting rid of the lyrical interference of the individual as ego";[46] and in Denise Levertov's counterstatement that "form is never more than a revelation of content."[47] Compared with these (among many other) contemporary perspectives, Zukofsky's insistence on "writing which is the detail, not mirage, of seeing, of thinking with the things as they exist, and of directing them along a line of melody" ("An Objective," 12) is but one instance of the constitutive dynamics between subject and object that are intrinsic to poetic praxis. Language is the only artistic medium that so fundamentally shapes its subjects, objects, and isms.

Some have even connected Objectivism to a multitude of kindred works, "from Sappho to Flaubert to Zen."[48] For example, Rachel Blau DuPlessis invokes an Objectivist ethos of disturbance and recalibration across a historically and geographically wide range of writers, including Robin Blaser, Coleridge, Robert Creeley, H. D., Beverly Dahlen, Dante, Tina Darragh, Robert Duncan, Nathaniel Mackey, Mallarmé, Alice Notley, Charles Olson, George and Mary Oppen, Pindar, Pope, Pound, Ron Silliman, Anne Waldman, Wordsworth, and Virgil (among numerous others, including Zukofsky).[49] Such capaciousness signals a mode of reading, making, and performing social change as central to the Objectivist legacy.

At the same time, however, such capaciousness quickly exhausts the capacity of Objectivism per se to refer to specific modes of practice and poetic forms, especially at the levels of close reading and cultural critique. Our work here concerns the relevance of the Objectivist ethos to poetic praxis in our time, and so we must grasp the most essential characteristics of this legacy that has so often been defined in terms of energetic oppositions against other literary movements, especially Symbolism and Imagism.

For example, Peter Quartermain holds that "Zukofsky was suspicious of symbolism because it is a language of disguise [that avoids] the thing, the object" (*Disjunctive Poetics*, 100). The contributors to *Nexus* situate the Objectivists "in contradistinction to both modernists (Pound, Williams, Eliot) and 'New American' poets (Olson, Creeley, Duncan)"[50] and consistently place Objectivism either "on the razor edge between the imagistic and the symbolic"[51] or "diametrically opposed" to Symbolism[52] because Objectivism drives away "the ghost of a symbolic gesture"[53] and "is clearest and most widely shared in its accounts of the evils it opposes."[54] Values antithetical to Objectivism (as articulated within *Nexus*) include the pursuit of the sublime and transcendence; recapitulations of nineteenth-century Romantic ideology; the prophetic status of poets and poems; and the ostensible triumph of will, reason, and liberal progress. Henry Weinfield[55] challenges these lines of argument as exemplified by Altieri's claim (in his first essay in *Nexus*) that Objectivist poets "seek an artifact presenting the modality of things seen or felt as immediate structure of relations," while Symbolist poets "typically strive to see beyond the seeing by rendering in their work a process of meditating upon what the immediate relations in perception reflect" (26). Weinfield's deconstructive critique (problematically) posits Objectivism as a form of late Romantic, constructivist Symbolism, contending that "one might say that it is rather the Objectivists who, far from disabusing us of our illusions, reinstate them—along with the pathetic fallacy" (204).

These and other distinctions between or among Symbolism, Imagism, Impressionism, Surrealism, Objectivism, and Nominalism were, in fact, addressed by Zukofsky, Tyler, Ford, and Taupin in the Symposium section of the 1931 "Objectivists" volume of *Poetry*. However, those conversational documents have so far escaped critical attention in the field concerning the subject of our argument here.[56] These Symposium paratexts—especially as they address a disruptive "system of correlated images having an inevitable dramatic pause [. . .] which is not subject to the continuous or historical premise"[57] and "a synthesis of real detail"[58]—ground our concerns here with sincerity, objectification, and contingency.

The Symposium is a collage of disagreements, interpretations, and translations,[59] beginning with one poem each from Parker Tyler ("Hymn") and Charles Henri Ford ("Left Instantly Designs") followed by *their* telling remarks that, we argue, influenced Zukofsky's evolving discourse on sincerity and objectification. Tyler and Ford invoke a poetics and praxis of contingent disruption that projects, and objectifies, "a system of correlated images" that contravenes "the hypothesis of continuous experience through time and space," thereby resisting sequentialist historicisms that would include, critically, heuristics of genealogy and of nexus. Tyler and Ford argue that the Objectivist poem

> is a gratuitous and arbitrary organism designed to contravene the hypothesis of continuous experience through time and space. It must

consciously eliminate the assumption of a continuous or historical type of experience by the projection of a system of correlated images having an inevitable dramatic pause [. . .] all that is desired is an experience which is not subject to the continuous or historical premise; the poem is an object. (287)

The notion that a poem can be an object capable of disrupting a subjective, continuous temporality is a significant contribution to Objectivist poetics overlooked by critics and scholars working in this field, including Burton Hatlen (as noted above).[60] This is perhaps due to Zukofsky's dislike for the poems by Tyler and Ford—"[these] young surrealists"[61]—compared with the "economy of presentation"[62] he so esteemed in Reznikoff's lines. Indeed, in the subsequent *Symposium* commentary revealing his wariness of Surrealism, Zukofsky (critically) frames his critique as "between two types of symbolism: the word as symbol for the object, and—*hallucination*. Objectivity and even merit may be claimed for the last."[63] The passage above from Tyler and Ford clearly provoked Zukofsky's consideration of a 'hallucinatory' type of documentation vis-à-vis Objectivism.

If these poets disagreed over the extent to which Symbolism, Imagism, Impressionism, or Surrealism might best inform the *direct treatment of real detail* (a notion that emerges in the Symposium), they at least agreed here upon a collaborative formulation. The Objectivist poem projects an ellipsis- or caesura-encoded system of correlated images, designed to contravene the hypothesis of continuous experience, via the "dramatic pause" that alerts one to the non-literary conditions of textual production. This intervention establishes the ontological status of the poem, its objecthood invoking the contingency grounded in a materialist reading of history. These gaps and pauses in experience are not so much reflective but an embodiment of the vast, lost catalogue of material conditions in which lives have been lived.

Zukofsky continued to reflect upon the relation of Symbolism and Imagism to Objectivism in his subsequent essay with René Taupin on André Salmon's poetry, the significance of which has also been overlooked in this field.[64] The *Symposium* concludes with three poems by Salmon—one of the early Cubists who belonged "to the generation which devolved from Symbolism"[65]—translated and discussed by Taupin and Zukofsky. Here the matter turns toward the problematic and persistent status of the image, which, they assert, may be productively reconfigured for Objectivist poetics and praxis through a "synthesis of real detail," characteristic of what they term "Nominalistic poetry":

Would the image no longer do? The real would: the poet was now obliged to find it in all its intensity, in its anxiety to be handled. The metaphor of Baudelaire, or even the metaphor of Mallarmé, was primarily qualitative; it expressed what consistently poor adjectives could not express. Nominalistic poetry is a synthesis of real detail, similar to the art of the primitives; and not of abstract or decomposed detail, like the impressionists. (290)

We emphasize the contributions of Tyler, Ford, and Taupin in order to place sincerity, objectification, and contingency in their original context, thereby highlighting the diversity of views and voices that shaped these priorities for Objectivism and Objectivist poetics and praxis. Tyler and Ford assert that Objectivist poems project a system of correlated images designed to contravene the hypothesis of continuous experience through time and space; thus the poem is created in one moment to pass through another, as an object of *radical contingency.* Taupin and Zukofsky consequently state their concern for a synthesis of "real detail"; hence Zukofsky's subsequent assertions that the entire matter involves active literary omission (or acting to omit the literary, as it were).

In his attention to these *Symposium* documents in two essays ("Program: 'Objectivists' 1931" and "Sincerity and Objectification") and their elaborations between 1931 and 1967, Zukofsky identifies "objectification [in] a poem, or a unit of structural prose, [that] may exist in a very few lines" because at "any time, objectification in writing is rare"—especially when the "good poems of today are not far from the good poems of yesterday."[66] In our reading of Zukofsky's pursuit of "historic and contemporary particulars" (12), we find less a consistent sequence or nexus (in the sense of a locus of events) than a rhizomatic, disruptive (i.e., less 'literary') documentation of contingent conditions that moves unpredictably, underground, and untapped.[67] It seems important to observe that Zukofsky's process of active literary omission, if in service to something termed 'Objectivism,' actually constitutes a radically subjective poetics that engages both aesthetics and historical materialism through international and interdisciplinary forms of social praxis. That process is highly individuated, with pauses to mark gaps in perception.

By drawing a distinction between two types of Symbolism ("the word as symbol for the object, and—hallucination"), Zukofsky doesn't move to replace literary symbols (with their capacity for cultural signification) with material objects (things made of ink and paper), but instead makes an argument for poetic expression in which a given, fixed symbolic value or meaning is untenable on the one hand and potentially useful as a unit of social meaning on the other: that is, the existence of the symbol itself and not what it represents is what matters. (A rose won't always represent love, but it once did.)

This acceptance of the symbolic evokes its *precarity*; it's merely and problematically reflective of material, contingent, and social conditions, rather than a continuous or historical premise of the subject. In other words, Zukofsky is less concerned with a poetics of personal experience (what Hejinian characterizes as lyrical closure)[68] than with a poetic praxis objectifying contingent social experiences that cannot be reduced to notions of historical continuity. As Tyler, Ford, Taupin, and Zukofsky argued, history and historicity are contingent upon an infinite number of finite, relational circumstances (or as Zukofsky put it in 1967, "A poem. The context based on a world"). Only sincere attention to real detail and particularity is (paradoxically) capable of constituting shared, lived experiences that might qualify as objective reality.

For this reason Zukofsky and his colleagues showed such poems to be objects embedded in a shared world. By recasting poetic sincerity as a *desire* (in the sense of the word as articulated by Gilles Deleuze and Félix Guattari)[69] to reflect social production rather than the affect of a bourgeois subject, the textual artifact or object is, if hallucinatory, at least in contrast to lyrically closed, expressivist poetry. And by reconfiguring poetic images as a function of contingent disruption (i.e., the conditions in which "inevitable dramatic pauses" occur) and contextualized social history rather than of symbolic convention, Zukofsky makes a clear distinction between Symbolist, Imagist, high-modernist poetics and nascent Objectivist values. Whereas Imagism amplifies cultural ideas associated with visual and literary symbols, Objectivism rejects such values in favor of ever-fluid social contexts required to evaluate the symbol. Consistent, static symbolic value (as an expression of culture, status, or ideology) is proportionally inverse to radical contingency.[70]

As late twentieth-century American poetry (Projectivism, Conceptualism, Language, Flarf, New Narrative, and so forth) shows us, the idea of what constitutes a poetic image has evolved from strictly visual symbols to also include speech acts—that is, from cultural emblems to epitomes of tone. A poetic image composed entirely of text (whether magazine excerpts, warehouse inventories, popular song lyrics) is capable of representing and documenting circumstances of shared experience—the poetics that Taupin and Zukofsky labeled "nominalist"—via a strategy of collage or pastiche. This development in contemporary praxis strengthens the poet's ability to explore the contingency that Engels locates in social relations, where "history must be studied afresh, [. . .] different societies must be 'examined individually,' [. . .] and the connections and gaps between the various structural facets are contingent and cannot be deduced in advance."[71]

That development also provides for the possibility of diverse lowercase objectivist writers preceding and proceeding from an uppercase Objectivist movement, in which shared aspirations produce as many kinds of poems as are possible in the conditions of their making. The rejection of images as qualitative symbols thus affirms their contingent disruptiveness and informs contemporary applications of Objectivist poetics to the praxis of documentation and witness that we see in the work of the many poets discussed in these chapters, such as M. NourbeSe Philip, John Seed, Rachel Blau DuPlessis, Robert Fitterman, Lisa Robertson, Heimrand Bäcker, and Beverly Dahlen among others—not forgetting the well-documented perpetuation of an Objectivist ethos by Language poets.[72] (And we trust readers will recognize the privilege of place given to Rae Armantrout's last word in our volume's roundtable.) Such articulations of solidarity, of course, naturally evoke the nexus of Objectivism articulated by DuPlessis and Quartermain, rhizomatically expanding across our not-so-new century.

In constructing this book we've imagined and encountered many challenges and potential *objections* to the project. We began our work in 2012,[73] when the 'turn to the object' was on many minds in the humanities, when object-oriented ontology and speculative realisms were coming under critique,[74] and when the close examination of subjectivity in poetic discourse was moving with greater acceleration toward renewed articulations of difference, diversity, and identity.[75] Today the function of objectivity in poetic praxis is once again a political issue; how is a poet to write 'objectively' in a socially fractured world, where oppression and subjugation make unwilling subjects of some if not all? As we write, American poetry (and, perhaps, even American literature) is making some small gestures toward recognizing the necessity of diverse, heterogeneous voices. A recent string of institutional literary awards to writers of color in an era of videotaped racial violence is most welcome. Among those many National Book Awards, Pulitzer Prizes, and so forth, perhaps the nomination of Claudia Rankine's *Citizen* as a finalist for the 2014 National Book Award for Poetry *and* the National

Book Award for Nonfiction warrants mention, since this institutional commendation may signal, not only growing attention from the literary elite to the consistent (and insistent) neglect toward marginalized voices in public letters and discourse, but a willingness to consider poetry as a genre or medium allied with nonfiction and therefore well suited to the work of documentation and witness, cultural intervention, and political agitation.

In this climate an anthology examining the legacy and continuing influence of a coterie of modernist poets (nearly all white heterosexual men) dedicated to a project of 'Objectivist' poetry may seem at first blush misguided, and we acknowledge that the relation of the so-called Objectivist movement to practicing poets of color and marginalized communities, even after this publication, remains underexplored. Aldon Nielsen's expansive work—concerning, among other lines of inquiry, the relationship of Rakosi's radical politics to the "too slowly shifting shades of racial metaphor"; Oppen's heartfelt alliance with the civil rights movement; and Zukofsky's complicated use of black dialect and racial epithets in his elegy for Patrice Lumumba and the victims of American racial violence—underscores the moral imperative these white poets felt toward communities of color.[76] Beyond Nielsen's recovery of the late Boston poet Stephen Jonas's investment in Objectivism,[77] and Nathaniel Mackey's citations of Zukofsky's notion that "we write one poem all our lives" and his famous dictum "lower limit speech / upper limit music" as inspiration,[78] the intermediary figure of Charles Olson is typically positioned as the most direct conduit of Objectivism per se for postwar poets of color like Amiri Baraka[79] (as he also often is, by the way, for post-1964 Canadians). If kindred Objectivist values of documentarian protest against legacies of racial, ethnic, and spiritual violence may be seen in the works of Robert Hayden, Lucille Clifton, Ramona Lofton, and Ed Roberson, for example, such contributions to a heterogeneous poetics and praxis 'after' Objectivism invite further study.[80]

In remembering Kocher's aforementioned rebuke, we find ourselves at a precipice, near the core of the lyric's "eccentric centrality"[81] to praxis—the function of *expression* in the making of poems. Leaving aside (if we can, for now) the thorny ontological issues raised by the "phantom" materiality of a poetic object, constructed as much by real social conditions as by ink and paper, and the more fundamental (and even thornier) question of whether a mind can be posited *behind* a text, we first ask: can a poet or maker actually escape sensible subjectivity and represent the "hallucination" of disruptively contingent historicity? Can a poet get *out of* or *away from* themselves when they write? And why would they? What grounds the subjectivity that guides our entry into poetical, critical, and political discourse? What do these articulations of sincerity, objectification, and contingency mean to poets today, writing in this era of late capital and globalized neoliberalism, where identity increasingly asserts itself as the primary political mobilizer of the age?

With these concerns at the fore, we return to Niedecker's deft challenge to Zukofsky's idealized notion of "rested totality" (that is, for him, an objectified poem) from his essay "Sincerity and Objectification" that she, the "imagist / turned philosopher" (23), studied in celebration and critique. After reading the February 1931 volume of *Poetry*, Niedecker wrote Zukofsky and enclosed some poems, including "When Ecstasy Is Inconvenient,"[82] offering the incisive riposte "who knows— / flight's end or flight's beginning / for the resting gull?" (25). (That critique anticipates, by the way, Simone de Beauvoir's remarkable pejorative in 1947 that "the serious man [. . .] loses himself in the object in order to annihilate his subjectivity. [. . .] The serious man gets rid of his freedom by claiming to subordinate it to values which [he would have] be unconditional.")[83]

We would also question the celebrated prospect of "thinking with the things as they exist" alongside Williams's aphorism "no ideas but in things," especially when such thinking privileges recognizable objects as containing inherent symbolic values—which are, as Bill Brown persuasively argues, shaped by essentialized post-Enlightenment subjectivity and linguistic-materialist construction.[84] We prefer instead a renewed and diverse poetics and praxis that recognizes fundamental misrecognitions about "the equivalence of personhood and subjectivity."[85]

Problematically, the use of terms such as 'object,' 'objective,' 'objectivist,' or 'Objectivist' to describe a poetic praxis inevitably invokes a variety of associations not limited to poetry; our above-mentioned disclaimer regarding Rand and Peikoff is symptomatic of this problem. One might even imagine Zukofsky, in an attempt to disfigure potential ideological projections onto a 'movement' required by a magazine publisher, arriving at an intentionally ambiguous notion of *embodied nominalism*. The histories of ontological and hermeneutical inquiry are as old as recorded Western thought, and the role of the subject in the production of 'literature' actually predates the poem as literary object, predates the invention of literary text, as for instance in Pindar's *Odes* (which incidentally conflate subjective and objective perspectives in helpful fashion).[86]

These facts open any inquiry into Objectivism to the question of what potentially constitutes a literary object in the first place—whether a choral recitation of Pindar in ancient Greece constitutes one, for instance. One might consider the poem as the site of action, behavior, and performance; as reflecting social realities, such as the existence of languages, customs, and laws; as (for Maria Sabina, for instance)[87] an immaterial and sacred form of incantation or prayer; as a material, textual, artifactual object; or, to paraphrase Zukofsky's ambition, as embodying (or 'objectifying') these realities. Our contributors understand Objectivist poetics to be a function of any combination of these forms of attention, and that relationships between subject and object in poetic praxis cannot be encapsulated by Objectivist tendencies any more or less than they may be by any other mode of aesthetic inquiry.

Of course, in light of the (*phantom* yet nonetheless) objective reality of social life and social structures, the goal of 'objectifying' poems was, and likely is, both mimetic and redundant—insofar as any act of poetic or literary production reifies the social conditions under which they occur, including conditions under critique. If you talk about or write within something, even negatively, your actions reinforce its existence. This reflection could likely relegate the Objectivist ethos to a moment in time, to specific registers of poetic forms and modalities stabilized by and contingent upon the conditions that produce them—style, form, subject matter, and so forth—and therefore undermining the possibility of any Objectivist poetry '*after*' Objectivism.

To conflate Objectivist poetics with the field of ontological study, however, is tantamount to supplanting poetry with theory, a move we (along with Bruns) hear and see Niedecker, Williams, and Zukofsky (among many others) warning us against. To emphasize the difficulty such a claim would encounter is to locate a distinction between subject and object that has been problematic since poetry's oral beginnings. If the social structures in which poems occur (whether Olympian festivals or Brooklyn poetry readings) also constitute objective, contingent realities, under which conditions then does poetic *performance* destabilize institutional claims of authority over *texts*? In what ways might praxis function as a disruptive, contingent, and regenerative network? Appreciative of Davidson's astute observation[88] that Zukofksy's 'hallucinations' of social objectivity echo Lukács's "phantom objectivity," we wonder: as we face the prospect of a digitized, atomized, and polarized era, how might the precarity of our shared lives guide our poetry, our poetics, and our praxis toward the posttextual?

The chapters that follow address these questions in measured, provocative, and sometimes counterintuitive ways through their individual and collective concerns with sincerity, objectification, and contingency within context of the movement's development and disjunctions from 1931 to the present. Whereas other volumes have charted the Objectivists' influence through forward-looking genealogies, tracing lines of convergence and divergence among distinctive schools—that is, from the Symbolists, Imagists, and Surrealists to the writers of the Beat Generation, the Black Mountain School poets, the New York School poets, and the Language Writers—we examine the diversity of contemporary praxis (e.g., Documentary Poetics, Conceptual Writing, Post- and Para-lyric, Concrete and Visual Poetics) and production (e.g., sequential and serial forms, sonic and image/text hybrids, discursive appropriations, and archival remediations).

Lastly, in light of the diversified ethos articulated here and in the February 1931 volume of *Poetry*, we have elected to revise the model of the single-author afterword (as exemplified by *The Objectivist Nexus*). Our collection concludes with a roundtable discussion, "Poetics and Praxis 'After' Objectivism," among several poets and critics[89] whose works engage the Objectivist legacy in the turbulent midst of the new and now. These choices emulate the polyvocalism of the 1931 Symposium—encountered here through a conversation about current practices of creativity and critique that renew the complexities of the past in terms of the difficulties of the present.

1

OBJECTIVIST POETICS, 'INFLUENCE,' AND SOME CONTEMPORARY LONG POEMS

RACHEL BLAU DUPLESSIS

The criteria for poetics that Louis Zukofsky proposed in his early essays offered central concepts to realist and left-oriented poets of the post-Pound and post-Eliot generation. "Objectification" and "sincerity" were ideas both precise and malleable; the poets inspired by this poetic ethos returned to these concepts throughout their lives, meditating upon them, and generating work that answered to these talismanic evocations. Zukofsky had outlined this modernist-realist aesthetic in his February 1931 issue of *Poetry* magazine: poetry as analytic work, featuring cuts of a material real focused by this documentary ethos, a fastidious attention to language as "matter," and a striking avoidance of mythopoetic surges. Neither "Program: 'Objectivists' 1931" nor "Sincerity and Objectification" were made as manifestos. Yet eminence grise Ezra Pound and editor Harriet Monroe were eagerly championing the reception mechanism of a "group," insisting that Zukofsky declare his thinking to be a manifesto for a movement rather than a statement of generative literary principles.

Although there will always be some debate on this point, the objectivist position is, in literary historical terms, a poetics without a movement. There may be objectivists, but there was, at the time, no Objectiv<u>ism</u>. The objectivist position links a radical (experimental) poetics to a radical (progressive) politics. And from these claims in poetics, like-minded poets found an articulation of some theoretical terms for their practice.[1] The objectivist "nexus" is, thus, both a set of concerns in poetics and a network of poets who related to each other via this general poetics. The historical "objectivist nexus" consisted mainly of key dyads active at various career junctures:

Reznikoff-Zukofsky; Reznikoff-Oppen; Zukofsky-Oppen; Zukofsky-Niedecker; Zukofsky-Bunting; Williams-Zukofsky; Pound-Oppen; Pound-Zukofsky. Some of the objectivist denizens never even met, or met quite late in life (like Oppen and Carl Rakosi). Some poets had angry, bitter as well as intense, or "perfectly nice," or mutually generative, or intermittent relations with each other. Be that as it may, it is useful to postulate a continuing "nexus" among poets who chose to draw upon this poetics and its implications.

However, this essay is not solely about poetics; it also concerns the biographical interactions between one of these dyads. As recent books on poetic friendship have proposed, interactional dialogue, relationships like mentoring, discipleship and resistance, events of mutual formation and group identity, but also dissensus, debates, and splits are all significant topics for a discussion of poetic careers.

The central "member" of the Objectivist "group"—had there been such a group—was Louis Zukofsky (1904–1978), who greatly affected George Oppen (1908–1984) and Lorine Niedecker (1903–1970), as well as taking Charles Reznikoff (1894–1976) as a model poet. However, Zukofsky was always the most adamant that no "Objectivist" group existed, that he wanted no part of it if it did exist, and that, like Peter in the New Testament, even if "accused" of this group, he would deny its existence. Yet independently of his wishes, his career remains linked to this nonmovement in various ways. Spoiler alert: there are a lot of ironies in the reception of Objectivist poets.[2]

What did the objectivist ethos generate in the late 1920s and early 1930s? To extrapolate from Zukofsky's and Oppen's earliest poems, one distinctive element is their deliberately ignoring, or distancing from, the "poetic" as an expectation for poetry, moving to a programmatic realist ethos. The "lens" became a photographic/filmic-materialist inducement to the selection, framing, combination, and juxtaposition of real-world materials extended by meditation. A number of Zukofsky's poems trump poetic tradition by realism—or at least by a drastic expansion of topics for poetry: the poem connecting ear hair to a flower; the poem about beds rattling at night; the poems about the washstand and the bathroom. Taking seriously these quotidian, ignoble materials conventionally beyond poetic notice creates a witty populist-inflected literariness. Oppen's published early work has similar a-poetic elements—elevator indicator lights so abstracted by visual description as to be simply language itself tinged by oddity and the jump-cut action shots of work and customers at a soda fountain, not to speak of the fundamental modular strategy of "discrete series."³ Objectification seemed to involve exacting antipietistic formal invention. And while both poets render poverty and economic crisis, Oppen rests on the irreducible and absolutist image (an impoverished man selling postcards on the street), while Zukofsky is far more prone to theorize and cite. His tour de force "singing" some of *Das Kapital* in 3/4 time predicts the three-step line of William Carlos Williams and constructs a Cubist-inflected Marxism. Their poems have topical resemblances: work on the river, cars, the beach. In mentioning geraniums, for example, Zukofsky frames the comedic, awkward rhyme and half rhyme of *millennium, geranium,* and *cranium* (he is charmed by the word), and Oppen, condensing an oblique plot in *you* and *him* and "two geraniums," makes an obscure comment on the world.⁴

The intense minimalism of *Discrete Series* and the almost baroque elaboration in Zukofsky's early poems do foreshadow greater differences of poetics under the objectivist rubric. Oppen's final *Discrete Series* poem notes one key difference: does art organize a "field" or is it part of that field?

> Written structure,
> Shape of art,
> More formal
> Than a field would be
> (existing in it) — (*New Collected Poems*, 35)

If, as Wallace Stevens proposed in *Harmonium*, one placed a "jar in Tennessee," does it organize that wilderness or does it become part of the wilderness? Does it shape the "slovenly" real or dissolve into the real? In Oppen the tension is unresolved (and a little tautological): the poem is indeed "more formal" (more objectified) than a natural field (let's say of the things that exist — no artifice about them, thus sincerity), but the speaker and poem also exist in the whole field of everything, including art. What is one's actual responsibility to each element? Objectification and sincerity are, cast in a certain light, opposite entities, contradictory goals, precariously balanced. Aside from the proleptic "field," a word suggestive of the link between projectivist poetics and the objectivist ethos, here the question of making a static or "formal" work ("objectification") is contrasted to registration of event happening as a situated person sees it (the "sincerity" of "existing in it").

Some of that sense of poised opposites also emerges from their biographical interactions. Zukofsky was four years older than Oppen; he had graduated from college and had an MA (George and Mary Oppen had simply left what is now University of Oregon at Corvallis), and he had precocious cultural range and incisiveness. Hence Zukofsky functioned as their pedagogue in poetry and poetics. The evidence in Mary Oppen's memoir *Meaning a Life* is warmhearted and appreciative; it constructs a picture of engaged young people in a supportive and exciting interior exile from family and social expectations.[5] Given that Zukofsky assiduously pursued a literary life and that Oppen stopped his literary production circa 1935 or even before, one result was that Zukofsky maintained no particular interest in or contact with Oppen from about that date. The feeling of falling away seems to have been mutual.[6] In fact, when Zukofsky says to Kenneth Rexroth in March 1936 that he rejected his ties with wealthy people in about 1930 [*sic* on that date], he undoubtedly means with Oppen, who, he apparently felt, had reneged on financial promises.[7] Therefore, except for their intense transformative early friendship, Zukofsky was always more interesting to Oppen than Oppen was to Zukofsky. Far more central to Zukofsky over his whole career were Ezra Pound, William Carlos Williams, Basil Bunting, and the less acknowledged Lorine Niedecker. It is even possible to argue that Oppen's desire to test himself within the world of action, skill, and politics was not only a critique of his cosseted, wealthy upbringing but also a rejection of the sheer literariness (and perhaps the different enactments of politics) of the Zukofsky world.

How does one theorize splits, revulsions, angers that seem so wholly "personal" (and/or economic), given a period of intense closeness, the eros of poiesis that Mary Oppen has recorded? How does one acknowledge not so much (in the current cant expression) "the hatred of poetry" but rather "the hatred between poets"? It is possible to note how generative some hatred or some polemical "dislike" of poetry actually is. There is a lot to dislike in it. (Marianne Moore's formulation in "Poetry" comes with a helpful lack of melodramatic staginess.) So, too, the mutual "hatred (or dislike) between poets" is fiercely generative. Dissensus is energizing; anger, however painful, is provocative. So when dealing with poets, one must interpret and not just deplore the painful, ugly explosions (as between Robert Duncan and Robin Blaser, Duncan and Denise Levertov) or game-changing decisions (as by LeRoi Jones) that realign one's sociality and political allegiances. To a later critic, the causes may be odd or even untraceable, and certainly such explosions have multiple motivations. After the magnetic eros of poiesis, they create antimagnetic force fields.

Fast forward about twenty hard years. In the period beginning in the mid-1950s, turning to Zukofsky was a way of declaring a generally Poundian poetics without having to cope with the increasingly obvious problematic of Pound's clear and continuing political and social allegiances—to fascism and to a nonpersonal anti-Semitism (as in "some of my best friends"). Zukofsky—like Pound then, an obscure, undervalued, intransigent, knowledgeable, hermetic, brilliant, cranky writer of a long poem and of influential essays in poetics—provided a way of affirming Anglo-American radical modernism yet sidestepping its most notable exemplar.

Given the long-ago relationship and then cooling between Oppen and Zukofsky, and the settled "divorce" (with whatever submerged feelings), nothing, circa 1958, could have been more surprising to the ambitious and frustrated Zukofsky than Oppen's reappearance in the United States as a serious poet.[8] There was some mutual reaching out between the families in 1958–1960, but the few encounters had a distinct oil-and-water quality. There were uncanny resemblances: in both cases a small family of three; an almost unreadable (or unparsable) intensity among those three in each case; the complexities of both wives having less visible yet personable artistic careers; the poetic ambitions of both men being (though differently) overwhelming. From Zukofsky's viewpoint, from 1947 on to the later 1950s and beyond it appeared as if his achievements in poetry were finally becoming acknowledged after a deeply felt, embittering neglect. He developed gratifying epistolary ties with, and the respect of, younger poets like Robert Duncan, Robert Creeley, Cid Corman, Jonathan Williams, and others (Robert Kelly, Jerome Rothenberg, and British poet Charles Tomlinson).

Oppen seemed (oddly) shocked that their old friendship and long-ago dialogue could not resume. But Zukofsky had no particular need of Oppen except perhaps as a member of the cadre of those who admired him, possibly even seeing Oppen as an irritant. Zukofsky resented the flowering of Oppen's second career—Oppen being a newer darker horse come up on the outside track when Zukofsky had staked his fame precisely upon being the dark horse of literary history.[9]

Between Oppen and Zukofsky, there were, then, strong differences that became pronounced, then acute, then insurmountable: economic differences occasioning resentment and suspicion, differences of political emphasis and action, differences in career trajectory. Most fundamentally, there were differences in the poetics of "objectification" and "sincerity" as proposed in actual texts, differences that I have, retrospectively, framed as versions of objectivist dissensus.

It is impossible, even in this poetics context, *not* to account for one of the biographical sources of resentment. The story is focused with distinct narratives around that most poet-ly of potential abrasions: the prospect of pub-lication. Oppen, in part fueled by his own intellectual, poetic, and career momentum after 1958, but certainly buoyed by the interests that his half-sister, June Oppen Degnan, maintained in his literary career and her desire to be making her own kind of literary mark, was able to broker the publi-cation of three objectivist and neo-objectivist books of selected poems plus the appearance of his own new work, *The Materials*, done by *San Francisco Review* (supported by June's wealth and fervor) and New Directions—no small plum of dissemination. For whatever reasons of regrounding himself in a talismanic poetics, of quite strategic reentry into the poetry world by constructing a reception context, or of recovering some almost lost poets, Oppen was reexamining "objectivist" writers—Reznikoff, Rakosi, William Bronk (a new entrant), and also Zukofsky.[10] Since Zukofsky already had a painful history of having manuscripts rejected by New Directions in at least 1940 and 1961, one can postulate his fascination with this publication initiative.[11]

However, the price to Zukofsky would have been high. First, he would be appearing in a context where some trace of the rubric "objectivist" as the suggestion of a former "movement" or formation was in play—some-thing he fiercely opposed. Second, he would be accepting a *selected* poems and discussing this selection with former "student" Oppen (of all people) as an editor standing between himself as poet and the press. Third, he would be agreeing to a representative set of shorter poems when for him many of his poems were singularities—or comprised one total oeuvre, indivisible. A *selected* shorter poems was proffered from Oppen to Zukofsky as a serious possibility in September 1962; a *collected* shorter poems was all Zukofsky wanted and all he would accept. So this negotiation in good faith turned bad around October 1962.[12] And finally Zukofsky was indeed published, not by New Directions but by Norton, when his short poems appeared in two paperback volumes accepted by poetry editor Denise Levertov and brokered by Robert Creeley and Robert Duncan.[13] The title (*ALL*) tells this story of pride and resentment in capital letters. By September 1963 Zukof-sky was very angry at Oppen for what he saw as Oppen's failure to accom-plish successfully what Zukofsky wanted, needed, and demanded after so many years of neglect.

Zukofsky's developing anger, a second resentment after the loss of in-come paid by Oppen decades before, folded into and exacerbated his already proud sense of being isolated, excluded, beset, sidelined, overlooked—even by his erstwhile friends. Their models of friendship—to make another theoretical point—differed considerably: Oppen sought the give-and-take, sparring dialogue in a fraternal (even rival-fraternal) relationship. Zukofsky's model of the exchange was of a superior (himself) and his willing foil, wingman, appreciative helper. That is, Zukofsky did not allow with Oppen what he himself had earlier sought from Pound—a fraternal relationship between equals—and he redirected the (anyway rapidly eroding) relationship with Oppen along the pattern of mentor-epigone.[14] In his own self-conception, Zukofsky was the better of the two poets by such a large margin as to make Oppen's positive opinion of his own work not simply derisory and ridiculous but downright insulting to poetry in general and to Zukofsky in particular. Oppen knew this. In a (typically) undated note, this direct address to Zukofsky shows his interior dialogue with an absent interlocutor: "But Louis, *you* think I haven't earned the poetry? It seems to me that I have."[15]

In this long-frayed former friendship neither, finally, talks to the other, although sometimes each will talk about the other, though in different ways (as to an awed and uncomfortable Charles Tomlinson).[16] The intimate, sometimes repetitive, sometimes staggering meditations and aphorisms that Oppen produced in his later career show that he never stopped talking to Zukofsky or talking about the originary Zukofskian terms 'objectification' and 'sincerity.' Oppen continued to mull, to respond to the statements, choices, and poetry of his long-ago companion-mentor, sometimes not in the most flattering terms, trying to measure a distance that now points to some contemporary uses of their work.[17] Finally, Oppen felt that Zukofsky had taken a wrong path into obfuscation and obscurantism, was misusing his considerable intelligence, and even was acting deviously at various moments.[18]

Oppen was also a fierce judge of the different uses, philosophically, practically, and poetically, that each made of those original concepts. He notes that "Louis' 'objectification'—tho he denied it—related back to Kant: the consciousness' act of objectification. [¶] I was, even in 1929 (discrete series) consciously attempting to trace, to re-produce, the act of the world upon the consciousness."[19] This is a fundamental difference—Plato vs. Aristotle, perhaps, or preformulated idealist vs. phenomenological pragmatist, or conceptual principles vs. historical situation and its demand for existentialist decision. This, as in "mine was a deliberate slide downhill, Louis a climb, up / Downhill is at least less prissy / Not only to say, but to be IN IT."[20]

The recent work by Zukofsky to which Oppen had access would have been *"A"* up through *"A-12,"* with the works of the 1960s (*"A-13"*–*"A-20"*) being freshly composed during this period (1960–1966), along with the homophonic Catullus translations (by Louis and his wife, Celia), dated 1958–1969. About both, Oppen had very critical thoughts. Some Oppen observations—devastating, acerbically droll, and provocative—reveal that he resisted the fundamental (playful/procedural) mechanism of the Catullus translations, noting that by prioritizing the sound of the Latin transferred to English, Zukofsky put words together without concern for their semantic bearing. Thus, to Oppen this work was untrue to both objectivist principles of sincerity (direct statement of an actual or genuine thought) and of objectification (efficient form).[21] However, one might counter that words treated as material objects—as dynamic matter—is at the heart of the Catullus and that the goal of that work is precisely objectification. Clearly these terms have their own interior fissures and interpretive possibilities.[22]

Although he had once been eager to reread the early parts of "A," Oppen made a stingingly critical remark on Zukofsky's career-engaging long poem: "Zuk's / A / the motor is running in neutral."[23] A reminder: when a gear is set in neutral, you can rev the motor by stepping on the gas pedal, thereby producing a loud "accelerating" noise, but the car does not and cannot go forward. It's a pretty devastating remark, resting on Oppen's key test of "A" between what Zukofsky has experienced and what he has simply elaborated with verbal dexterity and literary skills. A remark earlier on the same daybook page shows one definition of their differences with a touch of humble-brag: "I [Oppen] do not write a learned poetry—picking up tag ends of other people's knowledge. I write only of things that have been central to my life."[24]

As reconstructed in this essay, the friction between Zukofsky and Oppen in their later years was biographically generated but was also rooted in a fundamental difference in the interpretation of these two terms in poetics: sincerity and objectification. Zukofsky claimed that with "A" he had objectified crucial cultural materials and reformulated culture itself in the microcosm of his highly cultured, intellectual, artistic family and in the macrocosm of this poem as summa, in which that cultured, talented family plays a central role. Oppen, in contrast, felt he rested most thoroughly on "sincerity"—speaking about what he knew, had seen, had thought, an existential choice of a "limited clarity." Oppen felt Zukofsky was overly literary; Zukofsky (my projection or guess) thought Oppen's work was simply naive: "Another word I don't want to use is 'reality,'" Zukofsky says pointedly to L. S. Dembo; this could be a shrug in the direction of Oppen.[25]

One sees the vivid contrasts in their uses of these terms in poetics in the interviews they gave to L. S. Dembo. In April and May 1968 Dembo conducted individual interviews with four poets (including Carl Rakosi and Charles Reznikoff) under the rubric "The 'Objectivist' Poet."[26] At that point, Zukofsky had not yet written "A-22" and "A-23," but Celia Zukofsky's contribution of "A-24" had been assembled as a *Sprechstimme* collage from Zukofsky's total oeuvre, including his essays and plays. Zukofsky is squeamish when asked to discuss the overarching structure of *"A"* as a long poem (for one thing, it had not yet been completed), insisting that it is a congeries of highly focused specific materials, disclaiming the overall effect. He is also noticeably uninterested in recalling or working with the historical definitions of either sincerity or objectification, devoting only perfunctory—even evasive—attention to these terms, saying he wouldn't use those terms again (*Contemporary Literature*, 204), but that objectification had something to do with real things in the world and the craft to make the poem about those things (205) in order to produce an adequate structure (209) out of focused details—the detail being a synonym for sincerity (209). An objectivist is any individual person who, in Zukofsky's words, wants to be "living with things as they exist and as a 'wordsman,' he is a craftsman who puts words together into an object" (205).[27] He also reminds the listener that objectification—the poetic act—is the work of one singular person—not the rallying call for a group poetics (205). In contrast, Oppen discusses definitions both historical and contemporaneous (160), outlines the relationship of these terms to Imagism, distinguishes "achieving form" (objectification) from "moments of conviction" (sincerity), later described as a question of truth, close in his telling, to ethics (160–61, 165).

At a certain level of poetic-critical abstraction, the long poems of both Oppen and Zukofsky resemble—or can by critical finesse be made to resemble—each other. *"A"* as well as both *Of Being Numerous* and *Some San Francisco Poems* are saturated in personal relations among family members as a test of authentic life. In both Zukofsky's very long poem and Oppen's two shorter serial poems, the historical moment, the city, the ambulatory sense of passing among the sites of one's attention with meditative understanding all help to shape meaning. Both poets show a deep texture of citations whose varying sources might elicit discussion. And both are profoundly antimythic. Myth and transcendent nonsecular universals have almost no traction for them. Compare the long poem work of T. S. Eliot, Ezra Pound, sometimes William Carlos Williams (in *Paterson*'s lost-cause Jungian archetypes), H. D., Charles Olson, Ronald Johnson, Nathaniel Mackey, Anne Waldman, Alice Notley—to see how rare the purely secular long poem is. Where the poems differ texturally and acutely is in how they enact the loosely realist (antimythic) impulses; in Zukofsky this mode becomes procedural and baroque, in Oppen phenomenological and minimalist. This occurs because of a simple difference: to oversimplify drastically (and coarsely) about representation, Zukofsky's final allegiance was to the word and Oppen's was to the world.[28]

In "A" Zukofsky made a career-engaging work, declaring this goal when he was in his twenties, accomplishing that modernist "epic" in complicated and interrupted spurts through his life. The numerology of his cantos sends a procedural message: his 24 years as he began; the 24 count of the books of the Hebrew Bible; the 24 Bach pieces; the 24 books of the classic epic.[29] Numbers are a way of controlling the alternation between formalist ("A-9") and organicist ("A-12") sections. Such a long poem type—like *The Cantos* a sprawling, encyclopedic anatomy of erudition and ambition—always desires to change literature (and sometimes to prescribe for society).

For Zukofsky the two terms (*objectification* and *sincerity*) fused in the most fundamental building block of all language: the word. "A" seems to smash textuality to its components (as contemporaneous science smashed the atom). Words have historical and social (as well as sonic and visual) density: this is not a metaphor or a piety. It means that the work operates "thanks to the dictionary" and "the story must exist [as if holographically] in each word or it cannot go on."[30] Things (I mean "words") are clustered together in an almost nonnaturalized, often outré fashion. The work resembles John Chamberlain's crushed car sculptures: the material fact of cars for Chamberlain as the medium would be the material fact of words for Zukofsky. Then they are crushed together into a new form. A black hole/overwritten quality results ("A" is hermetic, compressed, even airless).

There was once a moment (according to biblical tradition) when "the whole earth had one language and the same words" (Gen. 11:1 NRSV), but that collapsed with the destruction of the tower of Babel; with his long poem, Zukofsky attempts to reverse the impact of the Babel story on humankind. Zukofsky's "A"—a pre-destruction Babel monument—reunifies "all" languages (in strange sameness/difference) and cultures into one; that "one" is composed of his two long poems: "A" and its aftermath, *80 Flowers*. Zukofsky spatializes time into monument. The poems desire monumentality: a wall constructed like towers out of the tiniest—and most intransigent—materials: words themselves. Form is based on acts of intense, often highly numerological construction. Cognition is based on acts of form.

Oppen, in contrast, temporalizes space. Events—as lines, words, phrases—occur on the page, gathering up a temporal momentum yet appearing endless, porous, suggestive, antimonumental. The source is an alternative objectification: saying only what you feel is known to you at the time you say it. This is an "as if" ethos; clearly his work is not a constant (projectivist) stream of thinking or seeing and registering, but it rests on adequation to a particularly charged moment or set of materials set forth in serial sequence. Any conjuncture of elements, if experienced authentically, becomes adequate for poetic meditation. Any of Oppen's serial works are anti-encyclopedic poems: summary soundings of specific conditions. That is, Oppen wants to register in word and syntax how the world hits the mind, ear, and eye: form is based on acts of cognition.

What is the impact of these two writers on later writers of the long poem? Theoretically speaking, this question involves a discussion of influence, a useful and yet quite volatile concept in literary study. For the word *influence* suggests a one-way street. Etymology offers something even stranger — "influence" is a flowing into — as if the person to be influenced were a kind of feminine vessel or vat. In fact, there is a lot of agency involved in "being affected by" another person. You choose. And you also shape the narrative of connectedness or contribute to it. In a nexus model of literary history, one sees poets returning to the work of someone or to the poetics of a certain group — in homage but also in contestation and resistance. The specific mix each person makes is specific and at least partly deliberate. Nexus (an ongoing constellation of intersecting [generally literary] formations) thus seems a more useful and functional descriptive term than casting poets in genealogical lines of descent. The "influence" model is rather hierarchic and patriarchal in a negative sense; it also suggests that "influence" is monolithic. A nexus is horizontal, rolling, dialectical, and more accumulative, more full of multiple contestations and links.

Thus to claim the monofocal "influence" of one person on another becomes a tendentious and overblown stance. Instead, poets synthesize important — and even contradictory — strands of work that went before them. Sometimes writers later than perceived "masters" may even fuse complex and apparently unbridgeable divides among several elders. The rhetorics, concerns, poetics, goals, distinctive stances, and exemplary elements of another poet get specifically articulated (or ignored) by you and remixed in your work, your poetics, and your poetic career. The synthesis involved in being affected by older "model" poets is an act of both humility and mastery. A later generation of writers will always take what they need from elders — even if what they need is contradictory and has led to irreconcilable differences for precisely those elders. Case in point: Zukofsky and Oppen.

In the magnetic relations of poets and in the dynamic antimagnetism of their dissensus in the aftermath of allegiances, such reckonings are the stuff of legend and poetic lore, but also of later use. The explosive relations between poets will sometimes implicate dissemination in a positive way. From such debates and abrasions come shards of possibility, mana, models of intransigence, and the potential for contestatory appropriation.

In this regard, I thought about myself and three other contemporary long-poem writers and friends, posing to all of us a very simple question—the uses, if any, of, or for, Oppen and Zukofsky in their long poems.[31] To speak personally for a moment, within my own work, in "Draft 6: Midrush," these two figures suddenly presented themselves to me as charismatic dream-avatars, a generative moment as *Drafts* began emerging into a sense of its terms and zone (c. 1987). Given the two writers, Oppen and Zukofsky, it's clear I am most, and most profoundly, influenced by Oppen in general attitudes in poetics, interests in the line, serial construction, ethics of sincerity, and form as cognition. Yet *Drafts* (c. 1,080 pages, closed in 2012 after twenty-six years) ended up—oddly to me—with a considerable parallel to Zukofsky's long poem: as a lifelong project, as, arguably, ending apparently (but not actually), as incorporating a number of genres, as having a generally secular attitude (this last shared with Oppen).[32] This all happened despite the fact that my history of reading Zukofsky (in 1987–1988, when this specific poem was written) had then been spotty and intermittent and did not in fact occur before the initiation of, or even during, a lot of the writing of *Drafts*. Further, as with my other interlocutors here, my interests in the long poem cannot be narrowed to these two "objectivist" options alone.

Beverly Dahlen's long poem *A Reading* (ongoing from 1978, now approximately 411 pages in print but probably longer in manuscript) has a clear goal of thinking with the things as they exist, a major objectivist proposition—but these "things" are often interiorized "streams of consciousness" (to allude to Dorothy Richardson's pioneering multivolume novel *Pilgrimage*). Dahlen, like H. D., has worked with Freudian free association to gain a method for continuous writing or at least for opening her writing space to chains of rich association, psychological, theoretical, and social.[33] In terms of poetics, this is a Duncanesque or projectivist ethos, marked by writing as continuous thinking—a spot where the objectivist and the projectivist poetics meet.

About the objectivists, Dahlen wrote (May 23, 2014):

I am not a big reader of Zukofsky, but I am sure I had read Oppen in the summer of 1978 when I began writing *A Reading*. I was then living in the hotbed of LANGUAGE poetry. They were mostly Z fans but of course I took the contrary position by beginning a poem (which I had no idea would be a *long* poem at the time. People have asked me since then why it is so short!) based on the Freudian principles of free association. I had been an admirer of Freud's since I first read his work when I was in high school. Also, the very first writing workshop I attended was taught by a professor who was decidedly influenced by Freud. So that was the beginning, not of *A Reading*, but of a method or technique for approaching writing.

A Reading is almost totally subjective. I love Oppen's work, but I am not, I think, influenced by it in terms of my own practice.

When I said *A Reading* was "almost totally subjective" I meant of course in contrast to "objectivism." I'm not sure how these labels help us understand anything. Lorine Niedecker, also classed with the objectivists[,] seems to me to be anything but. However, any poem is a construct and a material object. Given that it's made of language it is also a socially constructed object. All this seems obvious.

In her own self-characterization, Dahlen returns to the ground of sincerity and objectification strikingly (and with suspicion), while articulating ambivalence and affection for Oppen's work and a clear resistance to the enthusiasm for Zukofsky shown by her peers.

One of those peers was Ron Silliman, author of *The Alphabet* (a long poem of 1,054 pages in 26 sections, begun in 1979, written for twenty-five years), which fits into a set of four long works under the rubric of "a single poem" called *Ketjak*, this whole being "the sort of Russian-doll structure that I seem to keep reinventing."[34] It will include a work-now-in-progress called *Universe*, projected in 360 (possibly chapbook-sized) sections, the number of degrees in a full circle.

Silliman sets out his enthusiasm for Zukofsky (email of February 17, 2014). "I was first turned to LZ in 1966 through the *USA Poetry* TV show, best thing TV ever did for me. The only thing I could find [with his work in it] was the *Controversy of Poets* anthology, but I soon had '*A*' 1–12." He then tracks a relay of dissemination. "[Robert] Grenier got turned onto LZ through Creeley and the works that ended up in *Sentences* came out of that. He in turn spread it to Barrett [Watten] & Bob [Perelman] while in Iowa. So it was sort of a secret we all shared by 1970 or thereabouts. 'A' 22–23 sealed the deal, still the best poetry of the 20th century to my mind."

In this Silliman email, interestingly, we don't have a sense of what the incipient Language poets received from Zukofsky in poetry or in poetics, just a general challenge and a secret. However, this should not be underestimated as a motive in poetic formation; the challenge of decoding a secret, neglected work said to be too much for you might provoke you actually to read it. Pound's *Cantos* had had a parallel effect on people, as Bob Perelman notes in *The Trouble with Genius*. However, when Silliman describes his sense of process within the long poem, his words get more heuristic, involved in uncertainty, exploratory without a fixed sense of how it is going to come out: he talks of this feeling as "the middle."

Silliman:

> I knew at a young age—still in my teens—that I would write a long poem, but it took me nearly a decade before I actually began the work I am still writing today, some 38 years later. Some sections of this project—I call it *Ketjak*—have taken a long time to get under way: one section of *The Alphabet* took over 20 years from conception to completion. A section of *Universe* that I am working on presently—*Parrot Eyes Lust*—is something I have been thinking & dreaming about since my first false starts on the poem in 1973. Being unfinished is for me the norm—I am in fact always in the middle, rarely in a position to take a step back and say that this (or this) is the final shape of something, only building blocks toward an emergent *thing* that I call a poem principally because poetry is the art of language, and hence for me the category that contains all others at least implicitly within. [. . .]When I begin to sense that I am nearing the completion of any section of this project—maybe 50 pages out, perhaps just ten—I start to be aware of a rising tide of emotion not unlike the impending loss of a loved one. I often ride this emotion much in the way that a surfer rides a wave, and this directs me toward understanding what that moment of temporary closure might be. In my best writing, I give up all control to the poem: I'm barely holding on. But it also means that often I am working on passages, material, with no such sense at hand, not unlike a sailor who is out at sea, but unable to read the sky nor get any clues of direction from the horizon: sailing blind. In such moments, I have to trust in the process, in what the poem is telling me, and I have moments of enormous anxiety during these periods.

Interestingly, despite a strong sense of numerology and a strongly disciplined, even obsessive writing practice, Silliman's metaphor for the long poem process recalls some of Oppen's poetics and poems: the emotion is open, porous, anxious; the metaphors involve sailing an ocean. We here see different layers of objectivist influence: the topic of Language poetry and Zukofsky is a critical given, encompassing proceduralism, hermetic temptations, political resistance to hegemonic forms, a critique of ideologies embedded in language, structure, and convention that demanded critical-poetic rupture.[35] And Silliman is as emphatically numerological in his organizational strategies as Zukofsky is at times. But we also see other forces at work in Silliman's long work: his empathetic realist mode that insists on sincerity with an ethical grounding loosely recalls the work of Oppen.

Anne Waldman's *The Iovis Trilogy*, a long poem (2011; 1,013 pages) is built on the projectivist, Olsonic model; it is a poem of spiritual striving, political rage, gender commentary, and citations of documents (including letters to political leaders) and has a vatic, cross-cultural world reach. Waldman is situated in an important Beat-Projectivist tradition with its omnivorous accumulative sensibility, yet she is willing to situate herself with regard to Oppen and Zukofsky, even when they did not have the same traction on her career that we have seen in the other three poets consulted. That is, "influence" is an ongoing, rolling question of rereading oneself in relation to other poets, not only an identifiable affiliation that happens once and is sealed tight. It is a way of situating one's work in relation to a poetic field, a way of continuing to think about what such a work is and was, a turning of one's work to see its various facets.[36] In short, Waldman's comments clearly illustrate a dynamic poetic nexus, rather than "influence" as a model.

Waldman: "I wanted to meet the world and report it (field poet) with *Iovis* as my *upaya* (skillful means) a kind of sincerity that 'things are symbols of themselves' which is the great teaching of *Mahamudra* [. . .] seems some link there to a sought inherent knowledge of seeing [. . .] which is why we write the poem [. . .] and the poem is the symbol of itself as well." Here the word "sincerity" has taken on a larger-than-objectivist dimension and is buoyed by an ethnopoetic borrowing of mana. She then observes:

> Taking up the long poem was like taking up a gauntlet to challenge the idea that epic was exclusively a male form. What could hold handle transmit incubate resound digress permit transgress more than the long poem? What could demand attention and attempt to deliver

apotheosis, new form and language, declare ethos for writing in the first place (a ground zero charnel ground), stay difficult and "female" yet transcend gender more than the long boundary-less poem? What could include history, BE *'istorin, that practice of finding out for oneself,* and include Other.

Waldman's Olsonic impulse is clear from the italicized citation, but a critique of Olson also occurs, given the primary gendered challenge of making a work both affirmatively female and beyond binary gender. And her sense of a challenge to get beyond the Western tradition situates her poem as a cultural intervention critiquing such gendered genres as the epic.

But what about Zukofsky? He became, for Waldman, a model of ambition, able to work with domestic life as well as political life. "When I embarked on *Iovis* in the mid-1980s, the mysterious and difficult '*A*' was one of the ambitious texts on my mind. The scope, alone, was inspiring as I started BOOK I: *Iovis Omnia Plena,* thinking of "*A*"s 24 sections, perhaps for the hours in a day. Book I of *Iovis* clocked in at 25, with, in addition, *Both Both: An Introduction* and a Coda." "A-8" was particularly generative; the mix of history, labor relations, and (this next, also about Zukofsky, comes later in Waldman's email): the "network of barricades, gas & bullets, the ubiquitous JS Bach, cheese, film, Greensleeves, Bosch & Breughel, and much more. Where were we? The mind of the poet, and *all times contemporaneous in the mind of the poet.* A kind of permission." The permission is for hybridity of genre and topical inclusiveness.

The "contemporaneity" is Eliot's remark, but here one sees graphically how the existence of one long poem offers permission for another. Waldman continues:

> Paul Zukofsky's presence in [LZ's] poem was important considering my invocations of my son Ambrose as the epic's muse. [. . .] [*Iovis*] was written for my son, includes him, and for his generation and any future. [. . .] The initial pulse was the line in Virgil "Iovis Omnis Plena" (all is full of Jove) and the joke of everything impregnated with the seed of the Father. The generative '*of* Jove,' so that would be the rune to invade and expose and disclose. And how that played out in dailyness. And with a Buddhist vow to "do no harm" and the view of *pratitya samutpada,* or the interconnected co-arising of all phenomena that would link dreams, journal, the voice of the child and many others, histories, documents.

Her related comments about Oppen show the question of nexus and inspiration, not "influence" in a limited monofocal line of descent. It offers a graphic sense of the recombining that poets do when faced with elders. "I wanted to say something also about how 'Of Being Numerous' is gaze I'm profoundly haunted by—being such a New Yorker and all the years here since 1945 'glassed in dreams' / 'insanity in high places' the poem is more prophetic than ever!!!! War and the news is war [. . .] 'right view' is Buddhist tag."

Roman Jakobson says that the poetic *text* is based on selection and combination.[37] Poets' approach to poetic elders and influence involve selection and combination as well. All four of these long poem writers have in some way—but quite differently—accounted for Oppen and Zukofsky as they build an oeuvre and a poetics. There is no doubt of the differential claims made by their very long works, drawing from the "epic" complexity of Zukofsky to the serial long poems and modular structures in Oppen (as well as in Niedecker and Reznikoff). These specific writers I called upon (Dahlen, Silliman, Waldman, and myself) are interestingly pulled between the two modes of the long poem—something that can be seen, as well, in the contrast between Olson's very long poem and Creeley's serial long poems. Further, the poetics of objectification and sincerity is necessarily interpreted, torqued, and deployed variously by the work of particular poets drawing on Zukofsky and Oppen—such as the poets whom I consulted here. A poetics is never simply a closed historical artifact; it is a perpetually available set of possibilities. To claim the uses of prior poets by contemporaries is always to narrate a motivated relationship within frameworks (often trying vainly to make things fit consistently together), but it is also clear that these relationships of nexus are best narrated by emphasizing their own wayward scintillations and unique paths, their strange contradictions, their own magnetic eros and anger, and their own kinds of love and dissent.

2

"MORE FORMAL / THAN A FIELD WOULD BE"; OR, IMAGINARY GARDENS WITH VIRTUAL POEMS IN THEM

ON GEORGE OPPEN AND LOUISE GLÜCK

GRAHAM FOUST

In his essay "The Mind's Own Place," George Oppen offers a friendly amendment to Bertolt Brecht's question "What kind of times are they, when / A talk about trees is almost a crime / Because it implies silence about so many horrors?"[1] Oppen writes:

> There is no crisis in which political poets and orators may not speak of trees, though it is more common for them, in this symbolic usage, to speak of "flowers." "We want bread *and* roses": "Let a thousand flowers bloom" on the left: on the right, the photograph once famous in Germany of Handsome Adolph sniffing the rose. Flowers stand for simple and undefined human happiness, and are frequently mentioned in all political circles. The actually forbidden word Brecht, of course, could not write. It would be something like *aesthetic*. But the definition of the good life is necessarily an aesthetic definition, and the mere fact of democracy has not formulated it, nor, if it is achieved, will the mere fact of the extension of democracy, though I do not mean of course that restriction would do better. Suffering can be recognized; to argue its definition is an evasion, a contemptible thing. But the good life, the thing wanted for itself, the aesthetic, will be defined outside of anybody's politics, or defined wrongly.[2]

To be sure, Oppen's revision of Brecht's notion can be tied to the many instances in his prose, in his letters, and in interviews in which he speaks of a kind of unknown known (or a known unknown) as the source of poetry. Some examples (in chronological order):

Poetry has to be protean; the meaning must begin there.[3]

We, the poets, change the accents, change the speech. We change the
speech because we are not explaining, agitating, convincing: we do
not write what we already knew before we wrote the poem.[4]

It's true one sees afterwards that one has carefully and deliberately said
what he didn't know he was saying.[5]

The ear knows and I don't know why.[6]

According to Oppen's logic, if politics are (or should strive to be) a vehicle
for the alleviation of suffering, and if suffering is recognizable as such, then
what one wants from politics is what is already known. For example, I know
it is wrong for people to starve, and I recognize that people are starving,
which means I will then take pains to put into place a political situation
that will put an end to starvation. But poetry, it seems, works differently,
for, unlike politics, poetry is not, to borrow a phrase from Louise Glück,
"inscribed by the will."[7] As Oppen writes in his 1975 "Statement on Poetics": "I, surely, cannot hope to prescribe. I try one word and another word
and another word, reverse the sequence, alter the line-endings, a hundred
two hundred rewritings, revisions—This is called prosody: how to write a
poem. Or rather, how to write *that* poem."[8]

This statement follows Oppen's quoting from his own poem "Drawing,"
one of two titled poems from his first book, *Discrete Series*, in which two
practices involving marks on paper—that is, writing and drawing—seem
to intertwine:

Not by growth
   But the
Paper, turned, contains
This entire volume.[9]

The poem seems to speak of itself and of the series of which it is a part, but
in doing so it calls itself "drawing." Is "drawing" here an art object, or is
it the act of choosing a card or pulling water from a well? When speaking
of reading, we would normally say that we turn "pages"—and we're able
to see that here by way of the word "paper"—but in this poem we also see
an artist rotating her chosen surface in order to gain a fresh perspective or
an attempt at a different point of access, a movement that mimics Oppen's
slight twisting of a common phrase.

Oppen "distracts"—that is, he "draws apart"—and multiple readings of
this poem bring to light multiple meanings. ("Volume" could be a physical

book or an unspecific amount, "contains" could mean holds or controls.) Borrowing from "The Mind's Own Place," then, we might say that a poem, unlike Oppen's flower-related feeling of happiness, can be thought of as a *complex* and undefined human *action*, at least at its outset, though even a finished poem is, as Oppen says, "a knowledge hard to hold [. . .] a meaning grasped again on re-reading."[10]

What I want to do in this essay, then, is to reread a few already widely read Oppen poems, all of which happen to make reference to plants or flowers, in order to further explore his take on the strange relationship between the actual world in which poems exist and the virtual poems to which they give rise. In doing so, I also hope to show how Louise Glück (a very different poet, though certainly not an inapt one) has continued Oppen's investigation of this relationship in *The Wild Iris*, a book that sometimes seems to engage with—and often deviates sharply from—Oppen's work. I'll begin by looking at the first five stanzas of Oppen's "Technologies," which constitute a sentence that might be said to pollinate itself:

Tho in a sort of summer the hard buds blossom
Into feminine profusion

The 'inch-sized
Heart,' the little core of oneself,
So inartistic,

The inelegant heart
Which cannot grasp
The world
And makes art

Is small

Like a small hawk
Lighting disheveled on a window sill.[11]

In these stanzas, Oppen's speaker seems to assert that one mode of putting forth (the "inelegant heart" of art) is at once connected to and disconnected from another more visible one (the "feminine profusion" of a natural occurrence). More often than not—three-quarters of the time, let's say, given that summer is but one of four seasons—the "'inch-sized / Heart,' the little core of oneself" keeps closed and in doing so becomes strangely unlike itself: "small // Like a small hawk." The budlike "heart," then, is more like an animal than like a plant, and if it's small in the way a small hawk is small, then perhaps we're to assume that its smallness is both a relative and a difficult one. A hawk is a large bird, and in order to fit on a window sill (in order, that is, to fit into the human-made world), it must shrink itself by tightly folding its wings, an image that runs counter to the spreading that occurs when a flower blossoms.

"Tho I distract / Windows," writes Oppen a bit later in the poem, and indeed the window in the poem's first sentence is (if I may repeat the etymology of "distract") drawn apart in a curious way. Just as the poem's initial images keep jumping their sentence's discursive tracks by moving from plants ("buds") to the human body ("Heart") to birds ("hawk"), the word "summer" becomes something other once the window image at sentence's end is fed back into the poem's first line, for "summer" is also another word for "lintel," the top window part that runs parallel to the sill below it. What we first thought of as a *time* of blossoming becomes reduced to a decorative *space* just out of the hawk's reach, as the poem's first line can now be seen as also referring to something decorative—that is, to *images* of flowers carved in stone. Oppen's use of "inch-sized / Heart," which comes from the third-century Chinese poet Lu Chi's "The Joy of Writing" and perhaps describes the way small written characters help a "sheet of paper [to contain] the infinite," is then perhaps an ironic commentary on dissemination's difficulties.[12]

As has been well documented, "Technologies" was written out of a quarrel with Denise Levertov regarding "feminine technologies [as] a kind of medical pragmatism," and it may be that we see something akin to this argument assert itself in Glück's "Song," a poem in which a critique from outside the poem (fictional or otherwise) seems to shift the poem in a direction more interesting than the one in which it sets out:[13]

Like a protected heart,
the blood-red
flower of the wild rose begins
to open on the lowest branch,
supported by the netted
mass of a large shrub:
it blooms against the dark
which is the heart's constant
backdrop, while flowers
higher up have wilted or rotted;
to survive

adversity merely
deepens its color. But John
objects, he thinks
if this were not a poem but
an actual garden, then
the red rose would be
required to resemble
nothing else, neither
another flower nor
the shadowy heart, at
earth level pulsing
half maroon, half crimson.[14]

The poem's first sentence might be summarized as follows: "This particular rose is like a human heart with regard to its redness and in terms of what adverse experience does to it." The poem's second and final sentence then introduces an interlocutor, John, whose preference for "actual" gardens is encapsulated in the four syllables of line fourteen—"objects, he thinks"— the isolation of which helps us to also see the noun form of the action in which John engages, a fitting move given that John seems to prefer the experience of objects themselves to their treatment in and by poetic speech.

In John's mind—a mind given to us by the speaker's words—the poem blocks or taints the aesthetic experience of being in the garden. For him, noting the similarities between a flower and a heart—or even the similarities between two flowers—is, in a way, to look away from the flower, to pull away from the world at hand and eye. Perhaps this objection has something in common with a certain Objectivist poet's feelings on the matter, for as Michael Palmer writes with regard to Oppen's distinction between metaphor and image:

> By speaking against literary contrivance [such as metaphor], Oppen argues both for the possibility, or necessity, of an immediacy of poetic engagement or intervention, and against the "poetic," that is, against the devices of a passive and acculturated representation. He argues as well for a gaze turned outward, a responsibility of the self to find its realization, its form as thinking subject, in its relation to the visible and invisible things of the world.[15]

The "gaze" of which Palmer writes might best be articulated by the opening sentence of Oppen's poem *Of Being Numerous*: "There are things / We live among 'and to see them / Is to know ourselves.'"[16] And yet does this not in some way also describe what Glück's speaker does when she sees a flower and finds that it has something in common with the human heart? Or is hers rather the "gaze" turned *inward*, the self not finding its "realization" but rather losing its way by way of solipsism and pathetic fallacy? Were John not present in the poem, it would be all too easy to assert the latter opinion, but when we read the poem again, wherever we go there John is, and if there's no proof in the poem that his objection has anything to do with Objectivism, it's still very possible that Glück's own admiration for Oppen—which she's made quite evident in a handful of essays and talks—exerts on "Song" a pressure (in the form of John) that forces her to interrogate the very devices she deploys.[17]

Oppen often refers to a line from section 69 of fellow Objectivist Charles Reznikoff's *Jerusalem the Golden* as exemplary of the kind of poetry he sought to write (or at least as evidence of the kind of poetry he preferred to read). And indeed, "a girder still itself among the rubbish" (which Oppen, even in his introduction to Reznikoff's *Poems 1937-1975*, frequently misquotes as "the girder, still itself / among the rubble") does seem to oppose metaphor in favor of allowing a seen thing to simply be "itself."[18] If, say, William Carlos Williams's rock-splitting saxifrage in "A Sort of a Song" is a metaphor for the human imagination's ability to penetrate the world and thereby help the reader to it—the poem claims that metaphor is able to "reconcile / the people and the stones"—Reznikoff's girder is just a girder "among the heaps of bricks and plaster" in the ruins of another collapsed human creation.[19] As Joshua Clover writes: "If the girder must stand for something, it stands better for fact itself, the basic unit of construction. [. . .] Or let it stand for nothing else. [. . .] Things mean themselves so thoroughly it's crude and beautiful."[20] That said, one need only to move twenty sections backward from the girder in *Jerusalem the Golden* to find Reznikoff using a metaphor in a poem called "A Garden":

> About the railway station as the taxicabs leave,
> the smoke from their exhaust pipes is murky blue—
> stinking flowers, budding, unfolding, over the ruts in the snow.[21]

In this poem, Reznikoff compares automobile exhaust and cultivated flowers, two entities associated with human ingenuity, both of which we associate with our sense of smell. We think of flowers as smelling lovely, of course, and so the connection between flowers and automotive discharge is jarring: the exhaust doesn't smell like what it looks like. Similarly, what's jarring in Glück's poem is the sudden appearance of someone who doesn't approve of the vision of the poem that contains him.

John's presence in "Song" ruptures the poem, redirecting it in a subtle but profound way. We see evidence of this in Glück's use of the word "pulsing" where we might otherwise expect to see "beating." The heart and the pulse are related, of course, but we don't ordinarily say that the heart "pulses"; rather, the pulse is what's *taken*—we check it in order to gauge a person's health. In one way Glück's speaker's use of "pulsing" is a kind of check on John's opinion; the flower remains connected to the heart even after John's interruption, which means the speaker has managed to overrule her companion. That said, "pulsing" also points to a change of heart by serving as an indicator that the speaker has pulled back from her metaphor even as she clings to it, for by choosing "pulsing" over "beating," she recognizes that the flower's heart-ness is the result of her *abstraction* of the flower—that is, of her *taking* of it—and not a characteristic of the flower itself. Moreover, the pulse at poem's end is visible but not audible—the rose pulses "half maroon, half crimson"—thus foiling the sonic connotations of the poem's title.

Plants and flowers appear in Oppen's work more often than one might think. Even near the end of *Discrete Series* (a book we often associate with elevators, Frigidaires, tugboats, and so forth) we find in the poem beginning "Deaths everywhere—" a window box containing two geraniums that act as someone's "life's eyes" (his life-size?), suggesting that perhaps Oppen sees flowers as something more than just symbols for "simple and undefined human happiness" after all (*New Collected Poems*, 34). But if it's difficult to imagine Oppen anthropomorphizing a flower in the way that Glück does, a curious early poem of desire from this same book finds him engaging in what amounts to the very reverse of that activity:

> She lies, hip high,
> On a flat bed
> While the after-
> Sun passes.
>
> Plant, I breathe—
>   O Clearly,
> Eyes legs arms hands fingers,
> Simple legs in silk. (20)

Though the situation here might be described as a love scene, any sexual activity occurs either prior to or after the moment detailed in the poem, and we read not *of* entwined bodies, but rather *through* a tangle of time, language, and vision. For instance, "after- / Sun," which echoes "afternoon," suggests twilight—an amalgam of day and night, time and light—while "hip high" suggests that the woman is lying on her side *and/or* that the bed she is on is at the level of the speaker's hip. What's perhaps most strange about the poem, though, is the fact that the speaker refers to himself as "Plant." Oppen speaks to this in a 1968 interview: "My own presence is like a plant, just breathing, just being, just seeing this. [. . .] I was talking about eroticism, just internal sensations, like a plant [. . .] the closure of eroticism within oneself. [The poem is] two things, the tremendously sharp vision of erotic desire, together with a kind of closing of one's self, within oneself emotionally."[22]

That the metaphor isn't tempered by a simile (as in "Like a plant") heightens its strangeness, and the lack of an "a" prior to the noun makes "Plant" feel almost like a proper name, a possible companion for the capitalized adverb "Clearly," who seems to be addressed in the next line. Given that the poem ends by mentioning what the woman is wearing—that is, how she is *dressed*—it's possible that Oppen's vocative is a kind of quiet joke that also prefigures these lines from "Deaths everywhere—":

> Her pleasure's
> Looser;
> 'O—'
>
> 'Tomorrow?'— (*New Collected Poems*, 34)

in which we hear "To mar 'O,'" a more severe disfiguring of said poetic convention.

Nearly forty years after the publication of *Discrete Series*, Oppen forges another human-plant connection in a poem called "A Poem about the Garden," though this connection is somewhat looser:

> carpel
> filament the brilliant
> center pollen-gold
>
> crimson stirs in a girl's
> eyes as tho one had entered
> a flower, and become a stranger (299)

Oppen's garden is a place very different from—but perhaps no less erotic than—the room in "She lies, hip high," and one possible reading would assume that perhaps the poem is a memory fragment from Oppen's early years with his wife, Mary, and that the word "entered" is being used in the sexual sense. This would mean that the speaker is comparing the person with whom he's having sex to a flower, an act that in turn renders him "a stranger," a person alien to himself and/or his lover.

But another reading of this poem would simply entail a person looking closely at a flower and then into the eyes of a girl who is also looking at that flower. The speaker's own encounter with the flower itself is communicated to us by the poem's first stanza and by the first word of the second stanza, as his detailed description of the flower's interior and its colors would realistically require knowledge of the flower's characteristics prior to seeing it reflected in the girl's eyes. (That is, it would not be possible to identify, say, specific colors when seeing a flower reflected in that way, for any image in an eye takes on the color of that eye.) Shortly after the stanza break, we see that the speaker's attention has turned to "a girl's eyes," in which he knows there to be — but in which he can't actually see — the crimson of the flower that was observed previously. With a turn of the head — which we do not see but which we know must've happened — the speaker, whom Oppen fittingly abstracts into the impersonal pronoun "one," begins to feel "as tho one had entered / a flower." This feeling is linked to the flower's "stir[ring]," which means that having seen in the girl's eyes the reflection of a moving flower, "one" has had the accompanying sensation that he is the *cause* of its movement, as opposed to, say, a breeze or a bee.

Unlike the speaker of "She lies, hip high," the speaker of "carpel" does not identify as "Plant" but rather feels "as tho" *any given person* ("one") has managed to have a physical relationship with a plant beheld (and possibly even held) by "a" girl. (Oppen's "as tho" points to its own excessive extension, a move that's prefigured sonically in the poem's second line when it tempts us to stretch the two-syllable "brilliant," which comes close on the heels of "filament," into three.) Moreover, the cause of this feeling seems to have something to do with having seen an unintentional representation of the thing "one" feels "one" has entered. Were it not merely an analogical fantasy, "one"'s entering the flower would make "one" potentially visible to the girl, but the poem's final word lets us know that even as "one" feels like he has entered a flower and caused it to move, "one" also recognizes that he is rendered unrecognizable ("a stranger") — like some anonymous insect, like the wind itself — in the process.

A number of the poems in Glück's *The Wild Iris* are spoken by plants or flowers; the book's project, as Tony Hoagland says, "sounds preposterous."[23] And yet ventriloquizing a flower in a poem is really no more preposterous than, say, these lines from the second section of Oppen's "Image of the Engine":

> The machine stares out,
> Stares out
> With all its eyes
>
> Thru the glass
> With the ripple in it, past the sill
> Which is dusty—If there is someone
> In the garden!
> Outside, and so beautiful.[24]

Writing of Oppen's equivocal "if" clause, Burton Hatlen posits:

> On the one hand, the machine seems to "stare out" in the hope of seeing someone (someone *human* that is) in the garden outside. But at the same time it is this very observer in the garden who seems to anthropomorphize the engine, ascribing to it "eyes" and the power to "stare." Both meanings of the "if" clause, however, emphasize the *dependency* of the image on the human world. The machine, and the individual human being as well, find their meaning, indeed their very existence, only in and through the "other." [. . .] As we and our tools enter into relationship with the "other," and implicitly with a world that extends beyond our lives, the terms of our existence begin to undergo a profound change, giving birth to sudden beauty.[25]

In the Dembo interview, Oppen addresses the concepts of human as machine and machine as being when he speaks of an old fisherman who he says "refuse[d] to see a motor" and claims that "when the motor finally starts, it's different, it's itself, and it's very different from a lump of steel."[26] Anthropomorphization, then, is not limited to the making of poems but rather is a poetic device—an engine of imagery—with which anyone might approach the world. We know that we resemble machines in our finitude, but we also perhaps feel akin to them in our being "for" something. In the same way that an engine is not just a pile of metal, a human being is not just a pile of flesh and bone. Because of both their structure and their function in the world, machines come to share certain characteristics with humans, though these commonalities are of course only made evident by way of the human mind.

Glück describes the relationship between humans and flowers similarly in "The Red Poppy," one of her flower-speaker poems, though her poem begins with a *denial* of mind and an assertion of "feelings":

> The great thing
> is not having
> a mind. Feelings:
> oh, I have those; they
> govern me.
> I have
> a lord in heaven
> called the sun, and open
> for him, showing him
> the fire of my own heart, fire
> like his presence
> What could such glory be
> if not a heart? Oh my brothers and sisters,
> were you like me once, long ago,
> before you were human? Did you
> permit yourselves
> to open once, who would never
> open again? Because in truth
> I am speaking now
> the way you do. I speak
> because I am shattered.[27]

The "brothers and sisters" addressed by the poppy presumably have minds, but they do not get to speak them, though they are, like John in "Song," spoken for by the speaker of the poem. Put another way, though we are given impressions of these "brothers and sisters" (a group I would say includes us), the only voice we encounter is the voice of the mindless poppy, who is "govern[ed]" by its "feelings," one of which is its possession of a "heart," another name for the "glory" of its having opened itself to the sun, its "lord." For me, the poem's power resides in Glück's set of shifted properties, which lend the poem's inherent improbability a sense of order. This is to say that because the poppy has been given the power of speech, a natural occurrence (the opening of a flower) can be posited as an act of devotion, a natural object (the sun) figured as a deity.

Moreover, the poppy's assertion that it lacks a mind causes us to read its truth claim near the poem's end ("Because in truth / I am speaking now /

the way you do") as the product of *feeling* rather than of thinking, a fact that may then place the flower's claim in a particular light. Given that *The Wild Iris* makes some attempts to acknowledge its own artifice (perhaps most notably in "Song"), we may be right to assume that "the way" in which the humans in the poem speak (and so the poppy) is poetically. The poppy recognizes (or feels) connection in its disconnection; that is, it asserts that the humans to whom it speaks were once like poppies in some way because they were at one time not human (which may only be to say that they were not born). What's more, it assumes that traces of this nonhuman-ness must remain, an assumption that both justifies the poppy's claim to relation ("brothers and sisters") and attests to its powers of perception (that is, to its hearing the speech of humans as akin to its own). Formally, this trace is visible in the last three letters of the poem's final word, "shattered," in which the poppy's color can be seen but not heard (and perhaps we even see traces of Oppen in Glück's three uses of the word "open").

Flowers are not engines, of course, but they are certainly animated in their growth, their coming open, and their proliferation; moreover, they have historically functioned as devices for poets, who often use them to talk about other things. Only in a poem could a flower speak, and yet, like Oppen's engine, flowers could be said to be something more than the material of which they're made in that they communicate with us by way of the numerous connotations (both general and specific) that humans have bestowed upon them by way of, among other things, the "machines made of words" we call poems.[28] In the poem "Daisies," for instance—a poem that reverses the situation in "The Red Poppy," in which a single flower speaks to a group of people—a group of flowers collectively contrasts its poetic value with that of machines:

Go ahead: say what you're thinking. The garden
is not the real world. Machines
are the real world. Say frankly what any fool
could read in your face: it makes sense
to avoid us, to resist
nostalgia. It is
not modern enough, the sound the wind makes
stirring a meadow of daisies: the mind
cannot shine following it. And the mind
wants to shine, plainly, as
machines shine, and not

grow deep, as, for example, roots. It is very touching,
all the same, to see you cautiously
approaching the meadow's border in early morning,
when no one could possibly
be watching you. The longer you stand at the edge,
the more nervous you seem. No one wants to hear
impressions of the natural world: you will be
laughed at again; scorn will be piled on you.
As for what you're actually
hearing this morning: think twice
before you tell anyone what was said in this field
and by whom.[29]

In some way, this poem acknowledges the "preposterous[ness]" of which Hoagland speaks when the flowers warn their addressee—who seems to be a figure for someone considering the possibility of engaging in poetic speech—to "think twice" before mentioning what she is "actually / hearing," an echo of the "actual garden" that's said to exist outside of the poem in "Song." The daisies warn the potential poet that she could be mocked and derided for mentioning flowers in a poem, for they somehow find "machines"—which are "the real world"—more worthy of being spoken about. What's interesting, though, is that the addressee never gets a chance to take advantage of the daisies' initial permission—"Go ahead: say what you're thinking"—which means we only ever hear the daisies say what they *assume* the person would say had she been allowed to speak.

Rationally, we know the poem to be a human creation, but the lack of a human voice in this poem allows us to skirt that knowledge. Strangely, the daisies' monopolization of the poem's language *prevents* the addressee from having to speak of speaking daisies and yet also *allows* that very thing to happen. Though the "you" is warned about speaking of the poem and its source (and, moreover, never does), by poem's end we (who may well be the "you") have come to know both what was "actually" said (the poem) as well as the identity of sayer ("Daisies"), however improbable an occurrence that might be in the actual world.

In several of his essays, Allen Grossman discusses the notion of the "virtual poem," the poem that "the actual poem (the text at hand) postpones, as it were, forever."[30] One of his examples is Wordsworth's "The Solitary Reaper," in which Wordsworth's speaker comes upon a girl in a field singing a song that compels him but which he cannot understand. Grossman writes:

The represented speaker (who also represents and thus anticipates the reader)—the man who says, "Behold her, single in the field"—obtains the munificence of the unrepresentable girl's untranslatable song by the concession implied in the professed incapacity of his report (*his* song of another kind) to include the great song that "overflows the vale." The virtual poem, thus indicated but not represented ("Will no one tell me what she sings?"), imports a boundless version of human worth that the mechanism of representation defers, and thus recovers in human scale. (174)

"Daisies" in a way inverts or turns inside out the structure of which Grossman speaks in that a version of the "virtual" poem does make its way to us, though not by way of the voice of the "unrepresentable" person who stands at the meadow's edge. Instead, "Daisies" presents us with flowers who—unlike Wordsworth's narrator, who cannot grasp the words of the singer who compels him—both understand and speak for the silent person who is compelled by them. What's "defer[red]" in "Daisies," then, is not what the person says, but rather the person herself, who is never allowed a voice in the poem but rather is only ever ventriloquized, thus aligning her in some way with the daisies, who must themselves be ventriloquized by Glück in order for the actual poem to happen. The poem's "you" is only ever at the edge of the meadow, at the edge of the poem and the speaker, and so becomes "virtual" in the way that the Wordsworth reaper's song is. The flowers speak the words that the "you" could say (and perhaps would say), and yet the "you"—who it seems to me "represents and thus anticipates" both reader and writer—always remains more addressee than speaker. Can any reader say for sure what was said in this poem and by whom?

In her essay "The Idea of Courage," Glück discusses the concept of "ecstatic detachment," a phrase that seems to describe perfectly the condition of the speaker of "The Red Poppy" and, more generally, the poet at work. She writes:

No matter what the materials, the act of composition remains, for the poet, and act, or condition, of ecstatic detachment. The poems' declared subject has no impact on this state. [. . .] The poet, writing, is simultaneously soaked in his materials and unconstrained by them: personal circumstance may prompt art, but the actual making of it is revenge on circumstance. For a brief period, the natural arrangement is reversed: the artist no longer acted upon but acting; the last word, for the moment, seized back from fate or chance. Control of the past:

as though the dead martyrs were to stand up in the arena and say, "Suppose, on the other hand [. . .]" No process I can name so completely defeats the authority of event.[31]

Compare this with the assertions of Oppen's that I quoted at this essay's outset—not to mention his claim in "The Mind's Own Place" that "with whatever sense of vertigo, we begin to speak from ourselves"—and surely an affinity between these two writers becomes visible.[32] Elsewhere in Oppen, we encounter the kinds of confidences and anxieties that also manifest themselves in "Song" and "Daisies": this, from an early letter to his sister— "To write poetry means to correct and to re-write, which would require a perfectly firm conviction of what's good and what's bad, what's better and what's worse"[33]—and this, from one of his daybooks—"One revises a line, one alters a word, then one revises the punctuation, and then one alters the line division—after altering the line, one restores the original punctuation. [. . .] In all that, who tells you what is right? Who is there? Who taught Reznikoff, or Bronk, or Naomi [Replansky]?? who was there?"[34]

Language sounded out, ecstatically, in shatteredness; some firm conviction, even in a question; the hole in—which may be the whole of—whoever watches over us in poetry's imaginary gardens, a place "[m]ore formal / Than a field would be."[35] The poem "is not speech," writes Oppen, and yet "we have thought our way into what we wanted to speak of."[36]

3

"LISTENING'S TRACE"

READING LORINE NIEDECKER AND

LISA ROBERTSON

JENNY PENBERTHY

I began this essay with the vague and improbable notion that Lorine Niedecker and Lisa Robertson shared a poetic sensibility. Reading their early
work in tandem, I was startled to find that their sensuous, zany, disjunctive
lines were practically indistinguishable:

"Nobody attests a grove of titles" (Niedecker, "Synamism," *CW*,[1] 36)
"This gem's purple tint annuls flowers" (Robertson, *XEclogue*,[2] n.p.)
"When I'm alone it's an open day. I clouded myself on him"
     (Niedecker, "Domestic & Unavoidable," *CW*, 69)
"I need the pleasure of a naked pinch as speech looms on a dowdy
     edge" (Robertson, *The Apothecary*,[3] 18)
"A loop / of blue light shows white organdie ruffles herself"
     (Niedecker, "Stage Directions," *CW*, 35)
"Succinct flowers thrust gauche / grammars into the air" (Robertson,
     Debbie: An Epic,[4] lines 37–38)
"But I'm bound to the fears of my weathers. / Are you ready to
     release the evening?" (Niedecker, "President of the Holding
     Company," *CW*, 71)
"What foliage / is betterment. Dissolute it browses / the mists"
     (Robertson, *The Weather*,[5] 42)

Resemblances such as these occur frequently in Niedecker and Robertson's
early work and compel my investigation of contingencies of sound and style
and of affiliation between the two poets, as I search for traces of influence
and, inverting the conventional genealogical narrative, view Niedecker's
early work in the light of Robertson's.

As a young writer, Robertson had considerable exposure to Niedecker's writings. Three of her four years at Simon Fraser University (1984–1988) included a part-time assistantship in the Contemporary Literature Collection, Special Collections, run by Charles Watts, who gave her free access to the extensive collection of small press–published books and journals. Robertson has written about listening to the recording of Niedecker reading her poetry—SFU purchased the original cassette tape from Cid Corman in the mid-1980s.[6] Among her teachers at Simon Fraser University were writers Robin Blaser, George Bowering, and Roy Miki. I had just graduated and was teaching at SFU too. At Miki's request, I met up with Robertson in the fall of 1987 ostensibly to talk about George Oppen. Instead we talked about Niedecker, whom Robertson had not yet encountered. Robertson recalls:

> You strongly advised me to read Niedecker, and so I did—I bought *The Granite Pail*.[7] [. . .] Catriona and I then closely read Niedecker together.[8] We were both craving female antecedents—our fabulous avant-gardist professors, though friendly to feminism, did not construct balanced syllabi. Though George taught much Stein, thankfully. It was a matter of epoch. The fact that we read Niedecker and Barnes and Loy on our own made it more important, radical, than if they had been in the syllabus. [. . .] A little later I had the Jargon Society Niedecker[9] and read it carefully.[10]

A few years later, in 1993, Robertson's bookstore, Proprioception Books,[11] launched my *Niedecker and the Correspondence with Zukofsky 1931–1970*.[12] Robertson remembers our conversations in 1996 following my discovery of Niedecker's calendar poem, "Next Year or I Fly My Rounds, Tempestuous," at the Harry Ransom Humanities Research Center in Austin, Texas,[13] and she remembers reading Niedecker's "Progression" in 1998, when it was published for the first time in *Moving Borders: Three Decades of Innovative Writing by Women*.[14] That same year I gave a talk on Niedecker—at Robertson's invitation—for the Kootenay School of Writing's Objectivists series.[15] I recall my delight, five years later, when she agreed to give a paper at the 2003 Niedecker Centenary Celebration in Milwaukee.[16]

I piece together this chronology of Robertson's encounters with Niedecker's work as part of an attempt to measure the proximities between a 1930s Objectivist and a twentieth-/twenty-first-century poet. What did Robertson glean from Niedecker? Can we infer a deep acquaintance with Niedecker's early work subtending those very similar lines cited at the start of this essay? Robertson's introduction to Niedecker occurred via *The Granite Pail*, which omits all of her longer-lined, Surrealist-inflected early writing. *From This Condensery* also obscures the early work, partly by omission and partly by displacing what remains of it from the chronology and burying it near the end of the book among a miscellany of "Other Writings."[17] However, Robertson was always alert for women's work consigned to the margins, and she may well have attended closely to the hybrid genre of "Radio Plays" lodged in "Other Writings."[18] While no trace of the plays survives in Robertson's notebooks — instrumental in the composition of her poems — her early poems resonate with Niedecker's.[19] Here's an example from a poetic drama by each:

LADY M: Splendid ardour most obviously mine! April is a mere tuck in your shirt.

NANCY: You're menacing and delirious. Your face could go back. . . .

LADY M: Which brings me irrevocably to the sulking plums: The dusk is a perfect record. . . .

NANCY: Of the deadly metonymy of your hips.

(Robertson, *XEclogue*, n.p.)

and

SHE
It's hard to glutinize in leafless time.
HE
Who has unsettled you about this matter?
SHE
Oh – appetizers, upholders of the law . . . .
HE
Would you be traditional in buttering your bread?
SHE
Not if there were plums to placate the ardor.[20]
(Niedecker, "Fancy Another Day Gone," CW, 77–78)

A decade later, when Robertson read Niedecker's "Next Year or I Fly My Rounds, Tempestuous" and "Progression," both of which emerged in the late 1990s and first appeared in print *after* Robertson's early books, she must surely have recognized herself in the poems, as though she had already felt their influence. Later in this essay I consider the impact of these two poems on Robertson's subsequent work. In response to my recent probings after a genealogy of influence, Robertson recalls a specific Niedecker-influenced project:

> [M]y little poems "porchverse" [. . .] were typed out as a sort of daily shorthand note-taking on things seen during dog walks, around 1997 or 98. I kept an old manual typewriter out on the porch on Parker Street, to this end, for an entire spring and summer. There was much typing and re-typing of tid-bits, which got whittled down in the re-typing. Maybe the most directly Niedecker-esque exercise I've done (deliberately, that is).[21]

The recurring robins and the porch of *The Weather*'s "porchverse"[22] may gesture toward Niedecker's acutely observed and sounded "Easter":

> *Easter*
>
> A robin stood by my porch
>   and side-eyed
>   raised up
>   a worm (*CW*, 193)

But looking at the more than one hundred pages of "porchverse" manuscripts, one realizes that the "Niedecker-esque exercise" that Robertson refers to lies more likely in the repeated "whittling down": "porchverse" finally occupies nine sparse pages in *The Weather*, evoking a Niedecker from the familiar "condensary" (*CW*, 194).

Vectors of influence can be subtle and indirect, if not unconscious, often recognized belatedly — even by the writer. A careful tracing of Niedecker's poetics across Robertson's oeuvre leaves no doubt that Niedecker should be added to any future catalogue of Robertson's predecessors. Summoning the audacious spirit of both writers and finding further permission in an "Objectivist nexus" already "disturbed, torqued, or folded upon itself" in its narration of literary history, I propose that one of the core 1930s Objectivists be accessed by a reverse process of examining the work of a descendant.[23] The reach of Niedecker's experimental practice is productively registered via a reading of Lisa Robertson, a twentieth-/twenty-first-century heir of a literary inheritance not yet fully tallied. Seen through the lens of Robertson's poetry and commentary, overlooked features of Niedecker's poetics begin to enter the field of vision.

Like Niedecker, Robertson acknowledges that she "went to school to

Objectivism."[24] By the time she moved to Vancouver in 1984, the rediscovered Objectivists had become required reading for an avant-garde poetic and critical practice. The Kootenay School of Writing had relocated to Vancouver and become a hub for avant-garde poetry in the city. Committed to interrogating the intersections of language, politics, and class, the Kootenay School would include in its lineage the politically radical and formally experimental Objectivists. In 1985 the KSW hosted the New Poetics Colloquium, bringing writers from across Canada and the United States, among them many of the Language poets of the day, some of whom had helped restore the Objectivist poets to visibility. Indeed, the experimental and critical method of Language poetry owes much to the Objectivists. Robertson recalls that "part of [her] access to Objectivism was via the Language poets and their essays."[25] Poet Catriona Strang, fellow Simon Fraser University student, remembers, "For about a year or maybe a year and a half [Lisa and I] were both absolutely steeped in the Objectivists. [. . .] For me the Objectivists were Zukofsky and Oppen and I was pretty fierce about including Niedecker as well. [. . .] I was aware of Rakosi and Reznikoff too, as was Lisa."[26]

Strang attended Peter Quartermain's 1986 KSW seminar on Zukofsky; together she and Robertson read *"A"* and the essays in *Prepositions*, and according to Robertson, "We all read *Sulfur*, which was a steady source of Objectivism."[27] The KSW poets continued to program Objectivist events side by side with others; they were themselves part of "an Objectivist continuum," Canadian neo-Objectivists to add to the American poets listed in *The Objectivist Nexus*.[28] That Niedecker and Robertson shared an early exposure to Objectivist poetry and poetics is a significant point of contact. Their reactions to it and shifts from it are sympathetic and may offer the strongest accounting for the commonalities that I address in these pages. For each poet Objectivism was formative, even among many other influences.

Robertson's early work coincided with the period of recuperation of Niedecker's fugitive writings. For the KSW women poets in the late 1980s and early 1990s,[29] inserting feminism into the discussion was an urgent priority. The historical silencing of women writers was increasingly visible and irksome to the KSW women: they knew of Niedecker's troubled textual history[30] and of Emily Dickinson's. Susan Howe attended the KSW's New Poetics Colloquium in 1985, the year *My Emily Dickinson* was published, and two years later she returned to run a workshop and to address the occlusion of key features of Dickinson's practice in the standard print editions of her poems.[31] Robertson's *XEclogue* (1993) acknowledges the little-read but often-satirized Edith Sitwell as a "constant companion."[32] Alongside such unfolding revelations about the historical reception of women writers, the KSW women were engaged in their own challenge to their male-centered collective, who "tended to subordinate gender considerations to those of class."[33]

Niedecker would undoubtedly have measured her difference from the male Objectivists. Among her "historic and contemporary particulars" would have been a historicized awareness of the patriarchy. "A woman poet in America during the 1930s and 1940s was by definition marginal," says Burton Hatlen, but the margins, he argues, were a "freely chosen [. . .] liberating space," and the poetry Niedecker "wanted to write could be written only from the margins."[34] Her situation, however, was more differentiated and less romantic than Hatlen implies. She worked hard to protect her insider status, which, among other things, gave her unimpeded rights to listen in on and document local conversation—all within an acute consciousness of the effects of class and gender marginalization. While she seems not to have written under an explicit feminist rubric, we can infer a feminist outlook.[35] She self-identified as one of the "modern women" invoked in her 1933–1934 poem "Progression" (*CW*, 28), and her early work confronts normative gender relations—for instance, the role reversal in "After dinner the women smoke and the men retire to the front room" ("Domestic and Unavoidable," *CW*, 69). A profound recognition of marginality pervades her early work, visible, for instance, in her conscious foregrounding and materializing of the peripheral: paratextual apparatus such as footnotes, stage directions, and "sub-entries" become her primary material.[36] All but one of the voices in "Domestic and Unavoidable" speaks from offstage. Her critical appraisal of the embedded codes and conventions of her time is thoroughgoing.

Neither poet defaults to a feminist essentialism. Instead, across a half century, they develop distinct and complex feminist writing practices. The deep compatibilities of these may be traceable in part to shared predecessors. In the early 1980s, Robertson "spent a lot of time reading women modernists from the 20s and 30s. Djuna Barnes, Mina Loy, Mary Butts, Gertrude Stein." She recalls that Djuna Barnes's "use of archaic style strongly influenced me and gave me a lot of permission. And I read [. . .] all of Woolf, and every writer Woolf mentioned."[37] Second-generation modernist Niedecker (not yet on Robertson's reading list) found important models among these same women writers. She too found permission in Woolf—whose novels animating layers of consciousness Niedecker borrowed from the Fort Atkinson Library—and in Djuna Barnes, Mina Loy, Mary Butts, and Gertrude Stein, whom she would have read in *An "Objectivist" Anthology* (1932) and in the avant-garde little magazines such as *transition*, *Contact*, *Pagany*, and others.

Emboldened by such forebears, Niedecker and Robertson both begin their careers with "stylistic over the top-ness," woman poets claiming and relishing new terrain.[38] Robertson reflects that "many of my past [works] have foregrounded this declarative, manifesto-esque forward push."[39] Exaggerated language is the medium of the KSW women poets' exuberant challenge to patriarchy, deriving in part from their feminist activism within the KSW collective. The "Giantesses"—Robertson, Strang, Christine Stewart, Susan Clark, and Nancy Shaw—enacted the creation of an independent feminist state named Barscheit Nation, with a "Giantess" manifesto and other pronouncements that satirized, among several targets, masculine modernist enterprises, the Objectivists among them: one of their journals bore the name *Giantess: The Organ of the New Abjectionists* with an unmistakable chime.[40] The theatrical "New Abjectionists" pit grand emotion against lean control in a raucous and hilarious parody of Objectivism and more generally of the intrinsic gender-coding of language. Their foray into language experiment was raucous and hilarious but also a pointed exposure of the intrinsic gender-coding of language.

It is striking that Niedecker entered avant-garde discourse with similar declarative force. She writes to Harriet Monroe in an exalted, oratorical tone: "The effect of propaganda in poetic (?) [*sic*] form has the effect on me of swearing that I as a writer will portray my epoch and truthfully evoke life in its totalities" (February 12, 1934)[41] and to her friend Mary Hoard, with rhetorical fervour: "I have said a writer has no business with any writing whatsoever that is not an extension of his [*sic*] own wit to comprehend. [. . .] It is my conviction that no one yet has talked to himself [*sic*]."[42] As with the "Giantesses," there is a performative quality in her manifesto-like certitude and the heroic role she adopts as poet. This vigorous style carries into the poetry too, where the forthright is more often laced with wit and irony: "I love you magnificently. I've had every drop of blood from the moonstone put into a venture for you" ("Fancy Another Day Gone," *CW*, 73). For both poets, an intervention into male-privileged literary territory is facilitated by "splashy bravado," establishing agency and access.[43] It was a conscious strategy for Niedecker as it remains for Robertson, who "still strongly identif[ies] with the call to inflate everything, as a tactic—stylistic, ideological, you name it. It's really what I do—I inflate language."[44]

For both poets, the first-person pronoun connotes agency and is flagged as a male prerogative that is irresistible property for women's trespass. For both, their appropriation is larger than life and heavily ironized; they savor their use of the "I" objectified by history: "a seizing of the moment of the pronoun, a moment of agency that's enabled by an entire historicity, having to do with everything: family, community, economics, sexuality, etcetera."[45] Pronouns are abundantly present in their early work: in Niedecker's "Progression" (parts II–VIII) and "Stage Directions," for example, and Robertson's *The Apothecary, Debbie: An Epic,* and *The Weather.* Objectivism's particularizing, anti-universalizing thrust would further account for the women writers' attunement to the politics of pronoun use. In Niedecker's case, the early modernist woman writer's acute ear for pronouns may well derive from a sensitivity to the conventional, universalized "he" in writing of the time—a feature of Niedecker's own prose (see her letter to Mary Hoard on the previous page) and, as another example, of Mina Loy's.[46] The absent feminine pronoun would be overtly politicized along feminist lines, and then opened beyond questions of gender to broadly experimental notions of subjectivity.

For Niedecker and Robertson, this would occur in the context of a careful negotiation with an anti-expressivist, decentralized subject. Their forceful pronouns are chosen in full knowledge of Objectivism's repudiation of unselfconscious positionings of the ego and the lyric self. Certainly, as Robertson suggests, a critical reading of pronouns presents new opportunities: "Using the first person as an impersonal opening device, as a way of not pinning language to my experience but opening language to other experience, [. . .] led me to the idea that I could use this 'I' in a non-referential [. . .] way."[47] Such comments of Robertson's are a useful gloss on her own and on Niedecker's methodologies. The many antecedent-free pronouns of Niedecker's early poems resist a narrow range of reference. They disperse voices and thus redistribute expressivity and affect. In "Progression," parts II–VIII, the frequent pronouns offer few and uncertain points of identification; they are voices among many others, and the subjectivities evoked are multiple. Here and there in the works of each poet one thinks one has located an autobiographical "I," but the intuition turns out to be unreliable in a context where "I" has no centralizing, enunciative priority over other voices. It is the "I" of a subjectless text.[48] Even the gift-poem written for Zukofsky, "Next Year or I Fly My Rounds, Tempestuous" cannot be read unequivocally as an intimate lyric—"Sonnets from Portuguese but such a difference!" was Kenneth Cox's response[49]—because its pronouns are in continual flux. For example, the direct lyric address on one of the poem's pages reconfigures, with a mid-sentence pronoun shift, as reported speech: "Good deed, my / love. The ele- / ment of folk- / time. Nerves / are my past / monogamy, / said her arms / going farther. / Rock me out" (*CW*, 57). Subjectivity is a surface effect rather than a guarantor of representational unity. The result for Robertson and, I suggest, for Niedecker, is "an entirely pliable handling of perspective. No subject position, but a distribution of subjectivity as equivalently charged at any point."[50] These multiple nonreferential, nonspecific pronouns become in themselves a figure for subjectivity.

Niedecker's teasing critique of Objectivism—"Objects, objects. Why are people, artists above all, so terrifically afraid of *themselves*?"[51]—arises from her concern that its anti-expressivist ethos has proscribed the vital terrain of subjectivity. Exploring alternatives to a centralized subject and looking for other principles of relationship within the poem, she foregrounds subjective relations.[52] Subjectivities are a live consideration for Niedecker and one that is obscured by the habitual depiction of her as a solitary figure. Such tropes conceal the gregariousness of her life and writing. She may protect her outsider privilege, but she is also very much *inside* her local community, differentiating its voices and subjectivities. Her short story "Uncle," one of many instances, provides a snapshot of the sociality of community life that she encountered in the 1930s.

These early poems are the same ones she describes as "tending toward illogical expression" with a hybrid "Surrealist tendency running side by side with Objectivism."[53] For Niedecker, "impenetrability" or "unrecognizability"[54] was a defining criterion for poetry, a measure of the mind at work and a source of the "something else"[55] that she located variously in nontranscendent interventions: in difficulty, citation, abstraction, and, as I argue later, in stillness or silence. Robertson's remarks about distributed subjectivity help identify a further source of "otherness" in Niedecker's early poems—the nonreferential pronouns that "[open] language to other experience,"[56] the unidentified pronouns that are destabilizing and "somehow spectral or other."[57] Across a half century, they each experiment with pronouns to free the poem from the "predatory intent"[58] of the subject-centered poet and to access other "dimensions of interrelatedness."[59]

The resulting dispersed subjectivity is a condition for polyphony. Robertson describes *The Weather* as an attempt to create a "polyphonic, multiply voiced layered text, where the effect would be many voices overlapping."[60]

Niedecker's 1930s *New Goose* poems,[61] for example, register the multiple voices of the anonymous, orally transmitted Mother Goose poems. Hers are written artifacts with a readily evoked written history, but they also exist as sonically resonant emblems of intersubjectivity, artifacts with a popular community currency as spoken or sung poetry, poems passed from one mouth and ear to another, capsule histories, intimate exchanges, rhythms immediately intuited by the ear. Referring to the quoted voices that appear in many of her own poems, Robertson says, "I feel this kind of address outwards, to a populated history, [. . .] an opening, an acknowledgement that all the forms of language are hosted by generous predecessors,"[62] and again, "To act within language is always to act among others."[63] Similarly, Niedecker's hosts are her family, her local community, her friends, her friends' children, and the writers and characters of her reading: from the "verbal sharing" of phatic communion—an aspect of her early socialization[64]—to her archive of written and spoken voices. In fact, her entire oeuvre resonates with layered voices in experiments with subjectivity in language: "the entire thick history of linguistic conviviality."[65]

It's possible that Robertson's reading of "Progression" alerted her to its multiple voices and weather vernacular before she wrote her own *The Weather*. Certainly it was my reading of *The Weather* that alerted me to the polyphonic and citational in Niedecker's "Progression," the first of her surviving poems to be written after her contact with Objectivism. The poem has a dense intertextual history; it locates in their voices the power and privilege indulged by historic iconic figures, and it interrogates patriarchy and capital in relation to the marginalized local realities that she knew so well. Part I opens with a toast[66] to friends kept awake at night by the moral failures of their society.

> Here's good health, friends,
> and soothing syrup for sleeplessness
> and Lincoln said he thought a good deal
> in an abstract way
> about a steam plow;
> secure and transcendental, Emerson avowed
> that money is a spiritual force;
> the Big Shot of Gangland declared he never really believed
> in wanton murder;
> Shelley, Shelley, off on the new romance
> wrote inconsolable Harriet,

"Are you above the world?
And to what extent?"
And it's the Almanac-Maker joyous
when the prisoner-lad asked the pastor
"Who is Americus Vespucius?"
and an artist labored over the middle tone
that carried the light
into the shadow.
But that was before the library burned. (CW, 25–26)

Shelley chastises his abandoned first wife, Harriet, who is pregnant and thus very much of "the world." Niedecker casts scathing light on Shelley's specious question and makes subversive fun of hierarchies of knowledge and patriarchal myth-making. The quoted and reported voices—"said," "avowed," "declared," "wrote"—parlay duplicities that she satirizes before turning to the subtle palette of the artist.[67]

After part I, "Progression" turns from historical voices to contemporary. At the time of the poem's composition, 1932–1934, the Midwest was suffering the bitter effects of the Depression and an unprecedented climate crisis. "Solid fact" (26) ridicules the abstractions of the privileged in the opening of the poem: the observable evidence of summer weather foretells winter food rations—"you tell by summer sky / how you'll pare your potatoes next winter" (26). The poem tracks the seasons and their disruption—its calendar is skewed by drought. Simultaneously, it tracks the intersubjectivity of a community, primarily via weather talk. Robertson notes in her compelling essay "The Weather: A Report on Sincerity" that "weather is the mythic equilibrium of the social, rising and falling in the numbly intimate metres of the commonplace. The real knowledge of weather is indigenous."[68] Reading "Progression" with an awareness of Robertson's *The Weather* helps locate their shared understanding of the weather as a rhetorical system, "a soothing, familial vernacular [. . .] expressed between friendly strangers."[69] Niedecker's ironized sentences mimic rhetorical forms and rhythms long in use: prognostications ("if / dessert be fragile sky, trees pink-rust, crisp as pie / with a butter-crust, I ought to be going home") (31); aphorisms ("there's nothing like a good warm cow / when the wind's in the west") (28); prescriptions ("And doctor, / nothing so good I know for intricate rhyme schemes") (30); and weather report-ese ("wind: strong distance in closest places") (31). The content is associative and often illogical. "Home is on the land" (26) resonates with a mythologized and nativist "home" and "land," recalling the refrain of the "Star-Spangled Banner": "O'er the land of the free and the home of the brave." Recording vernaculars of weather—the sociopsychological rhythms and locutions of a community in a cultural and economic landscape, a community with a challenging present and a palpable history—Niedecker's poem satirizes the irrationality of communal thinking while knowing that it leaves the community vulnerable to exploitation. Acutely aware of its historical situatedness, the poem trades in Objectivist particulars, in thinking as it occurs in language.

"Progression"'s collocation of linguistic social structures also includes an intervention into genre and thus another significant point of contact between these two poets. For Robertson, genre offers a "tactical"[70] and productive entry into history and politics: the disruptions of the pastoral for *XEclogue*, the epic for *Debbie: An Epic*, the georgic and the meteorological and scientific writings of the eighteenth and nineteenth centuries for *The Weather*. I would argue that the same is true for Niedecker's "Progression," where weather prognostication—particularly in extreme conditions—draws on a long spoken and written history of superstition, faux science, popular wisdom, hearsay, guesswork, and coercion. Benjamin Franklin's best-selling *Poor Richard's Almanac* was a classic of the genre and a target for Niedecker in both "Progression" and "Next Year or I Fly My Rounds, Tempestuous." Published under the pseudonym of Richard Saunders and presented by the persona "Poor Richard"—the keeper of the almanac already a persona layered with historical reference[71]—*Poor Richard's Almanac* was published for twenty-five years between 1733 and 1757. Franklin, Niedecker's "Almanac Maker" (*CW*, 26), worked within the conventions of the genre assembling an annual calendar of months and days, holidays and festivals, farmers' planting dates, tide tables, astrological and meteorological forecasts, much of it sourced from other authors and all purveyed as "science" and essential knowledge. His iteration was also widely read for its instructional poems, jokes, and aphorisms, all goading the entrenched working readership toward further hard labor and forbearance. Its success as a genre continued into the nineteenth century in the form of *The Old Farmer's Almanac* and was still published in Niedecker's time. *Poor Richard's Almanac* had enormous circulation, but Franklin's loosely disguised authorship and commercial opportunism was pilloried by Melville and Hawthorne among others and, in the 1920s, by D. H. Lawrence in *Studies in Classic American Literature*.[72]

Niedecker's "Progression" registers with full satiric force the eighteenth-century almanac genre and the thought habits of its author-marketer and his susceptible readers.[73] Her critical disruption of the genre ventures further in "Next Year or I Fly My Rounds, Tempestuous,"[74] a repurposed pocket calendar with an oddly disjunctive format: twelve months distributed over twenty-seven pages. Niedecker's pasted-in, palimpsestic text erases another whose structure, content, genre, and design she vigorously denies. The original aphorisms, intended to coerce a submissive populace ("We are to be rewarded not only for work done, but for burdens borne, and I am not sure but that the brightest rewards will be for those who have borne burdens without murmuring"[75]), are lightly concealed by Niedecker's pasted-in sentences that disrupt the discursive meaning and its ideological import. In *Poor Richard's Almanac* itself the famed aphorisms are tucked almost subliminally into the columns and rows of tables that list the monthly weather forecasts, the times of sunrise and sunset, the phases of the moon, astronomical and astrological information, and so forth. Their words are dispersed between rows descending in a column within a grid of "facts": "Tis against / some / mens / principle to pay / interest, and / seems against / others / interest / to / pay / the / principle." Niedecker's "Next Year" duplicates the narrow column and enjambed sentence but simultaneously destabilizes the traditional practice by substituting the typical aphorisms and homilies for gnomic utility- and morality-free lines: "I can always / go back to / fertilization, / kimonos, wrap- / arounds and / diatribes" (*CW*, 48) and "The trouble / is: this stirs / a real mean- / ing. / Humanity / is engaged – / on equal burial" (*CW*, 52).

Between 1997 and 2000 Robertson worked on poems that were eventually whittled down and published as "porchverse" in *The Weather*. Throughout this period, Niedecker appears to have been, in Zukofsky's phrasing, a "presence in the air [. . .] however conscious or unconscious."[76] The early version of a poem called "The Cashier's Calendar," for example, was written on close to one hundred cashier slips, narrow (1.5-inch) strips of paper of varying lengths (6 to 18 inches).[77] Working with this material constraint, Robertson handwrote poems, often diagonally, across the narrow strip: "the joke of / luxury: / we saw a livid / shrub / in disciplined / abandon / love's the opposite / of futurity / wanting / this same / now / could this be / true?" Niedecker's calendar poem, "Next Year or I Fly My Rounds, Tempestuous," was surely a model. The drafts of these poems reveal a variety of compositional procedures: large notebook pages are filled with prose-poetry from which lines of poetry are extracted and numbered; the numbered lines are sequenced, then resequenced, renumbered, recombined, and so on. Subsequent typewritten pages have carefully cut-out words and lines with other pages assembling the cut-ups. Robertson says of the Dadaist cut-up as a compositional strategy, "These techniques change the thoughts one can have."[78] The large collection of "porchverse" drafts and recompositions constitutes research into the operations of language. In the notebook she has circled her statement "We go to poetry for information about how language thinks."

For both Niedecker and Robertson, poems are acts of the mind, complex acts of perception, organizations of mental energy. In her 1934 letter to Pound that accompanies "Progression," Niedecker cites Tristan Tzara as an influence, no doubt engaged by his ludic disruptions of language and linear thinking, his incorporation of readymade language material, and the cut-up.[79] For the work of both Niedecker and Robertson, collage construction is a fundamental device for "achiev[ing the] odd associations," instability, and layered, multiplied resonance of the lines quoted at the start of this essay. The singular focus proposed by "Program: 'Objectivists' 1931" may well have galvanized resistance in the vision-impaired Niedecker. Zukofsky notes that "strabismus may be a topic of interest between two strabismics; those who see straight look away" (269).[80] "Seeing straight" is a hegemonic notion that both Niedecker and Robertson confront: "a white dome logic" is at odds with the "wayside strabismic house" ("Progression," 28): the logic of the state capitol versus the off-grid multiple perspectives of lived lives. As she tells Harriet Monroe on February 12, 1934, she favors concentrated relationships between words: multiple, layered, symphonic, and nuanced along with simultaneous rhyming sounds discernible to the ear and to the eye. The "objects, objects" that Niedecker resisted are primarily optical. Likewise, for Robertson the visual image may be a starting point — "porchverse" begins with descriptions of her garden or scenes while walking the dog — but the outcome is often a sound-image, temporal, not fixed, in flux.

> As the robin as the
> songsparrow go as the robin
> as the songsparrow go
> as the robin as the song (from "porchverse," *The Weather*, 77)

A measuring of proximities between the poets must ultimately address Robertson's 2003 essay "'In Phonographic Deep Song': Sounding Niedecker,"[81] a study, I would argue, that launches Robertson's productive research and writing about sound and caesura.[82] The essay identifies the central place of sound in Niedecker's work; indeed, the essay is a reminder of this affinity between them. Both work at the micro-level of sound; they know syllables intimately: "I love syllables first. After all the research, I work through the ear," says Robertson.[83] Likewise, Niedecker's poetry, from its earliest manifestations, is grounded in the sonic.

Pursuing Niedecker's investment in sound further, Robertson finds there a registration of perceptual processes—of "listening [as] a compositional practice rather than [. . .] a mode of consumption."[84] Indeed, Niedecker's heightened attention to the acoustic world is not unlike her practice of transcribing dreams, accessing genuine automatic writing, and calibrating different shades or planes of consciousness. "Progression," only somewhat fancifully, notes that "the emotion of fall has its seat in the acoustic gland" (31).[85] The same practiced ear for her locale tunes into the intersubjective nuances of conversation and voice. Robertson crucially identifies this contingent space of listening and thought:

> Listening is passive in that it receives, and artful in that it complicates, transduces, the assumed binary of inner and outer, of subjective experience and worldly economy, of reception and extension. And here I'd suggest that passivity is an intensely figured grouping of agencies and techniques of reception, rather than an erasure of agency, a feminized naught.[86]

Niedecker's early declarative embrace of agency occurred simultaneously with her theorizing of a deep, inviolable commitment to silence as a critical part of the economy of poetry. She complained to Pound: "Words blare (Joyce) and bunch together desperately and there are no gaps, no groups of undirect and familiar words, no blurs for sub-consciousness or for that lull which holds everything without announcement by horns."[87] The silence on which she depends is not a conservative, nostalgic, antitechnological, or orientalizing[88] fetishizing of the natural but one intrinsic to a poetry attuned to its production in perception. Here Niedecker's argument for silence as an active potentiality is closely aligned with Robertson's own theorizing of the caesura in which "a thinking gathers, dissolves, moves."[89] These active, listening silences and caesurae occur at points of fragmentation or irresolution—intrinsic to a collage methodology—often within and/or following a short truncated poem, and at points where a strabismic perspective sees the tangential and the heterogeneous rather than the thing itself.

You see here
the influence
of inference

Moon on rippled
stream

"Except as
and unless" (CW, 228–29)

It is the spaces between substantives that offer radical possibility. The
ephemeral unseen and inaudible are part of Niedecker's sensorium; for example, in "Progression" the inaudible is an explicit part of the acoustic landscape: "I must have been washed in listenably across the landscape / to
merge with bitterns unheard but pumping." The "saw and hammer a hill
away" are audible but unseen — "sounds, then whatsound" (31). Sound
artist Salomé Voegelin questions how the artist might grasp the "invisible
thing of sound"[90] in a statement that is remarkably apt as an account of Niedecker and Robertson's poetics:

> [L]istening is a generative performance that works from the unseen,
> the oddities, what falls out of representation, reference, and positive
> truths and remains fluid, invisible, hidden. It is the performance of
> unnamed materiality that generates the world in its own truth, whose
> openness accesses plurality, ethics, thought, and consciousness as
> efforts of participation rather than as givens.[91]

Comments throughout Niedecker's letters attest to her desire "to do something with the language of poetry which had never been done before."[92]
Before writing *The Weather*, Robertson commented that she "was trying to
find a space in language from which a meaning I hadn't imagined yet could
arise."[93] Listening is a figure for this attentiveness "for what else might
sound; to hear that [. . .] which has as yet no articulation."[94] Niedecker's
porch poem "Easter" is an image for the attentive listening of both the poet
and the robin, a space of potentiality. She would never arrive at a final satis-
fying articulation of the "something else" in poetry that she was "trembling
on the verge of";[95] it remained definitively beyond her grasp. This is "sincerity," perhaps even an Objectivist "sincerity": a steady doubt of the actual
and a steady pressure on the possible. Robertson could be speaking for both
poets: "The wild joy of writing now has to do with deepening my capacity
to enter into and sustain an equivocation, a space of cognitive ambivalence
where, rather than promoting and defending substantive positions, I explore the spaces between the substantives."[96]

4

MACRO, MICRO, MATERIAL

RACHEL BLAU DUPLESSIS'S *Drafts* AND

THE POST-OBJECTIVIST SERIAL POEM

ALAN GOLDING

Enough to look at here / For the rest of a lifetime
—Rachel Blau DuPlessis, "Draft 85: Hard Copy"[1]

"Objectivist": the best-known and earliest definitions of the term come from Louis Zukofsky's early essays "Program: 'Objectivists' 1931" and "Sincerity and Objectification," which both appeared in the February 1931 special feature in *Poetry* that Zukofsky guest-edited. Zukofsky stresses "Objectivist" over "Objectivism" (a term he is careful to avoid) since "the interest of the issue was [. . .] NOT in a movement" but in certain forms and qualities of poetic attention. In his definition, "Objectivist" refers to the *"desire for what is objectively perfect, inextricably the direction of historic and contemporary particulars."*[2] Out of this desire, "writing occurs which is the detail, not mirage, of seeing, of thinking with the things as they exist, and of directing them along a line of melody."[3] What is commonly emphasized in this formulation is the first phrase, "the detail, not mirage, of seeing," accurate rendition of the image, but in the interests of my argument here, which requires a capacious definition of the term "things," I'd like to stress equally the second: "thinking with the things as they exist."[4] These are the features of "sincerity," moving toward, in the best-realized poetic work, what Zukofsky calls the "rested totality" of "objectification—the apprehension satisfied completely as to the appearance of the art form as an object," "writing [. . .] which is an object or affects the mind as such" (*Prepositions*, 194). Sincerity also involves the art of omission, of the cut or the gap that is central to serial form: "When sincerity in writing is present the insincere may be cut out at will and information, not ignorance, remains" (201). As a way of seeing and of embodying those perceptions in poetic form, then, Objectivist sincerity moves toward seriality.

In "'Recencies' in Poetry," the introduction to his 1932 *An "Objectivists" Anthology*, Zukofsky expands upon some of these principles in ways relevant to a major experiment in post-Objectivist serial form, Rachel Blau DuPlessis's *Drafts*. More than in his previous essays, Zukofsky emphasizes what he calls "context—The context necessarily dealing with a world outside" of the poem (207). The Objectivist poem-as-object is here "an inclusive object," "binding up and bound up with events and contingencies," socially embedded by definition (207, 208). George Oppen writes similarly, many years later, that the image as an "act of perception" is "a test of sincerity, a test of conviction" projecting "the sense of the poet's self among things."[5] This location of the poem in a social world was always implicit in Zukofsky's "historic and contemporary particulars," but it becomes *explicit* in his later formulation in a way important for thinking about DuPlessis's socially saturated work.

In the introduction to their germinal essay collection, *The Objectivist Nexus*, DuPlessis and Peter Quartermain review the basic principles of the poetics in question: "The term 'Objectivist' has come to mean a non-symbolist, post-Imagist poetics, characterized by a historical, realist, anti-mythological worldview, one in which 'the detail, not mirage' calls attention to the materiality of both the world and the word."[6] They go on to connect Objectivist poetics with serial form: "The Objectivists, with their decided sense of the line and their inventive serial organization, use the basic nature of poetry—its 'segmentivity'—to articulate social meanings."[7] "Seriality is a central strategy of the Objectivist poetry of thought and of its constructivist debate with a poetics of presence and transcendence" in ways that directly impact the *post*-Objectivist: "All writers absorbing the Objectivist example consider the praxis of the poem to be a mode of thought, cognition, investigation—even epistemology."[8] Beyond the obvious example of her own poetic practice, discussions of seriality or serial form run throughout DuPlessis's critical work, from essays on Robin Blaser and George Oppen to those on the long poem as a genre and on her own poetics. The following observation on Lorine Niedecker can stand for much of her theorizing specifically of Objectivist seriality: "In its segmentivity and sequencing, its deliberate fragmentation, and intense economy, its building a poem by accumulating moments of sincerity, and its materialist claims, [Niedecker's] 'Paean to Place' is written saturated with objectivist premises and practices. [. . .] It builds meaning by the cut of the fragments and the blaze of white space between the parts."[9]

"One of the mid-1960's inventors of seriality along with Oppen and (from another poetics) Jack Spicer," Niedecker "invented a version of seriality as a mode of reflective moments playing realist images and meditative pensiveness against one another."[10] At the same time, versions of serial form lie at the Objectivist movement's very roots: in Oppen's *Discrete Series* (1934), in Zukofsky's "Poem Beginning 'The,'" or in Charles Reznikoff's nineteen-section *Rhythms* (1918) and his twenty-two-section *Rhythms II* (1919).[11] Serial form is the Objectivist answer to the problem of the long poem—the problem of how it may be possible to write one in the twentieth century and the question of whether a long Imagist (or Objectivist) poem is possible. "I am often asked whether there can be a long imagiste or vorticist poem," Ezra Pound wrote in 1914, and his answer, with some qualifications, is that "I see nothing against a long vorticist poem."[12] Objectivist seriality (in itself diverse and by no means monolithic) came to provide one means by which such a poem might get written.

As an analytical tool, what DuPlessis and Quartermain call the Objectivist nexus is a "three-dimensional model of participation, production and reception over time" that "allows one [. . .] to attend to rupture as well as continuity, and to dispersion as well as origin."[13] But it is also a space of ongoing poetic practice, and as such is precisely post-Objectivist (or, in DuPlessis's term, "neo-Objectivist").[14] "The Objectivist nexus" thus provides a framework for thinking about poetry "after" (chronologically, and on the model of) the Objectivists, poetry that is part of the Objectivists' ongoing reception and legacy.[15] In *Drafts* DuPlessis continues the Poundian and Objectivist notion that technique is the test of a woman's sincerity, that an ethos and an ethics emerges from the writer's attitude toward materiality—that of the object world and of language. For DuPlessis, "this makes an ethic of writing emerge simultaneously with the making of language. The basic 'rule' of technique is that every single mark, especially the merest jot and tittle, the blankest gap and space, all have meaning."[16] We might note the materialist language here (mark, jot, tittle, gap, space), the connection of linguistic materiality to ethics, and the location of meaning in the small, even the microscopic. Every material textual detail has meaning in what DuPlessis calls the "through-composed" long poem—"for me a poetics is expressed philosophically via the detail"—and that constitutes one definition of what it means to associate technique with sincerity.[17] In this essay I want to explore some of the ways in which these post-Objectivist concerns with the material detail and its mystery, and with scale—the relationships among micro, macro, and monumental—play out through her long serial poem *Drafts*.

In her preface to *Surge: Drafts 96–114*, the final volume of *Drafts*, Du-Plessis returns us to some of the basic features of the project, "certainly a work saturated in an objectivist ethos" (13). This ethos is defined partly by an Oppenesque sense of "the mystery that has always generated the poem. Perhaps the words for this mystery are IT and IS. These poems have, at any rate, returned to those concepts as an insistent continuo—or obbligato."[18] Specifically, Oppen's "Psalm" offers the canonical Objectivist statement of this ethos, its "sense of the poet's self among things": "The small nouns / Crying faith / In this in which the wild deer / Startle, and stare out," lines preceded by the exclamation "that they are there!" with its awe before the mystery and strangeness of being (Oppen's deer have "*alien* small teeth" [emphasis added]), its "sense of the poet's self among things."[19] To return to DuPlessis: "The poem certainly wants to talk of the mysteries of 'it.' And 'she' [the title of Draft 2] is faced with that 'it' and with all of it."[20] The pre-occupation with IT IS, then, is a fundamental part of *Drafts*'s objectivist ethos. In "Draft 33: Deixis" DuPlessis cites "a statement by Louis Zukofsky [that] offers the poetics of this kind of examination of the smallest words."[21] The key part of Zukofsky's 1946 statement reads as follows: "'A case can be made out for the poet giving some of his life to the use of the words *the* and *a*: both of which are weighted with as much epos and historical destiny as one man [*sic*] can perhaps resolve. Those who do not believe this are too sure that the little words mean nothing among so many other words.'"[22] DuPlessis weaves references to the principle of the "little words" through-out *Drafts*, often in ways that call up Oppen or Zukofsky. As one example: "Little words, / worming into incipience. / 'The a.' / Then, half-contrary, / 'a the.'"[23] "The" (the title of Draft 8) and "a" are tied to DuPlessis's move away from the bounded lyric and to her earliest imaginings of *Drafts*: "(*No more poems, no more lyrics. Do I find I cannot sustain the lyric; it is no longer. Propose somehow a work, **the** work, a work, **the** work, a work otherhow of enormous dailiness and crossing*) [emphasis added]."[24] This chantlike repetition invites a reading of *Drafts* as a kind of "the-work" and "a-work" immersed in the "enormous" (Zukofsky's "epos and historical destiny"). But again, DuPlessis's own "little words" are other: "it" and "is." I'll focus the next phase of my discussion on the operation of those two words in *Drafts*, following along the line of one that "Draft 1: It" inaugurates.[25] Tracing this particular line through *Drafts* will allow me to foreground not just the pervasive presence of the material object, as fact, value, and idea, throughout *Drafts* but also its *foundational* presence at the poem's beginning and at each re-beginning.

Drafts has two entirely appropriate epigraphs, raising as they do questions of attention to minute detail and of the appropriate form for "ungainliness," the latter term from Zukofsky's "*'Mantis,' an Interpretation*": "Feeling this, what should be the form / which the ungainliness already suggested / Should take?" The first epigraph, from Clark Coolidge, reads thus:

> The minutest details of
> sunlight on a shoe . . .
> had to be scribbled down,
> and with *extensions*.[26]

Consistent with these considerations of "minutest details" and of the form their scribbling down and multiple "extensions" might take, the project begins with nonhuman subject and object, "Draft 1: It"—both material and grammatical object, and the key Objectivist pronoun. Subsequently, every Draft on the line of one, the beginning of every fold, that is, every re-beginning in medias res, uses the phoneme "it" in its title: "Incip*it*," "Spl*it*," "In S*it*u," "P*it*ch Content," "Veloc*it*y." (More generally, the use of "little" words as titles—"It," "She," "Of," "In," "Me," "The" in the first eight Drafts alone—establishes early on their importance for the poem.) At the same time, *Drafts* begins with a questioning of Objectivist premises, or at least the desire to extend them: "to reinvent 'attention' is narrow tho tempting," though one "reinvention" that DuPlessis does embrace is that of the page as a visual and performative site for self-reflexive attention to language (*Toll*, 4). "Draft 1" features multiple iterations of the phrase "it is," the linguistic, philosophical, and ethical foundation of *Drafts*. One such iteration, "I / is it," anticipates numerous later variations throughout the poem on Rimbaud's "je est un autre," but lays out early DuPlessis's preoccupation with the self's relationship to the object world, including the objects that are words (4). Reinvented attention will focus on the materiality of both language and the page, of "putt (pitting) the tiny word / litt / it / on stage in a 'theatrical' space / a / space white and open a flat / spot a lite on / it" (5). Why "pitting," "litt," "lite"? To highlight, sonically and visually, the omnipresence of "it." If one persistent intertext is Robert Creeley's formulation from *Pieces*, "it — / — it," there's another reference to Creeley, and to his well-known "As soon as / I speak, I / speaks."[27] For DuPlessis's "Object (pronoun) / squeaks its little song its bright white / dear dead dark," but at the same time "CANO"—"I sing"—so that "I" and "it" become equally the subjects or source of the long song that is *Drafts*.[28]

If "It"—as title and as pronoun—encodes Objectivist materiality, one aspect of that materiality in *Drafts* is its self-reflexiveness, a persistent "spoilage of / presence" (*Toll*, 3) in the work that differentiates it from much Objectivist writing (3). From the beginning, *Drafts* is occupied with the material conditions of language and of its own (and any print-based poetry's) production: "it's / framed marks that make / meaning is, isn't / it? Black // coding inside   A / white fold open."[29] In "Draft 20," another beginning—"Incipit"—focuses on "it is" in a way that connects "it" again to the poem's self-reflexiveness, its "aura of endlessly welling commentary // folding and looping over // Is" (*Toll*, 131). The large, upper-case boldface "**I**" links visually with a similar **T** five lines later to form

IT.

This passage gives us DuPlessis's commitment to "it is" as a kind of fate: "And that was it. / It sentenced me for life" (131). Thus writing from "it is" constitutes a baseline measure of the objectivist ethos of *Drafts*, while linking "it" to and opening "it" into moments of midrashic self-reflexiveness marks an extension of that ethos, as an ongoing theorizing of poetics enters into the poetry itself to a far greater degree than in the original Objectivists' work.

In "Draft 39: Split," the beginnings of the third fold, "'It' mark dots / down on the page" (*Pledge*, 2). It does indeed, and those dots, again reminiscent of Creeley's *Pieces*, help construct the seriality of the form. "It," like Zukofsky's "the" and "a," has a historical destiny (not to mention density): "but speak of how that 'it' emerged // it's 'there' it's 'where' it's never what // you think Might be" (2). "That 'it' emerged," among other sources, from a literary and philosophical history that is encoded in the iambic rhythms of these lines, and that includes one especially relevant iambic pentameter couplet, Charles Reznikoff's canonical image of Objectivist it-ness to which DuPlessis refers multiple times in *Drafts*: "Among the heaps of brick and plaster lies / a girder, still itself among the rubbish."[30] Also hovering here is what DuPlessis calls the "always palpable / stripped intransigence" of George Oppen: "No way seeing is-ness / no way saying it-ness / except resistance," that point where the Objectivists' ethos meets their variously left politics (*Pledge*, 197, 3). "It" moves as a kind of bass line through "Draft 39" via deliberately obtrusive rhyme: "it," "legit," "split," "bit" in one eight-line sequence. As always in *Drafts*, "it" is both material world and text, detail and plenitude, micro and macro, as we move from this comment on Beverly Dahlen's *A Reading*—"'Reading "it" / by the endless invention of "it"'"—into the quintessential encapsulation of what "it" means in and to *Drafts*: "Where 'it' // splits and doubles between the little (unspoken) and the looming // (unspeakable)"—the totality (*Pledge*, 11). "Draft 39" then concludes, in one of the many allusive summaries of the project, in a playful use of Williams's three-step line rendered iambically: "to cast a dot of matter forth // and, farther, farther, troll it out, // through cusps of darkling antecedent sea" (12). That darkling sea gestures simultaneously toward Arnold's "Dover Beach," toward Homer and the "darker, antecedent sea" that closes "Draft 1," and toward the possibility of the female-authored post-Homeric long poem, called up in "Draft 1"—as tongue-in-cheek imperative? As declarative?—via the use of Homer's famous adjective in "little girls little legs jump the wine dark line."[31]

The self-enfolded serial poem in multiple books has to keep concerning itself with (re)beginning, restarting every nineteen Drafts at its material base, "It." By "Draft 58: In Situ," her fourth beginning, DuPlessis is acknowledging the challenge of any "simple beginning, in situ, / that is, in the middle," as the poem confronts the impossibility, for her, of certain Objectivist ideals and of practices historically associated with the epic: "I just wanted simplicity, or relief, / wanted to list items" (*Torques*, 1, 3). However, "it lists [i.e., leans], it tilts—the it of all of this: / How account for it; how call it to account?" (5). Meditations on the traditional epic beginning, in medias res, break down in the face of political rage and human loss (a student suicide), as does the Objectivist impulse toward documentation or recording, the all-inclusive ambition to write a tale of the tribe, and the convention of the epic catalogue: "This was to be a straight-line list, / itemizing what was at stake" (1). Like "In Situ," the next poem in the line of one, "Draft 77: Pitch Content" begins the volume *Pitch: Drafts 77–95* by considering how to begin and by personifying the "it" that drives all of DuPlessis's re-beginning: "'*It wants to write. It wants me to / write it*, [. . .]'" in an epigraph from Hélène Cixous (*Pitch*, 1). After the epigraph, the first line of text has the effect of a Zukofskyan beginning, invoking both his little words and his long poem: "*A*," that line reads, and it's awfully hard for a reader of the Objectivists not to complete it as "A / Round of fiddles playing Bach."[32] In contrast to that social plenitude, we have "A / first page empty, blank and null"—the blank verso opposite this recto (*Pitch*, 1). For all that, however, sound and music do dominate this Draft that echoes "*A*," "the It / of impercipient vibrato"—here, "it" is all sound (4). In "Draft 96: Velocity," by contrast, "it" is all speed and motion—verbs like "pulse," "push," "surge," "plunge," and "sweep" dominate the first sentence. Zukofsky may well be present here also at the end of this last beginning, in a closing sentence that "*calls outright to A*," Zukofsky's key little word and the first letter (*Surge*, 26). The more visibly modernist presence, however, is Williams, not just in DuPlessis's use of his triadic line but in the reference to his great poem of (re)beginning, "By the road to the contagious hospital." In "Draft 96: Velocity" the figure for "it" is a swallowtail butterfly, "gripping down" like Williams's plants, babies, and new American poems: "rooted they / grip down and begin to awaken."[33]

Just as each volume of *Drafts* begins by returning to the ground of "it is," so each one closes with a variation on the ongoingness of poetic labor, of the work with "it is" that will end only with death: hence the doubled invocation in the last two lines of *Drafts 1–38, Toll* to "work until it tolls. / *And work until it tolls*."[34] *Drafts 39–57* moves toward these lines while linking "workplace" and "nekuia," mundane space of daily labor and necromantic poetic rite: "It is hard to know why / this site is so implacable / but it is, clearly it is" (*Pledge*, 221–22). *Torques: Drafts 58–76* closes with endlessness, with re-beginning, and with the citationality that forms one core aspect of DuPlessis's poetics. The volume's last page brings the invocation to "Begin! / Here! And Here!" while its last words appropriate the mail artist Ray Johnson on (self-)appropriation: "'My works get made and then chopped up, and then reglued and remade, and then chopped up again, the whole thing is really endless'"—reasserting, at a point of temporary closure (the end of the book), the open-ended constructivist nature of the work, something close to an infinite series.[35] Similarly, on the last page of *Pitch: Drafts 77–95*, "it" imposes itself yet again on the reflective poet: "Is this what I wanted to say? / It is said. Is it what I wanted? / It is what came out. // It chose me." Thus chosen, one can only continue writing beyond the ending, and "Draft 95," via the image of restarting a faulty watch, "ends" by anticipating the work ahead: "I knock it hard to start it up again, / hitting the table where I do my work."[36] The earliest parts of "Draft 1: It" date from May 1986, when "it? that? // plunges into every object / a word and then some" (*Toll*, 1). One hundred and fifteen Drafts later, in 2012, the poem is both concluding and ready to continue beginning with the Objectivist "it":

There are so many tasks. To start.

Up. Again.

Like this. The is. The it.

Id est:

So vector the crossroads once again!
Volta! Volta! (*Surge*, 160)

Thus, on "it is," the two little words that have driven it, and on another turn (volta), *Drafts* concludes in a (its) beginning, "closes without ending" (*Surge*, 1).

So, little words, big poem, a poem that consciously engages "the whole area of cultural ambition, to open up into the largest kind of space, the challenge of scope itself."[37] "It is" turns out to be crucially connected to "the challenge of scope" and of interpretation in this contemporary poetics of Mass Observation: "These are poems challenged by—moved by—the plethora. [. . .] Here is a typical situation: small to large, tiny to largest. It is about the plethora of stars, that vastness, and the dot or yod, the most minuscule mark. That *it is*. That we can read it" (*Blue Studios*, 214), As a simultaneously formal and social question, that of scale is insistently, though complexly, gendered in *Drafts*. DuPlessis is drawn, as poet and critic, to the creation of "large and encompassing structures *with a female signature*" (emphasis added), following on such female modernist models of ongoing, large-scale production—of "writing a gigantic oeuvre, a mound of oeuvre"—as Dorothy Richardson and Gertrude Stein ("An Interview," 404). Early in her critical career, she claims "in [one aspect of] women's writing [. . .] there is an encyclopedic impulse, in which the writer invents a new and total culture, symbolized by and announced in a long work, like the modern long poem"—a work motivated, that is, by "the thrilling ambition to write a great, encyclopedic, holistic work, the ambition to get everything in, inclusively, reflexively, monumentally" (*Pink Guitar*, 17, 9). At the same time, however, as a poem in the Objectivist tradition *Drafts* is also committed to a constructivist poetics of close attention to the immediate concrete detail or fragment, refusing any kind of panoptical perspective, a constructivist poetics that is also a *feminist* poetics of writing against the long epistemological, cultural, and literary tradition of coding the detail female. Around the time that DuPlessis was beginning *Drafts*, Naomi Schor offers a "feminist archaeology" of the detail in which she analyzes its "participation in a larger semantic network, bounded on the one side by the *ornamental*, with its traditional connotations of effeminacy and decadence, and on the other, by the *everyday*, whose 'prosiness' is rooted in the domestic sphere of social life presided over by women."[38] But Schor is equally interested in the redeeming of the detail as a site of value within materialist and realist modernism: "the ongoing valorization of the detail appears to be an essential aspect of that dismantling of Idealist metaphysics which looms so large on the agenda of modernity."[39] Thus an Objectivist poetics, in this view, becomes a way to undo the feminization of the "detail"; *Drafts* engages ongoingly with and in this gendered history and modernist degendering of the detail.

A foundational essay on the question of "scale" in women's long poems remains Susan Stanford Friedman's 1990 "When a 'Long' Poem Is a 'Big' Poem," in which she ventures "some generalizations about women's status as outsiders in relation to the genre and the self-authorizing strategies in which they have engaged to penetrate and transform its boundaries."[40] "In this horizontal-vertical discourse," Friedman argues, in which the long poem asks "big" or "deep" questions and does so at length, "vast space and cosmic time are the narrative coordinates within which lyric moments occur, the coordinates as well of reality, of history" (72). While I'd question whether Friedman's account of women's relationship to the genre of the long poem continues to pertain, it remains a compelling historical account: "Rooted in epic tradition, the twentieth-century 'long poem' is an overdetermined discourse whose size, scope, and authority to define history, metaphysics, religion and aesthetics still erects a wall to keep women outside" (723). Without using the term, Friedman refers here to the totalizing impulse; in response to that impulse, DuPlessis uses the serial form of *Drafts* to construct what she calls "an anti-totalizing text in a situation with totalizing temptations."[41] In the face of Friedman's accurate claim that the woman's long poem is no longer centered on a male hero's quest, *Drafts* maintains "the general aura of quest just as a baseline," though that baseline has its limits: "not hero, not polis."[42] But it does so in the interests of "a distinct demasculinization of the genre," of moving away from the long poem "as a masculine discourse of important quest-ions" while maintaining its scale and ambition.[43]

What are the different *kinds* of scale or ratio about which one could talk in *Drafts*? There is scale at the level of language, where DuPlessis mainly focuses on the micro: the serif, the tiny visual mark, the point (iota, yod). Then language is persistently felt as inadequate to the articulation of the macro, of enormity or plethora (both recurring terms in the poem). There is scale at the level of perception: what can be seen at the tiniest level as against a cosmic or astronomical scale, the microcosmic or the "micro-moment" and the macrocosmic. By the time DuPlessis invokes Blake's grain of sand in *Pitch*, the reader has been waiting for it for quite some time, while the term "micro-moment" lets us know there are questions of temporality at work too.[44] Scale in the area of genre or poetic method would set the monumentality of *Drafts* against the method of constructing this massive non-whole that "closes without ending" out of fragments, debris, "little stuff," bits and pieces, moments of what once was called "lyric."[45] Even the extensive notes to *Drafts* can be seen to participate in this ratio: "The note. The Note! a feminist task of the Scholiast!—the annotation, condensing enormous cultural pressures into a tiny meaningful margin, tracking around the monumental, following traces" (*Pink Guitar*, 130).

I want to think about the possibilities of an anti-monumental monumentality as one approach to what is, after all, at 992 pages one of the longest long poems of the twentieth and twenty-first centuries—large scale without monumentality as a way to claim, and as an analogy for, poetic authority without hierarchy.[46] Sheer mass in poetry, DuPlessis suggests, can itself constitute a cultural intervention, an obstacle that requires negotiation: "The modern/contemporary long poem often exists to put an unassimilable mound of writing between yourself and culture as usual; a large realignment of what you know and what you see takes shape in it."[47] At the same time, this "mound" is composed of the debris or rubble that forms one central motif in *Drafts*: "Perhaps the experimental long poem of our era smashes the epic into lyric shards as a social critique precisely of the totalizing ethos of the epic."[48] *Drafts* is both the practice of and "also a theory of debris," "*theory of the shard*."[49] We can map macro, micro, and questions of gender onto DuPlessis's concerns with monumentality and its shattering into rubble, a recurring term that will actually end up returning us to DuPlessis's Objectivist roots. I have written elsewhere on DuPlessis's complex relationship to Poundian monumentality, itself reduced to rubble: "my errors and wrecks lie about me. / And I am not a demigod, I cannot make it cohere."[50] In particular, "Draft 15: Little" contemplates the project and method of this millennial and monumental non-epic: "Not hero, not polis, not story, but it. / It multiplied. / It engulfing. / It excessive," "the little / stuff agglutinating in time, debris" (*Toll*, 102). The seemingly throwaway term "little" is here a poetic or formal and ideological commitment, with its own lineage running, as I have been arguing, through the Objectivists and—in the recurring image of "debris"—through Walter Benjamin. And here that "little" term "it" is linked simultaneously to the macrocosmic—"it" is what is multiplied, engulfing, excessive—and to the counter-epical agglutination of *Drafts* (including the accumulating moments of sincerity that cumulatively establish the Objectivist ethos).

The dialectical relationship between macro and micro is fundamental to DuPlessis's project: "This conflict or incommensurability of little and large and its unstable resolution [. . .] might be what incites anyone to write a long poem in the first place."[51] And the "conflict or incommensurability" finds its appropriate form in post-Objectivist seriality. "Draft 49: Turns & Turns, an Interpretation" is a poem formally and conceptually in dialogue with Louis Zukofsky's "'Mantis'" and "'*Mantis,' an Interpretation*" (the source of her epigraph on "ungainliness" seeking appropriate form, as it does throughout *Drafts*). The lineated essay "Turns, an Interpretation" poses this question-and-answer: "What is the form for motion, what is the form for dialectical shim, / for self-quarreling and readjustment—serious, humorous? / It's seriality: / its quick shifts and sectors, / its questions at each moment of articulation. [. . .]" Importantly for DuPlessis, the nature of seriality refuses resolution: "What single message from [Oppen's] 'Of Being Numerous'?"[52]

Via the trope of debris, let me return to Charles Reznikoff's couplet, from *Jerusalem the Golden* (1934):

Among the heaps of brick and plaster lies
a girder, still itself among the rubbish. (*Poems*, 107)

In ways centrally relevant to *Drafts*, this is partly a poem about the interconnectivity of singleness and plurality, "*a* girder" and "*heaps* of brick and plaster." More precisely, it is also about *distinctive* singleness, what one might call "it-self-ness," and its relationship to a *muddying* plurality, the indistinct "heaps" and "rubbish." Oppen repeatedly invoked this poem as an iconic, almost foundational or originary moment in Objectivist poetics—hence its notoriety—and always misquoted it, substituting "rubble" for "rubbish." In turn, DuPlessis consciously adopts this misquotation, returning to "rubble" as a persistent motif throughout *Drafts*: rubble as the shattered fragments of a broken whole, but rather more poignant, even elegiac a term than the more judgmental "rubbish." In one formulation we find "the girder   amid, between, among, above, / the rubble   under, on, from, next to, within"—little words making up what DuPlessis calls "prepositional debris" elsewhere in the poem.[53]

Monuments and their breakage recur throughout *Drafts* as a figure for the work's form, method, ethos, and cultural politics. Given "the monsters to whom / Monuments are built," it's no surprise to encounter the following faux cross-reference: "As for monuments— / see ambivalence" (*Pitch*, 56, 44). But these monuments don't survive intact; what survives is the trace, at least tentatively, somewhere, sometimes, even as it "makes no claims / that it will survive" (105). As well as the erosion of male power by time, the statue of Ozymandias to which DuPlessis alludes in "Draft 87" represents, as it did for Shelley, "monumentality / broken and scattered" into "trace elements," "which implies / not that trace / is outside of structure, but that it is / the shattered bits of former structure" (92). "Improbable Babel left in rubble, / This poem almost became its own erasure. / Almost blanked itself out," but was able to "let in fissure, fracture, broken shard" (129). This is the way, returning to the image of *Drafts*'s opening page, where handwritten capital Ns take the form of mountains, to "make the book an imitation mountain, but with real hard strata. Data": the poem made up of the shards of its own always already shattered monumentality, on the *scale* of a monument but with none of its features.[54]

5

JOHN SEED'S POETICS
OF THE PUNCTUM

FROM MANCHESTER TO THE "MAYHEW PROJECT"

ROBERT SHEPPARD

Objectivism—particularly as a poetic hygiene of concision and attention—
can be traced in the poetics of many writers of the British Poetry Revival
(1965–1978) and after, who turned away from the civilities and gentility
of the Movement Orthodoxy.[1] This poetics was often allied to a general
interest in the tradition from Pound through to Olson, the technical inheritance from Imagism to Projectivism, which, because retrospectively experienced, arrived at once in Britain, often without temporal discrimination.
There were some direct, though intermittent, contacts: Zukofsky visited
Gael Turnbull and Roy Fisher in the 1950s, for example, and writers as different as Jonathan Griffin and Charles Tomlinson can be found associating
with both the writers and writings of Objectivism in this period. Two particular British contexts are of some importance. One is the work of Andrew
Crozier in rediscovering Carl Rakosi in the 1960s (indeed, energizing him
to write again). The other was the existence of a British (he might have in-
sisted upon English, even Northern English) Objectivist poet, Basil Bunting. It may be no accident that his native Northeast (where he resettled after
a lifetime's wandering) was not only the specific site in terms of subject
matter and place of writing of Bunting's late masterpiece *Briggflatts* (1965),
but also the meeting place of admiring and younger Objectivist-orientated
writers, from Tom Pickard in 1960s Newcastle to Richard Caddel in 1970s
and 1980s Newcastle and Durham. And also of John Seed (who hails from
Chester-le-Street, near Durham), who summarized both the qualities they
admired in Bunting and the perceived deficiencies of the Movement Orthodoxy: "The crispness, the taut energies and clarities of *Briggflatts* were so
splendidly different from the dreary storytelling and slack attitudinizing of

what usually passed for poetry in post-war England that it is not surprising that a new generation of readers (and listeners) was dazzled."[2]

Whereas the original "discoverers" of Bunting took technical lessons from him—Pickard developed his musicality and alliterative verve, Barry MacSweeney learned the necessity of Objectivist concision in the service of an ever-impacted discourse—John Seed, coming later in the 1970s, found not technical devices (as we shall see, he learned these from other Objectivists) but a political and ethical attitude, one that he regarded as historical and specifically English. He cast to one side Bunting's own arguably protective privileging of sound over sense in his poetics ("*Briggflatts* is a poem: it needs no explanation. The sound of the words spoken aloud is itself the meaning") in favor of a reading that focuses upon content and, even more so, context.[3] (Bunting of course qualified his poetics: "I've never said that poetry consists *only* of sound.")[4] In his 1998 essay "An English Objectivist? Basil Bunting's Other England," Seed acknowledges the importance of Bunting as a link to American Objectivism, although as Bunting's activities were at the fringes of any literary culture, he shies away from asserting his *influence* as "an English Objectivist." Furthermore, "Bunting remained loyal to certain traditional literary conventions throughout his 'career.' If at times he uses fragmentation, disruption, shifting voices"—as in the section-by-section scene-shifting collage of *Briggflatts*—"he also uses traditional forms, such as narrative and ballad."[5] Seed notes parallels to Eliot: for example, "Bunting continued to share the animus of his generation against all that was represented by the terms 'Romantic' and 'Victorian,'" a huge contrast to Seed's own work, which, as we shall see, relates to the Romantic Shelley and the Victorian Henry Mayhew (119).

Seed identifies a contradiction at the heart of Bunting's poetics because "much of [*Briggflatts*] can be located fairly comfortably in the tradition of English landscape poetry," and Seed catalogues "Wordsworth, Gray, Hardy and others" as influences (120, 121). However, Seed, a historian of English nonconformism, recognizes a deeper, alternative history, embedded in choice of poetic territory and title for his epic, and one deeper than the orthodoxy represented by Eliot's traditionalist cultural poetics, conservative politics and practice in *Four Quartets*: "Bunting's allegiance to the Society of Friends and to the specific meeting house at Briggflatts had little to do with theological doctrine [. . .] and much to do about finding an anchorage in some kind of oppositional cultural tradition and in his own history" (122). Seed admires Bunting as a receptacle of an underground English tradition of nonconformist radicalism, specifically that originating in the ferment of the English Revolution of the seventeenth century, that Seed acknowledges in his own earlier, and later, work, as we shall see. Rather than a textbook of poetic techniques for the young poet, "*Briggflatts* is a profoundly English poem, though one which contests what dominant institutions have decided what 'English' and 'England' means" (216). "England" is a word that haunts Seed's own work as a contestable enigmatic sign.

Seed's earliest published poems are Imagist, sparse, "direct" treatments of things, without comment, with a strong use of space and (as time progresses) abrupt enjambment rather than euphony or regular metrics. In an untitled poem, we see what Charles Altieri identifies as the essential Objectivist way of measuring the world through acts of attention: "Objectivist poetics creates an instrument sufficiently subtle to make attention and care [...] ends in themselves. Attention, care, and composition become testimony to levels of fit between the mind and the world in rhythmic interactions that require no supplementary justification in the form of abstract meaning."[6]

In a subtle placing of lines, one of Seed's poems moves, without explanatory commentary, from the opening natural image of "winter sun silver over the waves," with its slight alliteration, to its final identification of (and with) the impedimenta of the industrialized seashore: "cranes silent along the dockside."[7] Images of the natural world and the manufactured world meet but resist merging through contrasting qualities of attention, in "the glitter of metal and glass / through the bright haze" (15). Page after page of the earliest poems in his *New and Collected Poems* (2005) (though usually without the slight sonority of conventional alliteration found here) abut the natural or the perceptual with the spectral traces of industrialized modern Britain. "Collage construction enables images to become a form of thinking," Altieri suggests; and the title of another poem, "Lindisfarne: Dole," presents a deliberate juxtaposition (even an inexplicable equation with its colon) of the ancient monastic island (which hints toward the conspicuously nonindustrial landscapes of Bunting's *Briggflatts*) and unemployment (which was rising in the early 1970s).[8] The poem itself contrasts the underemployed "walking, dreamless for hours" with the hard reality of "England's coast," which is as much a sociological construct as a geological feature: "England's coast this / Alien place," "Nightshift" observes (*New and Collected Poems*, 12, 33). A decade later, "During War, the Timeless Air," dated "England May 1982," is similarly situated, "At the nation's edge," in order to consider the Falklands War ("For a moment almost free"), where existential transcendence (the timeless air out of the time of war) is not unlike the inner freedom of the "dreamless" liminal perambulation of the dole poem (39). Care and attention are straining for political perspectives, but avoid "abstract meaning" in collagic thinking.

It is instructive to examine a poem addressed to an American Objectivist that deals with Manchester, a city central to Seed's work, despite his northeastern background. Adopting the same marginal convention used (and abandoned in later work) by Oppen, of capitalizing after line breaks while allowing for hanging indented lines without this convention, Seed, in "From Manchester, to George and Mary Oppen in San Francisco," begins in fragile *media res*, and clearly establishes urban deprivation as a shared theme with Oppen:

> this city has its beggars too
> Lonely and threadbare in bronchial gloom
> like the sparrows
> Imagining bread or Spring (43)

The notorious damp of the region is evoked well at the human level, the sparrows (not Bunting's dialect "spuggies" here) imaged and imagined as themselves imagining shorter- or longer-term respite. After an ellipsis, Seed alludes (in homage and identification) to Oppen's "Of Being Numerous" (1968), with its realization of the Crusoe-like human "shipwreck" of the singular being in the modern metropolis:

> [. . .] or the solitary
> Traveller   here and not here
> In the crowded night of streets (43)

The enjambment "solitary / Traveller" makes the isolated Romantic figure more so, as the capital on "Traveller," rather than being a mere metrical convention, raises the noun to a proper noun. Travel is not now "dreamless" but semipresent, transient, and the descent of "night" (a resonant word in Seed's work) invades the streets and crowds it (empty but populated with isolating vacancy). This "Traveller" is finally

> Dreaming each footstep
> Home
>
> indecipherable
>
> ache beneath the ribs (43)

The footsteps are only imaginary or aspirational, the whole process unreadable (words like "indecipherable" and "impenetrable" recur throughout

Seed's work), leaving only the desire as pain, but also reminding us of the bodily symptoms of bronchial disease, corporeal "gloom" (a determinant of poverty). The ever-rightward adjustment of the visual page, line by line, tilts the reading away from a discursive ending. "Indecipherable," the untranslatable, the inaccessible, could relate equally to the "dreaming," "the footstep(s)" or the "home" by prior syntactic linkage, or to the "ache," by anterior connection. In all cases the Oppenesque theme of the "solitary" (the word that is ranged farthest to the disappearing margin of our conventional reading page in Seed's poem) is a code that cannot be accessed (43). (A number of Seed's poems enact this by placing a solitary "I" at the end of a line.) What Burton Hatlen says of Oppen goes for Seed: "Oppen [. . .] perfected a poetry in which syntactic interruptions and suspensions open up abysses within which the unsayable resonates behind, around, and within what gets said."[9]

"For Oppen," writes Altieri, "sincerity is above all an ethical term."[10] Seed shares Oppen's perspective: "The potential he saw in 'historical and contemporary particulars' was a sense of social purpose without agitprop posturing" (9). The "gloom" and negative "night" reappear in Seed's later Manchester poem, untitled but dated "11 vii 1992" as, first, the "Architecture of solitude" but also as the "Continuous Victorian night," which embodies the ideology of Thatcherite Britain and looks back to Manchester's industrial past.[11] The poem is situated social commentary but without agitprop intent, as it rehearses the theme of "solitude" and expands the political and ethical associations of "night."

John Seed's 2013 book *Manchester: August 16th & 17th 1819* is a fascinating example of work written *after* Objectivism. *Manchester* is a "lost" manuscript, a poem written in 1973, at the beginning of his career, and provides a curious precursor to what I will dub Seed's "Mayhew project" of 2005 and 2007. Seed's techniques of appropriation, in both early and late works, are clearly derived from the practice of Charles Reznikoff rather than Oppen. Seed had purchased the 1965 edition of *Testimony* in the early 1970s at the Ultima Thule bookshop in Newcastle, one of the centers of the Northeast poetry scene. In his afterword to the book, Seed outlines the writing of *Manchester* and accounts for his *direct* communications with Reznikoff at some length. In July 1973 Reznikoff had replied to Seed's letter containing a copy of the poem (or part of it), not with a critique but with a series of practical suggestions for publication, even offering to send it to his publisher, Black Sparrow, though Seed thinks Reznikoff was merely being kind. Seed in return indicates that he had been using Reznikoff's *Testimony* in his student teaching practice, with schoolchildren in Hull, as stimulus for their own creative appropriations of local news sources. Seed saw Reznikoff's work as directly applicable as a method, in teaching others to write and think, and (as we shall see) in his own developing practice.

> I was very interested in how historical materials were used in *Testimony*. [. . .] Reznikoff's method was simple and direct. Working through thousands and thousands of court cases from the late nineteenth century for a law publishing firm in the 1930s, he occasionally spotted one that grabbed his attention. He then edited it, cutting away extraneous material but not significantly changing the language of his source, until he was left with a crisp concise narrative of an event or description of a situation.[12]

"The testimony," he continued, "is that of a witness in court — not a statement of what he felt, but of what he saw or heard," or — more accurately — read (51). This legal analogy is important, but Seed professionally works with documents of a different kind; a social historian since the 1970s, he was allied to the left-leaning "history from below" movement of that decade that followed the rich example of E. P. Thompson's *The Making of the English Working Class* (1963). Seed recalls: "The duty of the socialist historian was to bring alive the experiences and the consciousness of working people in the past, to retrieve an alternative people's history and an alternative cultural tradition."[13] Seed notes, similarly, "Reznikoff imagined a history of the United States as the testimony of many different witnesses, a chorus of voices" (*Manchester*, 52).

Seed's "testimony" concerned Manchester's "Peterloo Massacre," which he read about in Thompson's monumental tome, but he offers an ancillary contemporary motivation: "Maybe subliminally it particularly interested me because of the experience of being confronted by mounted policemen in and around Grosvenor Square on several occasions between 1969 and 1972. Thompson's was a text for the times" (42). Grosvenor Square was the site of the US Embassy, and the "occasions" were demonstrations against the Vietnam War.

Occurring before Manchester's Victorian industrial growth, the Peterloo Massacre was nevertheless a constituent event of the *making* of its working class. On that August afternoon in 1819, the Manchester Yeomanry were responsible for breaking up a radical meeting, attended by 60,000 men, women, and children, at which the radical Henry Hunt was speaking and at which the yeomanry attempted to arrest the great orator (and succeeded, eventually). The inept yeomanry were unable to control the now-riotous crowd, aroused by the death of a child. The more professional hussars were then dispatched to assist, but the yeomanry were largely responsible for the ensuing massacre, as the unarmed people fled. There were (officially) eleven deaths and over four hundred injuries, a hundred of them women. After as little as ten minutes, "the field was virtually deserted except for bodies, abandoned hats and flags, and dismounted Yeomanry wiping their swords and easing their horse girths," in Richard Holmes's colorful summary.[14] Such detail, reported by many witnesses, some from the national and local press, sealed the incident in the memory of nineteenth-century radicals and also supplied Seed with materials, the equivalent to Reznikoff's "court-cases," though Seed also may have used material from the well-documented trial of Hunt, thus bringing his practice close to Reznikoff's. According to Seed, many of the sources he used came from Robert Walmsley's book *Peterloo: The Case Reopened* (1969) (which is a heavily detailed but "contentious defence for the authorities," ironically enough).[15] Seed reminds us—quoting accounts that reference the many banners legible in press illustrations of the events—of the wide-ranging demands of the

> Reformers that day:
> About half-past eleven
> the first body of Reformers
> arrived at the ground,
> bearing two banners,
> each of which was surmounted by a cap of liberty.
>
> The first bore upon a white ground the inscription
> ANNUAL PARLIAMENTS AND UNIVERSAL SUFFRAGE;
> and on the reverse side: NO CORN LAWS.
>
> The other
> bore upon a blue ground
> the same inscription,
> with the addition VOTE BY BALLOT. (*Manchester*, 11)

There had, of course, been a previous famous poetic response to this repressive outrage against radicals and reformers, Shelley's "The Mask of Anarchy, Written on the Occasion of the Massacre at Manchester," which, against Shelley's wishes, remained a rallying cry without a rally, kept out of print by Leigh Hunt for almost as long as Seed's poem (but for a different reason: fear of prosecution). Perhaps only a poet of twenty-three would have dared to pit himself against the majesty and power of Shelley's assault, but in fact Seed did not know the poem at that time; his innocence of it shields his text from the risk of literary contamination. In any case, Shelley's removal from the events—"As I lay asleep in Italy"—could not be farther from the Reznikoffian techniques of documentary appropriation.[16] Seed relies upon the "testimony of many different witnesses" as sources and not on creating an imaginative response like Shelley's. However, Shelley also relied upon documentary evidence (and in the case of Hunt's *Examiner*, pictured on the cover of Seed's book, the *same* source as Seed). Shelley's "Troops of armed emblazonry" transform into "the charged artillery," which

> drive
> Till the dead air seems alive
> With the clash of clanging wheels,
> And the tramp of horses' heels. (39)

These are also described in Seed's poem, though in the first-person testimony of a survivor:

> I heard the bugle sound—
> I saw the cavalry
> charge forward
> sword in hand
> upon the multitude.
>
> I was carried forward
> almost off my feet,
> many yards nearer the hustings
> than I had been.[17]

The aim of the oppressors, in Shelley's allegory, is to make

> the fixed bayonet
> Gleam with sharp point to wet
> Its bright point in English blood.[18]

Referring to the same event, Shelley's "gleam" may be the equivalent of Seed's "glitter," but Seed has the upper hand in the treatment of the real thing; bayonets were not used at Peterloo:

> Their sabres
> glistening in the air
> on they went,
> direct to the hustings,

where Hunt was.[19] However, the contrast between the synecdoche of the alliterative bayonet, with its symbolic "English" blood and the matter-of-fact "I heard the bugle" or "on they went," could not be clearer, one part of Shelley's larger politico-poetic rhetoric, one lacking in care and attention to verifiable detail, the other a cooler, even conceptual, act of textual appropriation that leaves us not with the sonic compensation of verse ("Poesy") but with something that sounds familiar, like prose (which is why lineation is vital as a marker of an ironical and minimal poeticality) or prose's extempore cousin, speech.[20]

Speech is the documentary source of Seed's "Mayhew project," as I shall show, and this urgent first-person voice is rare in *Manchester*, but Seed has other tricks, relating to his "cutting away extraneous material." One section reads entire: "Hunt's white top hat," which emphasizes Hunt's trademark item of attire and his exposure on the hustings (*Manchester*, 18). This triumphant beacon of liberty (as it may have been seen) contrasts with the habilatory aftermath of the afternoon:

> over the whole field
> were strewed caps, bonnets, hats, shawls and shoes,
> and other parts of male and female dress,
> trampled, torn and bloody. (30)

Seed, like, Shelley, moves the poem away from the actual massacre, but while Shelley issues proclamations and prophecies, and concludes with the brilliant, stubbornly minatory, encouraging (and central) democratic truth "Ye are many—they are few" (*Shelley's Poetry and Prose*, 305), Seed moves (in part VI) to "*Night of August 16th*" and (in the concluding part VII) to "*August 17th*"—in other words, to the historical sequence of events and records. In *Manchester*'s part VI the city of Manchester under curfew ("soldiers posted") is apparently "in a state of tranquillity," but there are signs of continued unrest, though perhaps unreadable by the authorities (37). "Near a petty public house" were espied

> A new hat,
> a tea-kettle,
> some other articles of little value
> [. . .] displayed at the window,
> as is customary
> to display the prizes
> at walks or feasts [. . .]

This was to serve as a pretext
for their meeting together. (38)

This "custom," thus adhering to the word, not the spirit, of arcane and repressive regulations for the assembly of more than a meager number of
people, is potential precursor to an encounter with the authorities. In part
VII "The magistrates were assembled," not at a "petty pub," but

at the Warren Bulkely Arms,
before which the soldiery was drawn out
as that was the first point
against which the rioters had declared their intention
of making an attack . . . (39)

Seed's poem ends inconclusively, or rather, with ellipses that carry the force
of "to be continued," historically speaking. We might think it is the historian's duty to analyze cause and effect here, and the poet's to merely present
effect (and affect). Walter Benjamin realized his duty nicely in his *Arcades*
project (which Seed cites as an influence): "To write history means giving
dates their physiognomy."[21] This view unites Seed's ambitions as historian
and poet, although he acknowledges he was "doing something else" than
history. Benjamin's *Arcades*, as a "method of writing," like Reznikoff's, involved framing quotations, arranging them in categories, often juxtaposing
mutually illuminating examples, collage as a mode of thinking (*Manchester*,
46). Using the analogy of photography and the way Benjamin responds to
photographic evidence, Seed defines "something else": it is to make present
"the sense of another reality filtering through the language of historical
documents."[22]

Seed, until recently, has seldom offered his poetics for perusal, if by poetics we mean a speculative writerly discourse on the present (and future)
forms of his writing; as we have seen, he adheres fairly strictly to the central
tenets of Objectivism, references to historiography and Benjamin notwith-
standing. In "Sincerity and Objectification" Zukofsky defines the former
quality by saying, "Writing occurs which is the detail, not mirage, of seeing,
of thinking with the things as they exist, and of directing them along a line
of melody," while objectification relates to "the appearance of the art form
as an object."[23] Objectification is the formal process that allows sincerity—
Seed's historical "things"—to appear *in the poem itself*. William Carlos Williams's dictionary definition of Objectivist poetics reflects these aspects and
summarizes neatly: "It recognises the poem, apart from its meaning, to be

an object to be dealt with as such. O. looks at the poem with a special eye to its structural aspect, how it has been constructed."[24] The ocular metaphor suggests that the form as seen on the page might be of some significance, although Williams ends with an appeal to the intellect: "It arose as an aftermath of imagism [. . .] which the Objectivists felt was not specific enough, and applied to any image that might be conceived. O. concerned itself with an image more particularized yet broadened in its significance. The mind rather than the unsupported eye entered the picture" (582). The confusion between the eye and the mind—it is revealed in Zukofsky's hesitant "of seeing, of thinking"—reflects the tension in the poetics between the "thing" itself (with which Imagism was content) and the form of the poem-object that treats of this "objective—rays of the object brought to a focus," these "historical and contemporary particulars," this novel way of treating content and form.[25] The eye—the image—must be "supported" by the mind, a "thinking *with*," in accompaniment of, "things," a category that includes these particulars.

Tim Woods recasts the objectification and sincerity binary thus: "What this Objectivist poetics calls for, on the one hand, is a phenomenological concentration in its insistence that poetry must get at the object, at the thing itself, while on the other hand, it must remain 'true' to the object without any interference from the imperialist ego, dismissing any essentialism and calling for the 'wisdom' of love or sincerity."[26] As he explains, objectification involves an "ontological poetics," while sincerity involves an "ethical relation to the world" (33). Or again: "Sincerity is that aspect of aesthetic action that respects the particulars of an object," reminding us that "sincerity" is not detached, in this context, from text and text-production, while "objectification [. . .] is the 'formal' aspect, the poem as object-in-the-world" (146). Only objectification can body forth "sincerity." This is a more complex formulation than the conventional distinction between form and content; objectification is the process of bringing the poem as an object into phenomenological existence (through the active formulating engagement of the reader); Zukofsky's word "appearance" is suggestive of this irruption of the poem into existence (though again the ocular metaphor is trumped by the mind: "appearance" does not simply refer to the look of the poem on the page, however important that is for Seed and others).

Seed's poetics, as I have shown, hovers between and around the practice of the two US Objectivist writers we have considered, Oppen informing his lyric writing and Reznikoff informing his documentary works. However, the sense of the separation (but relationship) of historical particulars as

"sincerity," while objectification is achieved through a series of formal ma-
nipulations of those particulars, without egotistic intent, is notably stronger
in his documentary works, from *Manchester* to the "Mayhew project."[27] In
the 2013 "Afterword" to the former, Seed searches for a way of describing
that "something else" that he seeks by his framing of historical particulars, to create "the sense of another reality" and he reaches—not for Zukofsky's binary—but for Roland Barthes's distinction between "studium" and
"punctum," which he draws in *Camera Lucida* (1980).[28] Seed enthusiastically discusses the latter, and he returns to the elusive "something" when
he defines Barthes's term: "Through the individual photograph something
shoots out at the perceiver like an arrow, pierces and wounds him" (55). He
then quotes Barthes: "A photograph's *punctum* is that accident which pricks
me (but also bruises me, is poignant to me)."[29]

Seed says nothing about "studium." Barthes defines it as a quality of reception (or perception) of photographs, one which is culturally determined,
and may even be responsible for one's first interest in them, but this may
"require the rational intermediary of an ethical and political culture. What
I feel about these photographs derives from an *average* affect, almost from a
certain training" (*Camera Lucida*, 26). Never "delight or pain," it is a polite
interest; the name 'studium' suggests 'study,' which Barthes does not completely dismiss with his sense that this is cultured acquisition, an education
even, but more properly it indicates a "taste for someone, a kind of general,
enthusiastic commitment [. . .] but without special acuity" (28, 26).

Seed posits the question "Can a poem have a *punctum*?" but his whole
argument suggests that this is a rhetorical question, answered in the positive (55). "*Punctum*" is characterized by Barthes as "the second element"
that "will break (or punctuate) the *studium*" (26). It is "sting, speck, cut,
little hole—and also the cast of a die" (27). It is impolite, uncivil, but it is
not necessarily surprise or shock. In terms of photography, it goes beyond
a coded visuality, and beyond naming; it may involve a detail that manifests
itself in an image, "a detail" that "overwhelms the entirety of my reading,"
operating perhaps not unlike the luminous image of Hunt's white hat in the
single noun-phrase section of *Manchester* (49). Barthes uses the same gener-
ality as Seed: "This *something* has triggered me, has provoked a tiny shock,"
but ironically, "whether or not it is triggered, it is an addition: is what I add
to the photograph and *what is nonetheless already there*" (49, 55). Cognition
becomes recognition in an ethical movement that feels both inventive and
inevitable; Barthes relates it to the nondevelopmental quiddity, the instan-
taneity of the haiku, a poetic form with a clear relationship to the Imagist-

Objectivist tradition. "Punctum" is where sincerity meets objectification. It occurs at the moment where or when the text "think(s) with the things as they exist" and is simultaneously musicated in literary form, as it were. It occurs wherever or whenever the ontological sense that a poem successfully encapsulates the thing itself, is energized by the process of the poem coming into being as objective form, in the formulating act of reading (which is what Barthes's paradox of the viewer actively adding to the already present image is theorizing).

Barthes, by the time he wrote *Camera Lucida*, was very much an aesthete, and he is content to deal with his responses to certain photographic details (in a given photograph) that puncture and punctuate his *reading* (the folded arms of a black servant or the co-presence of nuns and soldiers in a war photograph, for example) without feeling the need to generalize. It might be useful to think of the abrupt enjambments of Seed's "Mayhew" poems as punctuational *puncta*, as ways of forcing the material to offer up its ghosts and their voices, as the trigger that motivates that *something* into *something else*. If, as Agamben says, "Poetry lives only in the tension and difference (and hence in the virtual interference) between sound and sense," then "enjambement is the only criterion which allows one to distinguish poetry from prose," which is especially crucial when the process of composition is—as in Seed's documentary pieces—to transform prose (or speech) into poetry.[30] It is capable of rising to the imagistic and majestic intensity of the *punctum*, as I have redefined it in Objectivist terms. Enjambment triggers the affective shock.

With Pound's minatory prohibition against breaking prose into line lengths ringing in his ears, Seed cautiously asserts: "It could be argued that merely breaking prose up into lines does something significant, whether we call it poetry or not" (*Manchester*, 63). Surprisingly, Seed cites not Reznikoff but the sociologist and educationalist Basil Bernstein (whose work would have been staple reading for Seed as a student teacher). Bernstein describes a classroom experiment (not too different from Seed's own teaching practice) which breaks up "continuous writing" into lines "like a poem. The piece took on a new and vital life" (63). Bernstein also apologizes and says that this was "bad aesthetics," but he calls it "the symbolic nature of space," which is a useful term for theorizing the spatial elements of poetic artifice. Like Pound and the Objectivists, Bernstein "became fascinated by condensation; by the implicit" (64). Bernstein observed: "The space between the lines, the interval, allowed the symbols to reverberate against each other. The space between the lines was the listener or reader's space out of which he created a unique, unspoken, personal meaning" (64). This passage, quoted from Bernstein's influential *Class, Codes and Control* (1971), was, Seed says, "enthusiastically marked" in his own copy (64). The poem is born as the reader is born *as a reader*, in the reading experience; it may result at least in the *studium* of the educative, but at most in the *punctum* of delight. While Seed alerts us to both Barthes and Bernstein, he does not make this connection explicit. Barthes himself likes the mild suggestion of the word "punctuation" in *punctum*, so, if we think of enjambment as the metrical equivalent of punctuation in syntactic and semantic structures—Agamben speaks of "the opposition between metrical segmentation and semantic segmentation" in poetry—the connection is apposite, even accurate (109).

Framing (selection) and recasting (lineating) are the chief modes of artifice, of formal manipulation, in Seed's documentary work, but they operate differently than Reznikoff, making much of this play between the two varieties of segmentation. The Mayhew books—arranged in two volumes, *Pictures from Mayhew: London 1850* (2005) and *That Barrikins: Pictures from Mayhew II—London 1850* (2007)—take as material the voluminous journalistic works of Henry Mayhew, which he published in his own newspaper and collected in four volumes, *London Labour and the London Poor*, between 1851 and 1862.[31] They are lively witness reports of the trials, tribulations, and occasional joys of the Victorian underclass, that body near-synonymous with the "unemployed reserve army of workers" that Engels describes as keeping "body and soul together by begging, stealing, street-sweeping, collecting manure, pushing hand-carts, driving donkeys, peddling," and comments: "It is astonishing in what devices this 'surplus population' takes refuge."[32] But whereas Marx and Engels fed off government reports and statistics to isolate the structural position of this group as vital to the operations of capital, Mayhew never theorized but relied upon his own witness reports and the testimony of the poor themselves. Most remarkably, he relied upon the skill of stenographers or shorthand experts to report—repeat—the spoken words, including the pronunciation and inflections, of the interviewees. Although stenographers would have been used in compiling the formal court proceedings Reznikoff used in *Testimony*, Seed's poems outstrip Reznikoff in the representation of the demotic; his poems only report the *speech* of Mayhew's interviewees (speaking in less formal surroundings than a courtroom), and they allow more flexibility than the occasional verbatim touches of *Manchester*. Both volumes of Seed's Mayhew project total approximately sixty sections, roughly divided into category of speaker by trade, occupation, or subject matter. Reading the poems is cumulative, slightly hypnotic; they feel choral, polyphonic, rather than lyric, as we encounter the series of flower girls, street entertainers, itinerant laborers, booksellers, and vendors of game, poultry, or fish; sometimes they are simply the poor, their voices isolated on the page, lamenting lost opportunity or the precarious situation of belonging to what Engels identified as capital's reserve labor pool.

Seed makes the point that he does not employ a single technique throughout, and the poems' techniques range from discrete lines with zero enjambment, presenting cries from street sellers demonstrating their professional language, from the hailing "Hi! hi!" of photographers, pleading for potential customers to "walk inside! walk inside! // & have your c'rrect likeness took," through to more complex representations of voice.[33] This isoverbalist presentation (three words to most of the lines) is at the opposite end of the scale in being a fixed mathematical measure.

> I hadn't a
> pinch of snuff
> for two days
> until a friend
> gave us a bit
> out of his
> box it came
> very acceptable I
> can assure you
> it quite revived
> me that's all
> I'm extravagant in
> I can't say
> but what I
> likes my pinch
> of snuff but
> even that I
> can't get (*Pictures*, 85–86)

Seed is forced by measure to employ violent and foregrounded enjambments and removes punctuation completely so that the representational aspect of the work is countered by the artifice, content clashing with form, the prose uneasily accommodated within the poetic structure so that readers never forget that they are reading a poem. Sentences end mid-line, without marking, and somehow this emphasizes the play of a relatively privileged register of speech ("extravagant") against dialect or idiolect (the odd use of the word "acceptable") as well as the purely ungrammatical demotic ("I / likes my pinch / of snuff").

Seed himself speaks of loosening syntax, grammar, restoring an artifice of *speech* as counters of authenticity and reconstruction "to bring alive the experiences": "My work of reading/writing was partly about undoing Mayhew's own work of rewriting and perhaps getting closer to his listening and recording," but he additionally "wanted the form to slow down the reader," to defamiliarize the reading experience and foreground artifice or "play," by the use of word count, verse forms, and the inescapable "visible form on white paper."[34] Where Reznikoff chops prose into line lengths, Seed revoices the material through restless formal investigation. They are after all "pictures" (like Williams's sequence "from" Brueghel, to which Seed alludes in his title) not voices, although the (self) portraiture and speaking are neatly poised:

> my father was
> I've heard say a
> well-known swell of capers gay who
> cut his last fling with great applause or
>
> if you will (*That Barrikins*, 129)

The pause at "or" separates the colorful demotic of praise and prepares the reader for the descending mood of the rest of the poem. "If you must know," the speaker begins; this is one of the infrequent occasions when one can hear the interviewee addressing the intrusive questioning of Mayhew:

> I heard
> he was hung
> for killing a man committing a burglary (129)

"In other words," she says, as though this were not clear enough,

> he was
> a making-cove what robs
>
> & I'm his daughter worse luck (129)

In Seed's "Mayhew project," quotation of the stenographic record is deformed and re-formed by Seed's selection and his lineated arrangement of the text into poetic structures. This operates a knowing ventriloquial trick as we imagine we hear the voices of the (almost) forgotten of history, recovered by Seed from Mayhew's commentary. Seed brings the voices alive only as form, with the force of Barthes's *punctum*. Oddly, this brings one back to Oppen, or rather Hatlen's apprehension that Oppen's "syntactic interruptions and suspensions open up abysses within which the unsayable resonates behind, around, and within what gets said."[35] Whenever we feel we apprehend the voice, hear it with our inner ear, the eye brings us back to the materiality of the page, to its literal objectification, the formal pull *against* historical particulars, leaving "the sense of another reality filtering through the [. . .] documents," the elusive "something."[36] Charles Bernstein's effusive, almost Shelleyan declaration that "*Testimony* tells the story of America's forgotten, those who suffer without redress, without name, without hope; yet the soul of these States is found in books like this," is also true of Seed's English "Mayhew Project": "the acknowledgment of these peripheral stories turns a wasteland into holy ground."[37] The poems stage a triumphant transformation of their materials, as they capture the particulars with care and attention, and body them forth in objectified formal structures that carry what Woods calls "the 'wisdom' of love or sincerity."[38]

6

MEANING IT

THE AFFECTIVE POETICS OF SOCIAL SINCERITY

JEFF DERKSEN

In a 1970 lecture Lionel Trilling, a former classmate of Louis Zukofsky at Columbia University in the 1920s, proposed that "a historical account of sincerity must take as its purview not only the birth and ascendancy of the concept but also its eventual decline, the sharp diminution of the authority it once exercised."[1] Such an account, Trilling admits, shows "the word itself has lost most of its former high dignity" (8). In leading up the waning of 'sincerity's' dignity, Trilling does, however, track the word historically, locating its emergence in the sixteenth century as a concept applied to things rather than understood as a human attribute. Trilling notes that in Dr. Johnson's Dictionary, 'sincerity' is "applied to things rather than to persons," such as a "sincere" (unadulterated) wine (13). Jane Taylor, however, locates an earlier emergence of the concept of sincerity within the nexus of the heresy trial, the Inquisition, and the authorization of torture in the thirteenth century: she "propose[s] that sincerity essentially arises in order to solve the problem of the forced confession."[2] Scrutinizing confessions from the thirteenth to the sixteenth century reveals, Taylor argues, "an evolving dialectic between external performance and internal convictions. Sincerity is necessarily a problem of performance" (25).

With regard to nineteenth-century uses, both Trilling and Herbert Read cite sincerity's strengthening as a form of publicity (and as the presentation of a bourgeois self in everyday life) with 1871's Rousseau's *Confessions*.[3] Rousseau famously opens the book with a direct address of his intention: "I want to show my fellow-men a man in all the truth of nature; and this man is to be myself."[4] For both Trilling and Read, sincerity coheres as a projection of such a direct address, emanating from a plain-speaking public subject who is able to precisely articulate (for them the subject is gendered) his historical, public particularity. However, beyond this particularity,

Rousseau illustrates, for Trilling, the emergence of the "psycho-historical concept" of the individual, of a new social subject made possible and produced in response to the "newly available sense of an audience, that public which society created."[5] That is, sincerity coheres when there is a public that recognizes sincerity as a form of publicity, which in turn produces the space for a "self, bent on revealing himself in all his truth, that is to say, on demonstrating his sincerity" (25). Susan B. Rossenbaum extends this relationship of the reception and production of sincerity to contemporary lyric poetry, where a "'confessional culture' influences habits of reading conventions of sincerity in the lyric" and "poets respond [. . .] to this climate of reception through their uses of the rhetoric of sincerity."[6]

However, rather than joining the performance and aesthetics of sincerity, Read separates sincerity and art: "All art is artifice, and therefore no work of art is sincere" (18). When artifice is immanent to art, sincerity is excluded—it cannot exist in an aesthetic construct. Read can then maintain the position that "sincerity [. . .] is a moral and not an aesthetic virtue" (18). Likewise, in Trilling's framework, sincerity has an uneasy relationship to aesthetics, and in art it is trumped by an authenticity "which implies a downward movement through all the cultural superstructures to some place where all movement ends, and begins."[7] Being able to cut through such determinations, authenticity "had come along to suggest the deficiencies of sincerity and to usurp its place in our esteem" (18). Authenticity is both a "criterion of art" for Trilling and the base of sincerity.[8]

More recently, art critic Boris Groys renders art, design, and politics together in relation to the production of sincerity. For Groys, self-presentation is consciously replaced by self-design, particularly in media. But self-design recognizes its artifice and reflexivity; therefore, "the main goal of self-design then becomes one of neutralizing the suspicion of a possible spectator."[9] Unlike the sincerity that Trilling and Read grant Rousseau's address, which has the potential to reveal the core of a subject, the production of sincerity and "the design of honesty" for Groys no longer comes, as it did for modernist art, when "the designed surface cracks open to offer a view of its inside" (43). The performance and design of a sincere subject are not obscured by an aesthetic surface or performance: the split between appearance and the self and the disjuncture among artifice, aesthetics, and authenticity here are finally set aside. There is no ideological surface to open up, no singular authenticity at which to arrive. Instead, today, "the effect of sincerity is not created by refuting the initial suspicion directed toward every design surface, but by confirming it" (43). Through this confirmation of aesthetics, Groys breaks the monologic transmission of sincerity from a subject to an audience and creates a sincerity that is relational.

Groys arrives at a form of participatory art—a practice he describes as predominant—that "weakens the radical separation of artist and audience to a certain degree" so that artist and audience are positions within a process that creates the conditions for the *production* of sincerity rather than the *representation* and *recognition* of it (47). In this Groys asserts the importance of the coproduction of sincerity and "shared political convictions" today—a model found in engaged participatory art as well as social movements.

Groys usefully locates sincerity outside of the psychohistorical subject and places it in the shared space of producer and audience.[10] Sincerity emerges as a social affect in relation to political and aesthetic conditions. Defined within the terrain of aesthetic and political acts, sincerity does not aim to regain its "high dignity," but it becomes a social affect among other intensities. Beyond art practices, and into a wider terrain of the social, as Ernst van Alphen and Mieke Bal argue, "Sincerity cannot be dismissed because, while not an integrated consequence and qualification of subjectivity, it is an indispensable *affective* (hence, social) process amongst subjects. Affect is understood here as intensities that are circulated among subjects."[11]

This short history of *sincerity* both relocates sincerity outside of the performance of a grounded yet hidden authenticity emanating from a bourgeois social subject and moves poetry away from the domain of the lyrical. Attention to how sincerity is aesthetically, rhetorically, and culturally produced and circulated casts it into a network of social and political relationships.[12] There is a double fold in this: the subject in this construct is more multiple than the one found in the model of surface and depth/outer and inner. Yet this multiplicity opens the subject to more subtle coersions, as well as other forms of affective countertactics and effective political coherences; that is, the subject becomes as complex and multiple as the social processes that shape it. Within the construct I am building here in relation to sincerity, poetry can produce an aesthetic-social complex that sets in motion what Lauren Berlant calls a shared "affectivity of the historical present."[13] Poetry that works through the denseness of the historical present, and the multiplicity of the subject, creates an attunement with the present as a long moment. This could be poetry's *contract* with the present as a temporally complex construct.

From Objectivist Sincerity to the Affect of Sincerity

Within this nexus of affect, poetics, and an intensity of the present, the Objectivists' legacy provides a compelling moment to read how a poetics of sincerity can approach the historical present as a social and aesthetic complex. Reading their poetry with the idea of a social sincerity and as part of an affective economy can help us today see their work as an engagement with the possibilities of the politics of affect in reaction to the constraints of a modernism tainted with Pound's politics and particular trajectories of poetry by the left. At an unstable moment in history—such as the late 1920s and early 1930s, when the Objectivists emerged—with competing utopic and dystopic horizons, how could a poem engage and register both the positive and negative possibilities of the present? How could this poetics both represent and respond to social conditions, but also produce and circulate shared political convictions?

I want to try to bring this reading of social sincerity into relationship with the Objectivist poets' rather open notion of "sincerity" that Louis Zukofsky introduced in 1931 with his famous essay "Sincerity and Objectification with Special Reference to the Poetry of Charles Reznikoff."[14] Objectivist sincerity, as DuPlessis and Quartermain point out, has been "perhaps paradoxically" productive, and it functions both as a structuring device in which the poem is "the arrangement, into an apprehended unit, of minor units of sincerity" but also a sincerity in the relationship of word to thing and by extension to the social based on "accuracy of detail."[15] This return to sincerity in relationship to things is not a return to the sixteenth-century notion of sincerity as a quality of things but is tied to Marx's definition of the commodity, a concept that sees things as radically social.

Objectivist sincerity works at the levels of the word and the poem and in relation to a social horizon. However, Stephen Fredman points to how the formal aspects of Objectivist poetry are in tension with the bourgeois subject: "If objectification opens the poems to multiple linguistic registers, then what about 'sincerity,' which would seem to imply a unitary personality that would be inimical to the kind of poetry Zukofsky values?"[16] Reading sincerity as an affect produced socially between social subjects (here the writer and the reader) negotiates the contradiction that Fredman notes here: if sincerity is not understood to only emanate from a unitary subject, but is seen as a shared affect produced by and circulating between social subjects, then the formal aspects of the poem are not harnessed to the adequate evocation of that authentic representation but are constructs in the "poem that establish as an affective encounter." Sincerity then is not directed to "adequately evoke the experience represented" but sets in motion the intensity of a shared affective situation.[17]

Charles Bernstein says something similar when he characterizes George Oppen's poetics as "this poetics of participatory, or constructive, presentness" that has as its horizon "the potential for social collectivity."[18] As numerous shifts in the way that social movements across the globe both imagine and organize themselves show us, building a shared politics without taking affect as a potential cohesive bond is not possible: this social imperative gives a renewed importance to sincerity and the poem. Now here is the more difficult part, the part I *really* mean (really *mean*): Can a poetics of sincerity be an affective challenge to the ways in which the ontological project of neoliberalism has inflected the texture of everyday life today and social relations between people (I mean this literally: between people, from person to person)? As Yahya Madra and Fikret Adaman specify, the ontological projects of neoliberalism "aim to reorganize the social such that all human behavior is governed through an interface of economic incentives." That has resulted in *"an epistemic shift* at the level of social subjectivity."[19] This goes beyond refiguring people as a *Homo economicus*, a subject who dances to the rhythm played by those famous hidden hands of the market, and sees neoliberalism as performative and governmental, descriptive and prescriptive yet never able to fully suture the subject, to rebuild it singularly as a *Homo economicus*.

Oppen's Affect

In his introduction to the collected poems of George Oppen, Michael Davidson contextualizes Oppen's early poetics as a turn away from "the aesthetic strategies of his modernist predecessors."[20] Of course, Oppen's most forceful rejection of that modernist history was his turn from Ezra Pound. Peter Nicholls productively locates this as both an ideological rejection of Pound's reluctance to speak of the tragedy of fascism and the gas chambers that the contradictions of modernism itself brought and as an aesthetic challenge: "At issue are not merely the *argumentative* habits of the older poet's work and the hectoring tone of the late stages of his poem [*The Cantos*], but, more important, what Oppen sees as a tendency to closure and solipsism."[21] I'd like to extend this reading of Oppen beyond the negation of closure that leads toward a formal openness as an end point, and beyond the immanent critique of the limits of modernism.[22]

This rejigs Oppen's poetics from the clarity of images brought forward from the Imagists (whom he criticized) or the "rested totality" defined by

Zukofsky for the Objectivists.[23] Rather than a goal of an honest or authentic relation to language, I read in Oppen's poems a sincerity toward "the materials" in a larger social and historical sense; here "the materials" of language, things, and the social are understood as processes in relation to the present and history. Neither the image, nor the poem, nor the social rests at a given clarity, even though Oppen's poems have an unadorned weight due to his focus on specific things (cities, streets, bricks, boats, tools, and so forth). There is still a contingency to that apparent clarity due to the syntactic torqueing that both opens and articulates (as in joining) image, context, thought, history, and the present. The poem, understood as social, cannot rest at a closure, for the social, as a process, never does.

For instance, the poem "Time of the Missile" from *The Materials*[24] shows how unsettled yet historical the clarity of the images becomes. The poem begins in a recognizable Oppen mode—on the waterfront with a view of both the spaces of labor and the city:

> I remember a square of New York's Hudson River glinting between
>   warehouses.
> Difficult to approach the water below the pier
> Swirling, covered with oil the ship at the pier
> A steel wall: tons in the water,
>
> Width.
> The hand for holding,
> Legs for walking,
> The eye *sees*! It floods in on us from here to Jersey tangled in the
>   grey bright air. (33)

The shifts in scale among the city, the massive ship, and human bodies works seamlessly and confidently to bring us to a particular place (the shore of the Hudson River with New Jersey in the background) where perception is asserted ("The eye *sees*!"). However, once grounded and scaled at the local, Oppen reverses this perceptual move and opens an ideological, and ultimately a geopolitical, perspective:

> Become the realm of nations.
>
> My love, my love
> We are endangered
> Totally at last. Look

Anywhere to the sight's limit: space
Which is viviparous:

Place the mind
And eye. Which can destroy us,
Re-arrange itself, assert
Its own stone chain reaction. (33)

The title's framing comes into play in this final movement—the total coverage of missiles in the Cold War's geography endangers everyone. Through small syntactic shifts, elisions, and conjoining (the two colons) the poem becomes more semantically associational: "sight's limit" again gives a human scale, yet with the colon used to hold "space" off at the end of that line, "space" is joined to "sight's limit" and also given the attribute of being "viviparous" (an unusual Latinate word for Oppen), of being reproductive. Yet syntactically "space" is also that "Which can destroy us." "Place" is syntactically a verb here, yet it flickers as a noun in relation to "space." So while the poem perhaps pushes toward perception, space, and visuality, the "stone chain reaction" brings back the Cold War missile discourse. Capitalism may have annihilated space by time, as Marx remarks, but Oppen here has missiles annihilating space. And, as in almost all of Oppen's later poems, this is enacted through a syntax that pushes at the edge of recognition yet pulls the reader in, or holds the reader in the poem through normative syntactic units that shunt and buckle.

Here I want to turn to a remarkable sequence in "Of Being Numerous,"[25] in which sincerity as a social affect is laced into a critique of how capitalism as a structure and a process constructs particular subjects. In sections 6 and 7, Oppen moves from an image of human proximity, coolly brings in "emotion," pivots obliquely on Robinson Crusoe's tale, and then uses a form of sincere address to invoke "being numerous." This section begins with the generalized statement "we are pressed, pressed upon each other, / We will be told at once / Of anything that happens. [. . . .]" (12). This could be a statement about the growing scope of news reporting, or even the growing importance of the media in bringing the Vietnam War into the living rooms of America. The sentence (which runs across two stanzas) continues: "And the discovery of fact bursts / In a paroxysm of emotion / Now as always" (12). The phrase "the discovery of facts" supports a reading of the line as a reference to the media, but then it is countered by the verb "bursts." This verb is a hinge here that allows a movement from fact to emotion: the discovery of fact "bursts," as it continues, and leads to "a paroxysm of emotion" (12). Latinate nouns stand out in Oppen's text and "paroxysm" here curiously doubles up on *bursts*: a paroxysm is itself a burst or an intensification of emotion or action.[26] Fact and emotion are in proximity here, "Now as always" as the next line states. In the framework I have been building, there is the possibility to read this as the relationship or even movement of fact, emotion, and affect, as an invocation of how facts create affects (or how affects deployed can make "affective facts," as Brian Massumi shows).[27] Facts are things, and like things they carry an affective weight or potential.

At the end of this sentence, the poem has a paratactic shift to Robinson Crusoe, with a mere four lines over two stanzas.

[. . .] Crusoe
We say was
'Rescued'.
So we have chosen.

These are key lines in that they set up the relationship of the "shipwreck of the singular" and the choice "the meaning / Of being numerous" that follows in section 7. Semantically these lines bring in a broader discussion of capitalist development and the social subject through the reference to Crusoe. Oppen would have been familiar with Marx's use of Daniel Defoe's tale of Robinson Crusoe, as Oren Izenberg demonstrates in his extended reading of this section of "Of Being Numerous."[28] Marx uses the figure of Robinson Crusoe both in the first volume of *Capital* and in *Grundrisse* to rail against political economists who naturalize capitalism through the essence of the individual. This individual is conjured up by Adam Smith and David Ricardo, Marx charges, "not as a historical result but as history's point of departure. As the Natural Individual appropriate to their notion of human nature, not arising historically, but posited by nature."[29] "This illusion," as Marx calls it, constructs a human essence that fits the economist's model of capitalism and creates an "absurdity" of a subject that is not a historical result. Marx's frustration with this "twaddle" is that a subject cannot exist before (or outside of) social relations.[30] Instead, Massimilano Tomba argues that "Marx aims at a *different* concept of the individual. [. . .] It is an individual that boasts a wealth of relations and waxes in power to the extent that the species does, an individual that 'embraces a wide circle of varied activities and practical relations to the world.'"[31] Tomba continues that the economists Smith and Ricardo, as well as Hobbes and Rousseau, are part of "the 'illusion' of the modern epoch [which] is that of a single, isolated individual which is treated *not* as a historical product, but as history's starting point" (28).

A history and context for the shipwrecked individual Robinson Crusoe, and "the shipwreck of the singular" in "Of Being Numerous" emerges here. By invoking Crusoe and using the single quotation marks, which indicate a generalization or even distrust of the word *rescued* (or, perhaps, signaling irony, which would reflect Marx's tone in his retelling of the Crusoe story) a reading of this section can be aligned with Marx's sustained argument for "social man." However, in "Of Being Numerous," Crusoe is invoked not solely as Marx's figure of the naturalization of capital but as a figure that gives a historical touchstone and a materialist gauge for the meaning of the individual and the numerous. Oppen's reference to Crusoe, a figure laden with social meaning through Marx's argument with the economist's use of him, along with the extended concept of "the shipwreck" that resonates throughout "Of Being Numerous," agitates the problematic *nature* of the social subject. The shipwreck of the singular (*and* the singular as shipwreck) is set upon by the subject constituted by multiple or numerous interactions between social subjects:

> Obsessed, bewildered
>
> By the shipwreck
> Of the singular
>
> We have chosen the meaning
> Of being numerous. (13)

From one angle, the initial "we have chosen" indicates that the route of the "Robinsonades" has been chosen—that the essential individual who is both naturalized by capital, and "rescued" and brought back to his natural economic relations, is the model for the social subject. I do not read these lines as a possible "discourse of the mind" relating to the conditions of choice, as Izenberg does; rather, in the narrative that sees Crusoe as "'rescued,'" a choice of the Robinsonades has been chosen.[32]

However, in the second use, "We have chosen the meaning / Of being numerous," a more affirmative reading is set; the numerous has been chosen over the Robinsonade. Syntactically, however, this entire stanza is slippery enough to yield other readings. Peter Nicholls, informed by Oppen's correspondence on this section of the poem, arrives at the proposition that "in a curious way, then, the 'shipwreck of the singular' and the 'meaning of being numerous' are not antithetical options, as might first be thought, but are rather mutually implicated possibilities."[33] I tend toward a meaning in a dialectical tension with the phrase "So we have chosen" (12). If we say that Crusoe was "rescued," then we have chosen to naturalize the Robinsonade essence of the individual, but the second instance of choice is an agency toward numerousness. This causal reading is troubled by the oscillation of the line "Obsessed, bewildered" as meditations on the choice, but I take it to indicate the act of choosing "the meaning of being numerous" over the obsession and bewilderment of the shipwreck of the singular. "Crusoe" effectively functions as a *problematic* in the poem, as a node that brings back a discussion of the subject in capitalism. All of this swerves away from Marx, for whom there would be no choice, as a subject is necessarily relational and numerous, and never singular: to propose singularity is to create an "illusion."

If we take one aspect of Oppen's poetic and political project to be the representation of the social subject during a time when an emergent neoliberalism begins the long retrenchment of the naturalized and autonomized subject, then his syntactic slips and paratactical shunts also reflect the trouble in representing this "numerous" social subject. Beverley Best proposes (vis-à-vis Kristeva) that "the collective subject in capitalism experiences a breakdown in the signifying function, the possibility of representing and articulating the social world in a particular (totalized) way."[34] In "Of Being Numerous" we also see the problematic of the representation of a collective subject in the capitalist mode of production as well as a break in the modernist tendency toward totalization. Oppen reaches back to Marx's initial critique and brings it forward into the urgent present as a question and a choice.

Earlier I pointed to Trilling's use of Rousseau as an exemplar of the sincere social subject. Coincidentally, Marx levels his critique of this subject, as it took shape in the eighteenth century, through both the Robinsonades and Rousseau. After mocking Crusoe as a figure used by the economists, Marx, in the same paragraph in *Grundrisse*, points to the naturalism in "Rousseau's *contrat social*, which brings naturally independent, autonomous subjects into relation and connection by contract."[35] Continuing his critique, Marx writes, "Only in the eighteenth century, in 'civil society,' do the various forms of social connectedness confront the individual as a mere means toward his private purpose, as external necessity" (84). Perhaps in this nexus of Marx's concept of the social subject and his criticism of Rousseau and Crusoe, a divergent form of sincerity—a social sincerity—that differs from the line that privileges sincerity springing from an authentic subject can be located in Oppen. Sincerity in "Of Being Numerous," I want to propose, can still be that form of attention to the relationship of language, thing, and social relations, as it also functions at another level: as a social sincerity that circulates between and through social subjects in an affective economy. The tone of *speculation* in "Of Being Numerous" continually draws attention to losses and possibilities between the singular and the numerous: the power in this series is that what is thematized in the poem is also enacted through an affective economy.

Charles Reznikoff: Documentary Practices and Affect

I want to now turn to the documentary poetic practice of Charles Reznikoff in order to make a connection to how Objectivist poetics, in a twofold relationship to the 'things' represented in the poem and to the historical present, engage with an affective economy. As I suggested earlier, the "thing" in Objectivist poems—whether it is a paving stone or the hull of a boat in Oppen, or trains, machines, tools, and guns in Reznikoff's *Testimony*—is not a stripped-down linguistic image functioning as an objective correlative to the stone in a street or a building; that is, the literary construct of the thing does not stand in for a subjective feeling produced in the reader. The function of sincerity at a level of poetics in Objectivism is to portray a thing or a place concretely and complexly through attention to the social relations both *in* and *around* the thing. This complexity of what Jennison calls "Objectivism's attention to highly differentiated social surfaces"[36] and the extension of the possibilities of the image brought forward from Imagism paradoxically creates a sincerity through the *unadorned* aspect of Oppen's poems and the redaction to a minimal, yet highly differentiated, aspect in Reznikoff's documentary works. Sincerity provides a poetics to approach the materiality of things and social relations that are represented and evoked in the poems at the same time it is an affect created *by* the poem.

The powerful effect of this twofold relationship in Reznikoff's documentary poems can be illuminated by comparing his poetics to the photographic documentary practices of the 1930s that his work was in dialogue with, as well as engaging his work in dialogue with contemporary reconfigurations of documentary practices attentive to the relationship of truth, uncertainty, and the role of affect. As Monique Vescia convincingly shows, *Testimony* can be read in relation to 1930s photo-documentary practices; however, the perspective that Vescia builds can be broadened when we move past a national framing of Reznikoff's practice. Vescia argues that "Reznikoff's desire to present a multiplicity of viewpoints is, I believe, less of an aesthetic project than a social one and thus in tune with the goals of the American documentary movement, which sought to include all aspects of the nation in its record."[37] The multiplicity of views presented in the texts Reznikoff selected and redacted for *Testimony* are of a nation, but they are also a documentary of specific geographical, gendered, racialized, and class relations in capitalism at that time. The accumulative effect of *Testimony* is an indirect but withering critique of social relations, and the relation between subjects, in American capitalism at that time. Seen from this angle, sections of *Testimony* share the attention to details of the lives of working people and to the ways that ownership, race, and law play out on those bodies that are also vivid in Engels's *The Condition of the Working-Class in England in 1844* and in Marx's "The Working Day" chapter in volume 1 of *Capital*.

For instance, in the *Testimony* section "Children" (itself within the section "The South (1891–1900)"), the majority of the narratives of cruelty, injury, death, and calamity involve work. Within that section, one of the poems directly details working hours:

> The factory hours were the ordinary hours of the state —
> eleven and a half to twelve hours a day.
> He had been put to work at eight or nine years of age
> And now had been working in the mill more than two years:
> All day in the cotton mill
> Filled with its machinery whirring at high speed.[38]

Like Marx, Reznikoff relies on the reportage and testimony of others regarding children and labor to build this image of how children's lives are shaped (and often crushed) by the conditions they live and work under. But unlike Marx, who breaks an objective position (and does not control his emphatic satire and disgusted irony — even though he often relegates them to parenthetical remarks), Reznikoff builds a case against the cruelty of capitalism through his original selection from legal reports. Reznikoff activates an affective relationship through his minimizing editing — redactions that materialize the language of the testimonies, lifting them out of the legal frame of court transcripts, and that address the subject in the poem as a subject *in* history. The sufficient — and palpable — particularities in these poems do not *transcend* to a universal perspective on capitalism but, in their sweep, do critique it structurally. The poems stand as pure (as in minimal) and intensified (hence affective) tales of the specificity of the conditions that capitalism builds. And they also provide hardened particularities about life in America at that time.

The sincerity that circulates in these poems is the interface with the source language (the legal testimonies) as a necessarily *rich* language (for it is embedded in the social relations of the moment) and an affect created by the stripping down of the original text. But affect is not aimed at the "victims" in these short poetic narratives. The poems do not allow for an empathetic identification with the people in the poems; however, as with Marx's chapter, there is a sincerity in the laying out of the conditions of their lives as a form of critique and — more important — the building of an affective engagement with the subject in history. The coolness of the poems in their descriptions of the injuries, debased bodies, and ruined relations, and the construction of the serial poem that emphasizes the repetition of these conditions, amass a portrait of a condition. The cruelness that the subjects of the poems suffer is distinct and particular, but the larger structural cruelty is that they are shown not to be agents of history. The affective accrual reflects this political condition and puts the reader in proximity to it.

Through research, through redaction, and through a serial ordering, Reznikoff created a vast counternarrative that develops a political effect through its affective economy of "objectivity" and sincerity. *Testimony* was received tepidly by the left in its time, and as Vescia points out, the first volume was seen as Reznikoff's "reluctance to take sides in the class war" (*Depression Glass*, 31). Yet in reading *Testimony*, class war (and other linked social struggles) accumulates as central both to the history of America and to everyday life in capitalism. In building this, Reznikoff demonstrates an astounding insistence rather than a reluctance. The ethical urgency of "taking sides" works through an affective register rather than through constructing a representational certainty. Reznikoff pulls back from having the intervention of authorial subjectivity through sematic statements, but turns to other poetic means to convey conviction. Class relations — and the relations of gender, race, ownership, and geography — unwind through historical and geographic particulars that attest to the difficulty of representing *processes* through documentary practices.

There is, however, one instance where, as with Marx's asides in "The Working Day," a sense of outrage is ironized in *Testimony* and breaks the surface of the narrative by addressing the legal framework and racism. One poem describes a racist attack on a "Negro's house" that was shot up, wounding the man and igniting his cotton — fleeing the danger, the wounded man ran to the house of his neighbor, who was "a white man." The racist gang followed and shot a hole in the neighbor's door. The poem, through Reznikoff's editing, ends with a rare direct comment on justice:

> Justice, however, was not to be thwarted,
> for five of the men who did this to the Negro
> were tried:
> for "unlawfully and maliciously
> injuring and disfiguring"—
> the white man's property.[39]

As this is quoted within the testimony rather than an interjection from Reznikoff, it does not step outside of the documentary poetic methodology of *Testimony*. However, this laconic and caustic irony is an instance where Reznikoff's selection fits with both testimony as a restriction and an Objectivist poetics, as this concise statement from Reznikoff (in a 1968 interview) shows: "By the term 'objectivist' I suppose a writer may be meant who does not write directly about his feelings but about what he sees and hears; who is restricted almost to the testimony of a witness in a court of law; and who expresses his feeling indirectly by the selection of his subject-matter and, if he writes in verse, by its music."[40] Selection based on research; a seriality akin to montage; a redaction based on paring back details that obscure the relations at the core of the social narrative; and an editing based on a musicality of the poetic line: these are the politicized aesthetic of his documentary.

The questioning of documentary practices that the artist and theorist Hito Steyerl has pursued over the last decade provides a framework for the importance of an "affective and political constellation" in documentary practices that can illuminate what is enduring in Reznikoff's practice. Merging Foucault's definition of "governmentality" with documentary truth production, Steyerl identifies a form she coins "documentality," which relates to *Testimony*. For Steyerl, documentality can be the type of truth construction that Secretary of State Colin Powell participated in when he fabricated a set of truths to justify the invasion of Iraq in 2003; or it can be, conversely, the type of documentality that attempts to "thwart and problematize not only dominant forms of truth production but also of government, for instance in the attempts of the group Kinoki [Kino Eye] to create the Soviet Red Cinematography."[41] Pointing to the historical distrust of documentary representation, Steyerl arrives at an emphasis on, and recognition of the necessity of, affect in the representational economy of documentary, an economy shared by both social uncertainty and the challenge to documentary truth production. Steyerl points to the documentary image (and specifically the "poor image," an image whose truth value can be challenged due to its quality, yet an image that circulates electronically with ease) as having the potential to "possibly create . . . disruptive movements of thought and affect."[42]

This phrase is remarkably accurate for the poetry of both Oppen and Reznikoff. Steyerl locates the possibilities of documentary in a constellation similar to what I have suggested operates in their poetries, where a contingent affective economy forms among the poem, its possible publics, and the present (and in the case of *Testimony*, how the relations of the past mediate the present): "In this sense, the only possible documentary today is the presentation of an affective and political constellation which does not even exist, and which is yet to come."[43] While this temporality may seem utopian—invoking the *yet to come*—Steyerl's insistence on affective alliances and constellations gives us an insight into a poetics of affect that moves beyond the surety of the image, of the word, and of the document toward a sincerity that brings aesthetics and politics together. Such a poetics can link with "the investments and incoherence of political subjectivity and subjectification in relation to the world's disheveled but predictable dynamics"[44] without itself being predictable.

7

AGAINST OBJECTIVISM

CLAUDIA RANKINE'S *Citizen*

AMY DE'ATH

Serena, in her denim skirt, black sneaker boots, and dark mascara,
began wagging her finger and saying "no, no, no," as if by negating the
moment she could propel us back into a legible world.
—Claudia Rankine, *Citizen: An American Lyric*

In an essay on William Carlos Williams and the politics of form, Carla Billitteri invokes Walter Benjamin's concept of the aura and critique of New
Objective photography in order to characterize the auratic telos of Objectivist poetics. In reading Williams as an Objectivist (against the more usual
exclusion of his work from that frame), Billitteri's aim is to show how, in
contradiction to their insistence on the political refunctioning of the artist,
Objectivist poets upheld a "poetics of authenticity" reflected in the perfected form of the poem. She points to the existential and epistemological authority implied by Louis Zukofsky's method of "thinking with the
things as they exist," George Oppen's claim that poetry is a "singular 'test
of truth,'" and the politically conservative—yet strikingly concordant—
aspects of Williams's "intense vision of the facts," whereby the poet's perceptions are objectified in perfect poetic form.[1]

Thinking about what has come 'after' Objectivism, therefore, is made a
more complex task by the opacities, contradictions, and redirections that
characterize Objectivist poetics. But Billitteri's argument that "political engagement openly clashes with aesthetic inclinations" (44) is perhaps nowhere more reflexively and conscientiously explored in Objectivist poetry
than in Oppen's work, and it is to some astute readings by the poet Rob
Halpern that I will briefly turn in order to propose that the difficulties—
in Halpern's reading, the erotics of failure—that marked Oppen's poetry
throughout the 1960s, and to some extent Objectivist poetics more gener-

ally, must be set against another position regarding questions of perception, representation, and the relation between subject and object: the experience and ontology of the black subject.

To this end, I want to propose that we could look back on Objectivist poetry through the contemporary frame of Claudia Rankine's remarkably successful 2014 book *Citizen: An American Lyric*, a sequence of poems in which blackness is implicitly linked to the notion of experience that takes place outside, or beneath, the structure of social life, and where the ontological status of the black subject *as a subject* is pulled into question. If, as criticism of Oppen's work has shown, the subject's sense of historical agency, sense of crisis, and knowledge of oneself depends in his poems on the encounter with radical alterity, and with the world of matter, then how is the premise of such a poetics—a product of its time, and still dependent on an Enlightenment understanding of subject-object relations that tends toward an unexamined universalism—challenged or perhaps entirely refused by a book like *Citizen*, where the problem is not the relation between subject and object but the ontological preclusion of subjecthood within a global history of antiblack structural violence?

More complex than they may at first appear, the oft-quoted opening lines from 1968's "Of Being Numerous"—"There are things / We live among 'and to see them / Is to know ourselves'"[2]—represent the beginning of an extended period in which the nature of the encounter between subject and world was the focus of constant scrutiny in Oppen's work. This would involve contending with ontological crisis as Oppen, a Jew who between 1936 and 1941 was also a member of the Communist Party and spent most of the 1950s in political exile in Mexico, strained to comprehend the atrocities of recent history and the contemporary Cuban missile crisis. At the same time, however, his epistemological "search for truth"[3] became a search for "something outside of history": perhaps most important, and as Halpern's writing on Oppen does much to demonstrate, truth might be glimpsed or felt in an encounter with "the mineral fact," the impenetrable and mute "fatal rock," which signifies at once concrete matter and abstract metaphysics and extends the frame of temporality from historical time to geological time.[4] Thus, while truth or knowledge in "Of Being Numerous" seems to move dialectically between the part and the whole, from "The absolute singular // The unearthly bonds / Of the singular" to the "unmanageable pantheon,"[5] Oppen would reject dialectics and the historical materialist view of history he had held previous to his notorious thirty-year abstention from writing. As Peter Nicholls suggests, a Levinasian sense of relating to the other "as the quintessential expression of the ethical" may help to define the sense of social obligation in a poetry that Oppen himself—stringently separating aesthetics and politics—would have refrained from naming as "political."[6]

But even for this most philosophical and apocalyptic of Objectivists, for whom the radical contingency of material history went hand in hand with profound doubt concerning the centrality of the subject's status as an agent of history, the object always implied a subject—and one whose presence was perhaps paradoxically emphasized under the threat of geological obscurity and impenetrable matter. Halpern characterizes this sense of crisis as a "domestic dysphoria" surrounding "what it means to act in the world, and what it means to be acted upon," a dilemma revealing "a crisis of masculinity, and a catastrophe in the very idea of historical agency."[7] Succinctly capturing Oppen's desire for an encounter with the "mineral fact" of the object-world, Halpern notes that

> Oppen's passion—inseparable from patience—begins with a pathos of distance, an attitude toward knowledge that hangs on the ability to distance oneself from the object of encounter—*differentiation*—so as not to turn it into oneself. [. . .] But while distance may be necessary to point and see—and indeed, such distance is the condition underlying crucial lines like "There are things / We live among 'and to see them / Is to know ourselves'"—Oppen also seeks to breach this distance, courting its collapse in the veracity of the encounter so that one can doubt no longer. (60)

Keeping in mind Oppen's desiring subject, who seeks both to retain and to close the gap between himself and the object he perceives, and whose fearful sense of threatened agency and radical contingency is set against the scale of geological time, let us turn to Rankine's *Citizen*. Here, by contrast, we find a speaker who describes the inevitability of sighing by reference to a continuity and a field of impact between her body and the world where, "truth be told, you could no more control these sighs than that which brings the sighs about."[8] The sigh seems forcibly extracted: "Perhaps each sigh is drawn into existence to pull in, pull under, who knows"; and a new section continues: "The sigh is the pathway to breath; it allows breathing. That's just self-preservation. No one fabricates that. You sit down, you sigh. You stand up, you sigh. The sighing is a worrying exhale of ache. You wouldn't call it an illness; still it is not the iteration of a free being. What else to liken yourself to but an animal, the ruminant kind?" (60).

The monologue of the fourth section of *Citizen* centrifugally spins from

this involuntary sigh. It constitutes a scene of somatic negativity that resonates across the book, as if the worrying, aching mood of the sigh were
carried in the consistently frequent "you" of the book's second-person address, a mode to which much of this prose poetry is firmly confined.

Rankine's short, measured sentences, the consistent seriality of her stanzas and sections, and the introspective or "ruminant" character of her observations might *seem* to bear resemblance to the writing of Oppen's "middle
period," especially when we compare their poetry as forms of durational,
serial, and recursive writing that foreground a disconnection with, or distance from, the world and others. Here is the succeeding part of the fourth
section of *Citizen*: "You like to think memory goes far back though remembering was never recommended. Forget all that, the world says. [. . .] Don't
wear sunglasses in the house, the world says, though they soothe, soothe
sight, soothe you" (61).

Consider this soliloquy alongside section 13 of "Of Being Numerous":

> They are shoppers,
> Choosers, judges; . . . And here the brutal
> is without issue, a dead end.
> They develop
> Argument in order to speak, they become
> unreal, unreal, life loses
> solidity, loses extent, baseball's their game
> because baseball is not a game
> but an argument. [. . .][9]

The formal and tonal similarities are clear: both speakers are disturbed by
an abstract, generalizable world at the same time as they comment on their
separation from it; short sentences are anxiously punctuated by superflu-
ous commas and repetitions (most emphatically in "soothe, soothe" and
"unreal, unreal"); and both examples evidence a grappling with existential
questions about the imperative to "forget" memory (Rankine), or about a
loss of reality and "solidity" that slips away when the rhetoric of communication, that is, "Argument" and speech, takes hold (Oppen).[10]

And yet, while we might note similarities and parallels between these
lines from Oppen and Rankine (indeed, between Rankine's oeuvre and
Objectivist poetry more generally), it is important to understand why such
formal similarities cannot be read as such, why they are not the same thing;
and thus why, for example, Rankine's feminized speaker derogatorily compares herself to "an animal, the ruminant kind" (ruminant animals regurgi-

tate and rechew their food, hence the phrase "chewing the cud"), while the subject of Oppen's writing reliably substantiates Billitteri's description of an "auratic" Objectivism. As Oppen, likely thinking of his wartime comrades, writes, "I cannot even now / altogether disengage myself / From those men" ("Of Being Numerous," 171), his experience of war is also what forces his poetry to face "the great mineral silence," a lofty force that "Vibrates, hums, a process / Completing itself" (179).

But how might we best understand the significance of the difference between these poetries, and how could we respond to it as readers and critics? Dorothy Wang's recent critique of reductive modes of reading specific to Asian American poetry provides a useful starting point. Wang posits the hypothetical (but all too recognizable) claim that the Asian American poet John Yau and the British American poet T. S. Eliot display the same formal techniques when they question the idea of a stable subjectivity:

> The fallacious assumption here is that because Yau and Eliot both seem to be making similar poetic (and metaphysical) moves, these moves are formally and substantively identical. But Eliot and Yau are *not* actually doing the same thing in their poetries. Given how radically different their persons, subjectivities, histories, contexts, and so on are, there is no way that their projects of destabilizing subjectivity are the same. Nor can the resulting poems be the same. Poetic subjectivities and poetic practices are not interchangeable.[11]

Wang's point is strikingly simple, but as her clear delineation of identity as a historically produced category implicitly rejects the essentialism of conventional identity politics, it can help us to propose a number of distinctions between Oppen's and Rankine's poetries. Where one assumes a universalist and arguably transhistorical position—albeit an outlook brought into focus by the conditions of modernity—in which all subjects are equally negated by the object-world, the other situates itself historically in an antiblack world, where blackness names an ontological category produced by slavery, and in which the black subject never actually enters into subjectivity, perhaps since, in "the afterlife of slavery," as Jared Sexton writes,[12] blackness names not a subject but an object. On the basis of these positions, it is possible to reframe Wang's reasonable and suddenly obvious assertion to propose that since Rankine's poetic practice implicitly challenges Enlightenment conceptions of the subject, it also challenges the premise of any project interested in destabilizing subjectivity. In other words, the intellectual project of *Citizen* throws the universalism of the following lines from "Of Being Numerous" into sharp relief:

> But who escapes
> Death
>
> Among these riders
> Of the subway,
>
> They know
> By now as I know
>
> Failure and the guilt
> Of failure," (174)

The failure and "guilt / Of failure" that Oppen laments here, so intrinsically tied to a popular idea of death as the great equalizer, is no doubt linked to his acute sense of crisis following the contortion of 1930s communism into Stalinism, the traumas of World War II and the Holocaust, and his political exile in Mexico.[13] Yet assuming that the implied answer to the rhetorical question "But who escapes / Death" is *nobody*, these lines can feel outdated in the face of the increasingly obvious reality, in an era defined by the proliferation of wageless life and surplus populations, that death is profoundly unequal. It is perhaps with depressing hindsight, or through something like Freudian *Nachträglichkeit*, then, that the performative quandaries of Oppen's writing—a self-consciously ethical poetics produced from the subjective position of a Jewish man who had lived through some of the worst atrocities of the twentieth century—may help us to understand the contradictions propelled by Objectivist poets more generally. And because Oppen's work registers the gap between a "real politics" and a poetic practice, between a set of intensely particularized and often traumatic experiences and a quest for a quasi-objective knowledge or truth, it can give us a better bearing on what Billitteri refers to as the Objectivists' "conflicted record" or, referencing Benjamin, their "unwavering reliance upon an aesthetics of reception predicated on the achievement of a poetic form which would facilitate the 'contemplative immersion' of the reader in the poem."[14] It is thus perhaps a horrid irony—given the ontological preclusion of blackness from the lifeworld of human subjectivity on which I will later elaborate—that in Oppen's case such authenticity is guaranteed by what he calls "anti-ontology."[15] As Nicholls has underlined, consumerist and war-hungry American culture was, for Oppen, "mired in 'rootless speech,' a language which has no relation to being (it is 'Anti-ontology'), and which betrays any sense of historical 'continuation.'"[16]

But if this "poetics of authenticity" assumes a subject negated by the object-world, then what we might read as its refusal—or "the refusal of what has been refused"[17]—in Rankine's practice avoids the moralism potentially associated with correcting or reminding the white poet or reader of their structural advantages, because such reading does not take place along an ethical register. Rather, I want to suggest that the horizon of *Citizen* is set against a different striation of historical time, one that contests the Objectivist historical imaginary altogether. In this way, Rankine's work can be read as a refusal of now conventional (and often white and male) modes of linking politics and poetic form, given that these critical modes depend, at least initially, on a basic opposition of subject and object that *Citizen* challenges.

After Objectivism?

It may thus seem rather obvious to propose that Rankine does not write *after* Objectivism. Indeed, to ignore this fact risks obscuring the very capacity of poetry that Zukofsky and Oppen held as most important: the articulation of social meanings through the poem shaped by the historical moment in which it is written: a matter, as Zukofsky wrote in a 1953 letter to Lorine Niedecker, "of what was in the air at the time."[18] Perhaps it is no surprise that Zukofsky's description, in 1931, of a writing "which is the detail, not mirage, of seeing, of thinking with the things as they exist"—a "rested totality" achieved by "the resolving of words and their ideation into structure"—retained its capacity to describe an oppositional force in poetics for decades. The idea of the poem as a crafted object that could represent or mediate an entire structure of relations, while also casting off transcendent flights of fancy (in Zukofsky's words, that "*symboliste* semi-allegorical gleam"),[19] holds an enduring appeal—augmented by a promise of clarity—for a materialist or Marxist poetics. But it is not necessary to assert that Objectivism has indelibly or comprehensively shaped contemporary poetry in the United States—a scene of tremendous heterogeneity and racial diversity—in order to acknowledge that Objectivist poetry has been a crucial influence among a wide array of poetic practices in the twenty-first century.

For Jennifer Moxley, Oppen's *Of Being Numerous* "connects 'things' to both self-knowledge and structural assumptions," leading her to ask a series of questions about labor, commodities, and value: "What are we made out of? Of things? To believe so confirms the labor theory of value. [. . .] Or is it rather that *our* value is constituted by the number of things we make?" and subsequently, "But what if those whose labor produced the things cannot live among them?"[20] While Moxley's *There Are Things We Live Among* pursues a more anecdotal, diaristically contemplative route in its answer to these questions, as opposed to taking up value in the strictly Marxist sense, her approximate rehearsal of the Marxian critique of alienation leaves out Marx's critique of the labor theory of value—which, importantly, shows us that value is artificial, and not determined by the amount of labor congealed in a commodity. On this level, Moxley does not depart from the orthodox 1930s Marxism that was so influential for Zukofsky and Oppen. At the same time, the taut aestheticism of *There Are Things We Live Among*—which frequently delves into explicatory asides, close reading exercises, and phenomenological ruminations on object relations, deliberately engaging the forms of fetishism it seeks to highlight—risks playing into current depoliticizing tendencies in literary studies that, echoing formalist aspects of New Criticism, seek a return to textual surfaces, to the "innocent" pleasures of reading, and to the very *literariness* of Literature.[21] But this is precisely the kind of critical gesture that a dialectical Objectivism would refuse. As Ben Hickman, writing about Zukofsky, notes:

> Since the first essays on the Objectivist poets by Hugh Kenner and Cid Corman there has been an anxiety among commentators to decant the poets associated with the movement from the revolutionary cultural milieu that gave rise to their unique fusion of modernism and left-wing politics. [. . .] Zukofsky was, at least at one time, a poet interested in a good deal more than subverting "New Critical close reading," which is constantly and anachronistically presented as the great aim of his work.[22]

As if to counter such small claims for poetry, Jeff Derksen's *The Vestiges* foregrounds a dialectical movement between the concrete and the abstract, invoking Oppen's serial forms in order to suggest an aesthetic-political anachronism between Fordist and post-Fordist modes of value production. *The Vestiges* oscillates between expressive and critical language, ironic imitation and sincerity, in its attention to globalized production: "The quiet diplomacy / of a world connected // by things used / every day and made / elsewhere. Easy."[23] The result is an abstracted lyric that provides a kind of tracking critique of the material movements of various capitalist circuits. While *The Vestiges* attentively reproduces the steady rhythms and durational patience of *Discrete Series* and *Of Being Numerous*, the equalizing force of the object-world, so central to Oppen's poetics, is meticulously substituted here with processes that denote movement: hardened labor is shipped out of the global South, social reproduction in Calgary "circles" the Albertan prairies, a pipeline is built through indigenous territories, rain in the Brazilian coffee belt causes stock indexes to plummet.[24]

In this way *The Vestiges* could be read as a dialectical attempt to represent the unevenness of social relations within a post-Fordist global economy and a system of capitalist abstraction that is nevertheless *historically real*: in other words, concrete and objective. Oppen the poet seems to linger here not only as methodological and politico-philosophical informer, but through a shared sense of crisis and vulnerability, an anxiety also shared by the queer politics of Halpern's *Disaster Suites* (2008), and through many stages of Rachel Blau DuPlessis's "life poem," *Drafts* (1985–2010), sections of which directly respond to *Of Being Numerous*. But where in the contemporary scene of politically committed poetry does *Citizen* stand?

Citizen begins with a series of events described in the second person: a nun deliberately overlooks, or fails to notice, as a white schoolgirl cheats from your exam, later presuming to thank you with the words "you smell good and have features more like a white person"; a close friend keeps accidentally calling you by the name of her black housekeeper, eventually stopping but never acknowledging her mistake; your neighbor calls the police on the "menacing black guy casing both your homes," who turns out to be your friend who is babysitting and taking a phone call outside; a mother and daughter arrive at your row on a United Airlines flight, see you in the window seat, and are visibly perturbed, murmuring, "This is not what I expected," and:

> A woman you do not know wants to join you for lunch. You are visiting her campus. In the cafe you both order the Caesar salad. This overlap is not the beginning of anything because she immediately points out that she, her father, her grandfather, and you, all attended the same college. She wanted her son to go there as well, but because of affirmative action or minority something—she is not sure what they are calling it these days and weren't they supposed to get rid of it?—her son wasn't accepted. You are not sure if you are meant to apologize for this failure of your alma mater's legacy program; instead you ask where he ended up. The prestigious school she mentions doesn't seem to assuage her irritation. This exchange, in effect, ends your lunch. The salads arrive.[25]

The "you" of *Citizen* is both an address and an implicit "I": as much as it conversationally invites the reader to imagine an experience, it also underlines the durational, cumulative, reliably familiar—in short, permanent—qualities of this experience for a particular, racialized "you" or "I." The experiences invoked here are specifically *not shared*; they are often illegible to the individuals they are caused by or involve. The implied "I," then, is distinctly antiuniversalist and signals a different order of lyric isolation; one that is imposed rather than exploratory, that registers privately and sometimes in disbelief—"What did you say?" the speaker asks at one point (14)—at the racist logics it encounters. In the passage above, for example, the conditions under which lunch happens seem to close in on the speaker, whose agency only emerges negatively as the annulment of the event of lunch: "This overlap is not the beginning of anything," and "This exchange, in effect, ends your lunch" (14).

While a privately noted refusal such as this affords the speaker little relief from a situation that continues to unfold regardless of the speaker's investment, it nevertheless suggests a cognitive withdrawal: a detached, isolated thought process that seems to split the situation in two. As the woman's overbearing sense of access to the social space of the conversation is accompanied by an apparent failure to understand both the structural implications of her hereditary privilege and the insult her comments carry, Rankine's own commentary on the situation is implicit in the speaker's tone as she or he describes the conversation. The arrogance of the woman's obliviousness is already clear in her language—we can guess that her dismissal of the "minority something" plays into predictable reactionary criticisms of affirmative action as politically correct faddishness—but Rankine's narration brings out the more generalizable overtones of this depressing situation. The speaker's distance from "the woman you do not know," and uncertainty about the absurd possibility that an apology might even be expected from her or him, is compounded by the other woman's childish sense of entitlement: "the prestigious school she mentions doesn't seem to assuage her irritation." As in much of *Citizen*, the affective pull of the exchange is heightened by a tonal evenness disturbingly imbued with the quotidian currents of structural racism.

It is crucial to emphasize that *Citizen*'s black speaker does not simply provide an example of thematic and formal "difference" as she or he addresses a contemporary context of antiblack violence and racist microaggressions. Rather, the literary and social properties of the book are products of their specific temporal and spatial contexts, and *Citizen* joins contemporary writing by Dawn Lundy Martin, Fred Moten, and M. NourbeSe Philip, among many others, in addressing a crisis of racial representation as one outcome of a structure of domination in which the implicitly white subject is constituted—at the level of the social and the symbolic—by the negative impression of blackness, where to be Black is to be racially marked by the system of chattel slavery.[26] One of the most resounding publications in North American poetics to address this crisis is undoubtedly Philip's *Zong!*, a book-length documentary poem about the slave ship *Zong* and the "destruction" of its "cargo"—150 of whom were thrown overboard so that the ship's owners could claim insurance for their loss. Restricted (by scant historical evidence rather than conceptual procedure) to the language of the 1783 case report, *Gregson v. Gilbert*, *Zong!* has been variously defined as testimony, a poetics of witness, conceptual poetry, musical score, and excavation of legal text. Visually the poem resembles the late twentieth-century paragrammatic fragmentation of concrete poetry of Canadian poets such as bpNichol and Steve McCaffery; but as Susan Holbrook notes, Philip "engages a similar technique with very different motives and effects." Unlike Nichol's "search for the alternate and hidden logics in language," Philip's paragrams tend *not* to "resolve themselves back into the rational."[27]

The "organic division between the rational and the crazy" is refused by Martin's and Moten's work too.[28] Like Rankine, these poets understand the persistence of antiblackness in forms both plain to see and maddeningly obscured. "How to know what violence is? / Always inches from disappearance. From swelling into unrecognition,"[29] writes Martin, and as I have argued elsewhere, her recent poetry approaches a kind of treatise on the black female body as it is "framed by modernism," in the process documenting an experience of the *denial* of experience.[30] Her 2015 book *Life in a Box Is a Pretty Life* ventriloquizes eugenicist racist vernaculars and emphasizes the phenotypical aspects of racialization, unfolding at the level of private psychological experience at the same time as it apprehends antiblack misogyny and modernist aesthetics as coextensive structures of oppression.

Martin's inward-turning prose lyric, and committed focus on the forms and modes of racist violence both physical and psychological, sets her work in contrast with the more outward-looking black optimism structuring Moten's poetic-critical project. Declaratively rooted in the black radical tradition, Moten's affirmation of "a social and historical paraontology" theorizes the forms of insurgent black life that precede—indeed, are the precondition for—the structure of domination set in place by the transatlantic slave trade. For Moten, this fugitive social life moves amid the undercommons of an already integrated totality,[31] and his by turns deconstructive, Deleuzian, and Marxian project emphasizes "the normative striving against the grain of the very radicalism from which the desire for norms is derived," a strife that "is essential not only to contemporary black academic discourse but also to the discourses of the barbershop, the beauty shop and the bookstore."[32] In Moten's poems this strife often manifests as a tension between social struggles and personal dilemmas on the one hand and the movement of an everyday black vernacular on the other. Circular syntactical arrangements, internal rhymes, and lulling rhythms propel the poems onward in spite of these deep violences and quotidian oppressions, at times against the poet's wishes: "I belong to that sound / all the time, everyday. how bound I am / by music!"[33] Thus, while Moten's writing arguably shares an ontological investigation with *Citizen*, the complex tenor of its black optimism—impossible to properly explore within the confines of this essay—may sit in discordance with the often pointedly flat mood of Rankine's prosody.

My point in skimming all too briefly across these works is to highlight the simple but significant fact that Philip, Martin, Moten, and Rankine are all deliberately explicit about situating their poetry in relation to a history of black thought. Indeed, it is hard to see how the assimilating, new formalist kind of reading that Wang describes could be performed on their poems with a straight face. Philip, for example, cites Lindon Barrett's argument, in *Blackness and Value*, about the significance of the prelinguistic "shout" to black creativity, and she directly compares her project to the way southern novelist Walker Percy explores "a state of amnesia in which the individual, his or her subjectivity having been destroyed, becomes alienated from him- or herself."[34] Moten and Rankine reference black writers, musicians, and philosophers—often simply by inserting their names—in what might be read in the context of a dynamic discourse in black studies around the politics of naming,[35] while Martin's approach is different insofar as she invokes overarching themes of black thought (for example, the relation between blackness and humanity, house and field, incarceration and beauty) yet often declines to attach these ideas to specific figures. None of this is to say that the influence of a (white) avant-gardism is precluded in black poetry—indeed, Tyrone Williams has compared the "field aesthetics" of *Zong!* to an Olsonian open field poetics[36]—but that, consciously and often deliberately, these poets may be more interested in setting a history of black thought in relation to present social antagonisms: in a wry invocation of the "good black subject," one of the few names to conspicuously appear in *Life in a Box Is a Pretty Life* arrives in the line "Only Will Smith has been spared."[37]

At a moment when endemic unemployment, mass incarceration, and racially motivated and state-sanctioned police murder of black men and women are increasingly met with rioting and protest that lay bare a deep history of black oppression and revolt, the force of Rankine's critique and the aesthetic experience it engenders—enough to provoke criticisms that *Citizen* is not poetry but sociology[38]—is drawn in no small part, then, from Rankine's self-conscious positioning of the text's historicity, perhaps most powerfully achieved through the book's collage of striking visuals. An image of the white, blond Danish tennis player Caroline Wozniacki, with towels stuffed in her top and shorts in a racist imitation of Serena Williams's figure, appears in the book alongside images of contemporary work exploring blackness and representation by the Kenyan–New York artist Wangechi Mutu, the young Nigerian artist Toyin Odutola, and Carrie Mae Weems, as well as two Glenn Ligon paintings and J. M. W. Turner's 1840 painting *The Slave Ship*. These images—as well as citations drawn from Frantz Fanon, Homi K. Bhabha, Patricia Smith, Frederick Douglass, James Baldwin's *The Fire Next Time*, and Ralph Ellison's *Invisible Man*—not only position Rankine's text within an illustrious tradition of black thought that cumulatively pulls into view a systematically obscured totality but serve as a reminder of the enduring complexities of black representationality as it responds to, or indeed precedes, a persistent and world-historical antiblackness.

Objecthood

As I've intimated already, my reading of *Citizen* is informed by the theoretical tendency in black studies known as Afro-pessimism. This "intellectual disposition," in Jared Sexton's words, "posits a political ontology dividing the Slave from the world of the Human in a constitutive way,"[39] thus requiring an ontological status of *social death* for the black subject. Arguing that Marxist cultural theory's focus on the wage fails to account for gratuitous violence against black bodies, another of Afro-pessimism's key theoreticians, Frank B. Wilderson, explains antiblack violence as "a relation of terror" that stands in stark contrast to the rational/symbolic wage-relation defining the subject of Marxist discourse.[40] In this paradigmatic framework, blackness is an ontology of social death necessary in order for the Human (and its Enlightenment notions of freedom) to maintain its libidinal safety in the realm of the symbolic, and we might see how *Citizen*'s critique *could* be read along similar lines—that is, as a suggestion that that which is excluded ontologically from the premises of linguistic or symbolic meaning makes no sense in the language of structure.

Interestingly, this reading would not square with emerging materialist accounts of contemporary antiblackness that are beginning to develop through the work of critics such as Chris Chen and Jodi Melamed, and that build on earlier work regarding racial formations and "racecraft" by scholars who include Howard Winant and Barbara J. Fields. These positions are varied, to be sure. But they all make use of contemporary analyses of structural unemployment, expulsion from the formal economy, and vulnerability to state violence in order to consider processes of racialization through the Marxian concept of surplus populations and in terms of the dispossession of the commodity labor-power. A materialist account of antiblackness may therefore hold that expulsion from a structure of oppression (most pertinently, waged labor) does not mean that one's life does not remain defined by that structure.[41]

The difference between these theoretical frameworks is not a point of inquiry for *Citizen*. But it does hold relevance for how we read—*and attribute cause to*—the social and psychic patterning of objectivizing violence indexed by this book. While that question necessitates a longer discussion, we might at least say for now that since Afro-pessimism, Marxian analyses, and *Citizen* consistently emphasize the negation of the black subject dropped from the radar of social life, *Citizen* could be read as a Fanonian poetics. Indeed, the book seems to echo the premise, first put forward by Frantz Fanon, that the singular process of racialization that produces blackness as a category does so by marking blackness as that which is relegated to objecthood.[42] Consequently, Rankine's black lyric "I" is apparently incapable of containing a subject as such:

Sometimes "I" is supposed to hold what is not there until
it is. Then *what is* comes apart the closer you are to it.

This makes the first person a symbol for something.

The pronoun barely holding the person together.[43]

Appearing within an extended serial monologue, the rhythm and tone of these lines implicitly compose a second movement within the book, following on from a more narratological, documentary-style series of encounters with racist "microaggressions." They seem to describe a process of subjecthood brought into being by forcible insistence: "I" will hold "what is not there until it is." Like a failing version of Pascal's "kneel down and you will believe!"[44] the pronoun of *Citizen* is shown up as a liberal construction— an affirmation of a subject designed by multiculturalism and understood in terms of difference rather than domination, a subject that increasingly falls apart at the seams "the closer you are to it." The first person, then, is "a symbol for something," as opposed to *someone*, even as the following line suggests that this construct of blackness is a thing depended upon; indeed, as numerous critiques of the politics of recognition have shown, in Western democracies certain racialized subjects are only granted visibility—and legal and cultural validity—within structurally circumscribed limits.[45] Clearly, the trouble with subjectivity here is fundamentally distinct from the problem of the lyric subject that has provided such productive grist for antisubjectivist avant-gardes, from Ezra Pound's (nevertheless emotion-charged) "direct treatment of the 'thing'" to Christian Bök's exaltation of words by and for machines.[46] This is an avant-garde that, as Wang has argued persuasively, is almost always implied as "the provenance of a literary acumen and culture that is unmarked but assumed to be white."[47]

Seeming to insist on this very distinction, Rankine is emphatic a few lines later: "Drag that first person out of the social death of history, / then we're kin,"[48] she writes, in language more directly confrontational than in other, ostensibly documentary and descriptive sections. While these words reverberate with Orlando Patterson's influential 1982 book, *Slavery and Social Death*, they might more precisely be a reference to Hortense Spillers's writing on kinlessness and enslavement. Spillers's emphasis on the "bitter Americanizing" dimensions of slavery points to how the violent loss of indigenous name and land in the Middle Passage and the New World functions additionally as metaphor for a range of human and cultural displacements, not least the severance of blood ties by a patriarchal order of slave ownership where any new child's human and familial status remained undefined. Spillers describes this "enforced state of breach" as a "vestibular cultural formation where 'kinship' loses meaning, *since it can be invaded at any given and arbitrary moment by the [sic] property relations.*"[49]

It does not seem too far a stretch to suggest that *Citizen* springs from a contemporary version of this same threat, as a book composed in part by scripts for situation videos dedicated to the memory of Trayvon Martin, James Craig Anderson, and Mark Duggan. Elsewhere *Citizen* responds—usually through intimate language—to racially determined topical events: Hurricane Katrina, the 2006 World Cup, or the Jena Six assault,[50] the latter of which Rankine finishes by alluding to the seemingly inevitable fate of the young black male, who is shown, in this particular sequence, to lack "positioning which is a position for only one kind of boy face it" and for whom "the fists the feet criminalized already are weapons already exploding the landscape and then the litigious hitting back is life imprisoned."[51] Here Rankine's assertion that to be young, black, and male is to be automatically criminalized recalls Moten and Stefano Harney's depiction, in *The Undercommons*, of the settler-fort and the surround, insofar as the circular grammar of "the position of positioning which is a position" suggests what Moten and Harney call "the black before" of the surround, black life as that which *precedes* civil society and the systematic violence necessary to preserve it, and which therefore means "we cannot represent ourselves. We can't be represented."[52]

Indeed, while Spiller's rendering of "property relations" can quite literally denote a whole range of state apparatuses and abstract structures of late capitalism—a configuration that Sexton characterizes as an emergent global apartheid set to exclude domestic black populations via the prison-industrial complex, ghettoization, and displacement[53]—"property relations" means *psychic* property too. In *Citizen* the scale of this exclusion becomes condensed into single, isolated psychological experiences and events and expanded again via the curatorial accumulation of a particular order of experience, giving each episode of the book a synecdochal intensity—an example, perhaps, of Sianne Ngai's conceptualization of a visceral abstraction—not so much an Objectivist expression of metaphysical truth, more a singular physical experience felt with the weight of an abstract totality.[54]

Later, Rankine kaleidoscopically conflates and redefines the optics of subjects and objects in a script for a situation video about the racially motivated murder of James Craig Anderson, captured on closed-circuit television. Here the lifeless, machinic murder weapon—a pickup truck—seems to possess more subjective agency than Anderson, who is depicted as the passive recipient of racist violence: "In the next frame the pickup truck is in motion. Its motion activates its darkness. The pickup truck is a condition of darkness in motion. It makes a dark subject. You mean a black subject. No, a black object" (93).

For Wilderson, this particular scene might figure as a metonym for a condition of ontology, one in which blackness is "a position against which Humanity establishes, maintains, and renews its coherence, its corporeal integrity,"[55] a structural position of nonrelation brought into being by a gratuitous violence that is symbolic rather than political/economic. And as these lines throw other parts of the book into relief, it seems clear that *Citizen* is above all interested in the relation between subjectivity and "an American Lyric" for a subject who has not, historically, been guaranteed. Since the pickup truck "makes a dark subject," and then a "black object," we might even say that Rankine's language of conditionality and activation presents a challenge to G. W. F. Hegel's conception of universality—the "universal content everyone must activate within himself"[56]—as well as his framing of the problem of how philosophy must activate itself too: the Hegelian assertion that philosophy cannot take account of its own movement in a way that is separate from, or prior to, that very movement itself.[57] As Sexton notes, black ontology presents a problem for "the thought of being itself" ("Social Life," 7) and thus for critique, since we can no longer presuppose "the system in which subordination takes place" (10).

Coda

Underpinning the Objectivist concerns with the particulars of everyday life, with the material of the world, and with "form and technique as a conscious activity of intellectual labour," as Andrew Ross puts it, we might regard the double edge of what Ross calls the "moral [. . .] imperatives of sincerity, authenticity, and conviction"[58] as Objectivism's enduring contradiction. If the Objectivist poem is a mission in demystification, an effort to cast off that "symboliste semi-allegorical gleam," it also appeals to an epistemological authority that, in Zukofsky's and Oppen's work at least, acquires added layers of existential, and paradoxically *re*-mystifying, authenticity. With this strange philosophical contradiction in mind we might consider how *Citizen* obtains its force as a mode of critique and as an address to institutions of power, not because it implicitly rejects certain late modernist proposals and principles regarding form and craft—though it emphatically does that, and in the process asserts its own significance and self-reflexivity as a literary work—but because its refusal is linked to another articulation of a politics of refusal: one that pertains to the very basis of philosophy itself. It thus seems fitting to observe that Rankine's poems do not merely "raise questions"; they make political statements. They come down on a side. *Citizen* does this by attesting to the history of black subjection and its origins in chattel slavery; the effects of state-sanctioned antiblack racism; the potential for ambiguity in casual racism; the shocking clarity of casual racism. More specifically, the formal mechanisms and social content of Rankine's poems provide a complex commentary on the processes of mediation through which "race" is ascribed after the "post-race" Obama era, such that we might read this book as an attempt to articulate, as if across a spectrum of legibility to unintelligibility, the terrain of a social field in which "race" functions as a structural force that exerts itself via economic exploitation and expropriation, via disciplinary state apparatuses, as well as through less concrete codes at an institutional and personal level and through the gratuitous, often state-sanctioned, violence visited upon black bodies. As such, *Citizen* is an answer to the incredulity of Serena Williams, who cannot believe the umpire's five bad calls against her in the 2004 semi-final of the US Open—even as this answer might be that Serena, like all African Americans, does not live in a legible world.

In this way, *Citizen* maps an antiblack structure of domination and a set of historical conditions through which the Objectivist subject (which is to say, any nonblack subject) is constituted, too. What can it mean to read poetry 'after' Objectivism if the poetry in question asks us to think beyond the humanist binary of subject versus object? To be sure, much contemporary black poetics is informed by and borrows from a field poetics, a breath and a line, that was itself significantly influenced by the rhythms and vernacular of black literature and culture (albeit often without acknowledgment). But, as becomes especially clear in Oppen's work, objects—and the threat they pose—mean something so fundamentally different from what objects and objecthood have meant to a long history of black thought in the afterlife of slavery that we would be hard pushed indeed to claim that contemporary black poets are writing *after* Objectivism. This is not to position Oppen or Zukofsky as villains of antiblack racism—as if structural conditions were a matter of the intentional or conscious acts of individuals[59]—but to argue that it would be a disservice to contemporary black poetry to ascribe to it "predecessors" who are not predecessors. At the same time, it is also true that the politicization of the subject-object divide, out of its simplicity, may allow us to reread the Objectivists not only with admiration but with a sense of pathos for the things they were unable to confront. Reading 'after' Objectivism will thus mean taking *Citizen*'s ontological claim about the history of racial capitalism seriously, perhaps in order to respond to Cedric Robinson's insistence that "for the realization of new [poetic] theory we require new history."[60] This project seems especially urgent for the white reader and critic, positioned on the opposing side of this relation of domination, given that blackness is an experience to which she has no access. When the negativity of much black poetry is persistently neutralized by a liberal framework of a "poetics of identity" that literally and metaphorically ghettoizes black poetics,[61] celebrating its difference is surely less important than implementing its critique, which—in a nation-state that has made the dispensability of black lives abundantly clear—implies that we must read a book like *Citizen* historically, as new history.

8

WOMEN AND WAR, LOVE, LABOR

THE LEGACY OF LORINE NIEDECKER

JULIE CARR

The title for this essay came to me in a dream. I was a student in a class on feminism. The teacher was political philosopher Wendy Brown. We were looking at images of the second-wave feminist movement: women marching together, waving signs, chanting slogans, looking amazing in their T-shirts and sunglasses. It's not like that anymore, someone said sadly. What do we do now? Brown agreed. It's not, she said, for us to fight a war. To be a feminist in America now one must turn to labor and to love.

I know what my dreaming self thought Brown meant: that we have to labor, regularly and doggedly, for the equality of women, not just here but everywhere. It won't be a glorious battle; it will be work, and like all work it will be hard and sometimes frustrating, confusing, and dull. At the same time, we have to *learn to love* (the title of an interview with Brown I'd just finished reading was "Learning to Love Again"). This means we have to learn more about what love means for us in the personal/political sphere(s). We have to learn how to structure a society grounded in love, which is to say, in desire and vulnerability and care. (This second point is how I understood the recent work of Brown's partner, Judith Butler.)

But the irony was not lost on me while dreaming, nor when awake. Love and (certain kinds of) labor have always been within "women's domain." Not just the labor of birthing, though that comes immediately to mind, but also domestic labor, factory labor, farm labor, office labor, teaching labor, healing labor: all the laboring that women have done and still do, often underrecognized, unpaid, or underpaid, often while caring for children, sometimes without much or any help from those children's fathers, or (at least in the United States) from the state.

And love—we know what (heterosexual) love and its ideologies have done to women and girls under patriarchy, which is why, when my five-year-old says, with a slightly theatrical spreading of her arms, "Love is the most important thing!" I wince a bit.

But, I would argue, it's precisely because of these ironies, because of the way that *love* and *labor* have so often meant forms of oppression for women, that Wendy Brown is telling me to think about these terms: to reignite them in some way—and it's precisely because of the relationship they bear to war and violence too.

This essay is about the legacy of Lorine Niedecker, a poet often thought of in terms of labor, for famously, unlike many well-known poets of all generations, she was not financially well off, nor was she supported by an academic or professional job. And unlike many of the middle- and upper-class women of her generation, she was not supported by a male partner either. She worked—first as a proofreader, later as a manager of modest vacation properties she'd inherited, and finally as a cleaning woman. Moreover, she wrote often about labor and class, about the daily tasks of laundry, lawn mowing, wood chopping, and cooking, and also writing—about the ways in which class differences assert themselves in our streets and homes. As Margaret Ronda puts it, "Niedecker center[s] [her] poetics on a structuring concept of *labor* as animating force governing social processes, forms of bodily being and knowing, and aesthetic creations."[1]

Less often noted, but as predominantly, Niedecker was a poet of war. As Eleni Sikelianos writes, "Lorine Niedecker [. . .] quietly recorded the presence of things that fly through the air and explode in body and mind." Sikelianos finds "the disjunctiveness of a world gone to war" not only in the references to wounded dismembered soldiers, or to blasts, gases, and bombs (the London Blitz, the atom bomb), but also in the pieced-together forms of Niedecker's long poems. Sikelianos suggests that Niedecker reaches toward a kind of healing of the ruptured world by way of form, as her serial poems construct "wholes" out of severed parts.[2]

Not only is Niedecker a poet of labor and a poet of war (her two most frequently used nouns are "war" and "work," reports Elizabeth Willis); she's also a poet of the intimate relationship between the two.[3] She understood the soldier as a worker, and understood too the ways that capitalism depends on war as one of its most productive industries, even as war's human cost is paid primarily by the poor. In poems such as "Bombings," "Tell me a story about the war," and "1937," she reveals this damaging dynamic. And when she pairs such poems as "They came at a pace" with "I doubt I'll get silk stocking out" (*New Goose*); or "The number of Britons killed" with "Old Hamilton hailed the man from the grocery store" (*New Goose* manuscript) she seems to be using proximity to speak to the ways war and labor (or class) intertwine.

But how does one speak of "love" in Niedecker's work? The subject of romantic love, at least, seems more often avoided than explored. Rather, Niedecker is nothing short of sardonic in her assessment of gender relations, whether she's considering the ways girls present themselves as objects of desire "with their bottoms out" ("Not feeling well") or thinking about the subjection of women in marriage, such as in the poem "So you're married young man," where she writes, "She needs washers and dryers / she needs bodice uplift / she needs deep-well cookers / she needs power shift," or in "I rose from marsh mud," where she describes a bride as a "little white slave girl / in her diamond fronds." Despite the loving gesture of her "Poems for Paul" (and perhaps through the child to the father), there is very little even here of direct expressions of love or affection.[4]

So how *does* love show up in Niedecker's work, and how might this love be a response to the destructions of war she is so keenly aware of throughout her career? Interestingly, love becomes thematized most directly in Niedecker's *handmade* projects—works that were also, not incidentally, gifts, two of which bookended her career: *NEXT YEAR OR I FLY MY ROUNDS, TEMPESTUOUS* (mid-1930s, for Zukofsky) and *Homemade Poems* (1964, for Cid Corman). Indeed, we often refer to handmade objects as *labors of love*. They take so much time—"unnecessary" time, since a machine could usually do it quicker—that one has to *love* the work to bother with it. But also, homemade objects speak directly of intimacy, for they bear the mark of their maker's hands as they reach toward a receiver. These works are *labors of love* in a third way too: not only does the handmade object resist the numbing and distancing effects of capitalist production, but also handmade work becomes for Niedecker, as for many poets who have followed her, a way to resist the estrangements and destructions of war and other forms of violence.

Before we look at examples of this dynamic in Niedecker's work, I'd like to gesture to the present by talking briefly about the contemporary phenomenon labeled *Craftivism*. Craftivism, as the name implies, is a form of activism rooted in craftwork. Needlepoint, knitting, book making, sewing: these traditionally female activities have been reclaimed by contemporary, often female artists who see in that work an opportunity for resistance. That resistance functions on various levels and has various targets. Craftivism often stands against patriarchal aspects of the art world (and thus, by extension, of culture in general), which has traditionally devalued the aesthetic labor of women throughout history. It stands more generally, and perhaps wishfully, against global capitalism's factory-made objects and the objectification of the human that capital enables.[5] For the crafter, the handmade object resists the "commodification of all aspects of life,"[6] not only because it offers a nonalienated form of labor but also because it invents a new/old temporality, a sensed slow-time that is in itself a transformed mode of life. As Ann Cvetkovich writes, "The craft of slow living [. . .] take[s] up the manual labor often associated with working-class and precapitalist ways of living and working. [. . .] As a practice, and not just an ephemeral feeling, crafting is not the homology or first step or raw material for some form of political change beyond it. It is already a form of self-transformation."[7]

But significantly, craftivists have also often brought their work to bear directly on war and its ravages, as a form of art as protest. As Kirsty Robertson writes, describing the works of several female artists:

> In the work of artists such as Barb Hunt of Canada and Maria Porges of New York, antiwar statements are made through the juxtaposition of the softness and warmth of wool with the form of bombs, guns, and landmines. Both artists knit or felt weaponry out of pastel-colored wool. The Toronto artist Barbara Todd makes quilts out of suit fabric in the shape of fighter jets to demonstrate the links between capitalism and the military, while the Dutch artist Marianne Jorgensen organized a collaborative project to make a bright pink tea cozy for a military tank [titled *Pink Tank*]. ("Rebellious Doilies," 195–96)

Some of this work—such as *Pink Tank*, the work of the Revolutionary Knitting Circle; the post-Newtown antigun violence group Moms Demand Action, which early on urged its members to make T-shirts, mugs, hats, and other handmade objects as a way to voice opposition to lax or absent gun control laws; or, even more recently, the organizers of the 2017 Women's March, who encouraged marchers to knit and wear "pussy hats"—emphasizes the collaborative and democratic nature of crafting, while placing "textiles [. . .] at the forefront of a political practice" (185). In these works, the handmade thing, despite or because of its often soft, delicate, small, and intimate qualities, directly opposes militarized violence.[8]

In thinking about the labor of love as antiwar document in Niedecker's work, it's important to look back as well as forward. Elizabeth Willis has written at length about Niedecker's affiliation with William Morris and the Arts and Craft movement he founded at the end of the nineteenth century. Willis traces that affiliation in Niedecker's letters and especially in the poem

Niedecker wrote about Morris in 1969, "His Carpets Flowered." As Willis notes, the Arts and Crafts movement of late nineteenth-century Britain (unlike its development as high-end furnishing and design in early twentieth-century California) "shifted the paradigm of art production in several important ways."[9] Like the craftivist movement of today, the Arts and Crafts movement helped to dissolve boundaries between high and low art, between such things as knitting, weaving, embroidery, and furniture making and such activities as painting and verse writing. Furthermore, Morris, like John Ruskin before him, tied the labor of craft, and aesthetic labor of all kinds, directly to the liberation of the maker and thus to a utopian vision of redeemed social life. In this vision, articulated in Morris's utopian novel *News from Nowhere*, all people will be involved only in what Morris called the "difficult easy labor" of working physically and with creative faculties fully engaged in a barter economy freed from the exploitations of industrial capitalism.

Morris thus draws a direct link between the handmade object and the liberation of people from what he called the "continuous and unresting" "war" of the class system. As he wrote in his 1883 lecture "Art under Plutocracy": "That system [capitalism] is after all nothing but a continuous implacable war; the war once ended, commerce, as we now understand the word, comes to an end, and the mountains of wares which are either useless in themselves or only useful to slaves and slave-owners are no longer made, and once again [. . .] nothing should be made which does not give pleasure to the maker and the user, and that pleasure of making must produce art in the hands of the workman."[10] Only when the class system is abolished will the beautiful handmade object be once again the norm, but at the same time, the presence of beautiful handmade objects will help bring about this desired end. For Morris believed that encounters with beautiful objects create longings for more such encounters, igniting the intense desires necessary to motivate revolution.[11]

And thus Morris, like Niedecker, ties class struggle and exploitation directly to war and violence, seeing the former as an example of the latter. One response to this violence (one *immediate* response, that is, because after reading Marx in 1881, Morris firmly believed in the eventual abolishment of the class system) lies in experiencing, as producer and consumer, the handmade and freely circulating object.[12] Elizabeth Willis describes a similar vision in Niedecker: "Niedecker clearly saw the abjection of the poet within American culture, but she also saw it countered by the dizzying freedom of working with others almost entirely beyond the bounds of the market economy, in the realm of barter and free exchange."[13] Niedecker's poem "His Carpets Flowered," which draws much of its material from Morris's letters, illustrates these shared ideals, as it moves between descriptions of crafting ("I designed a carpet today"; "to get done / the work of the hand"; "Good sport dyeing / tapestry wool") to political critique ("now that the gall / of our society's // corruption stains throughout"). For both writers, then, the handcrafted object (and the poem as an example of such) becomes a mark of resistance to the violence of labor and class under capitalism.

Niedecker wrote *NEXT YEAR OR I FLY MY ROUNDS, TEMPESTU-OUS* on scraps of paper, which she then glued to the pages of a pocket calendar from 1935, pasting her poems directly over the homilies the calendar originally displayed. The resulting poem, perhaps more than anything else, is about time; specifically, as Elizabeth Robinson has noted, it's about two temporalities in competition with one another.[14] The first, materially represented by the calendar itself, is ordinary chronological time, clock time, countable, progressive, linear time, maybe factory time; the second, announced first by the poem's title, is circular or cyclical time, the temporality of the natural world, or of the poet who sees herself as contiguous with that world, and perhaps also the temporality embraced by lovers who resist the normative narrative of romantic relationships.[15] This alternate, resistant temporality—resistant not just to calendar time itself but also, one could say, to all the institutions that rely on its predictability and regularity—replaces the squares by which the calendar counts its days with *rounds*, which the speaker *flies*, as a bird flies her rounds gathering fragments and scraps for her nest.

Thus Niedecker establishes her claim on nonlinear time simply through repurposing and retitling the calendar. She makes it even more explicit in the opening poem, which reads in its entirety: "Wade all life / backward to its / source which / runs too far / ahead."[16] Life is figured as a fantastical river, an endlessly looping fluidity with a source both before and behind us. To "wade" through life, one must enter this looping, rather than progressive, movement; one must "revolve," as the next poem tells us (42). "The satisfactory / emphasis is on / revolving," begins that poem, and then Niedecker introduces what I see as the poem's secondary but related theme: romantic love. "Don't send / steadily: after / you know me / I'll be no one," the poem concludes. Reading this as advice to the lover (and admittedly, there are other ways to read it), one might paraphrase: "Don't send for me, don't pursue me because as soon as you think you 'know' me, I'll simply dissolve, becoming no one." But is this a statement of self-protection or of preference?

As Rachel Blau DuPlessis has argued, to be "no one," to exist in relative anonymity, was for Niedecker a political choice. With anonymity comes a deep connection to the "folk," to the collective, and to art as the voice of the collective. With anonymity too comes a way to preserve integrity, for it is a form of withholding, of resisting full participation in a world whose values one does not share. As Niedecker wrote just a few years later,

> Scuttle up the workshop,
> settle down the dew,
> I'll tell you what my name is
> when we've made the world anew (*Lorine Niedecker*, 87)

"Her anonymity," claims DuPlessis, "is then a utopian gamble; she'll have a name when social and political changes begin to transform the class and gender materials which she spent a lifetime analyzing."[17] If we accept this argument (and I find it convincing), we might then read the end of this fragile and ambiguous second poem of *I FLY MY ROUNDS* less as an attempt to protect identity or selfhood and more as a claim to the freedoms of anonymity. To extend this just a bit, I'd say that the claim to anonymity is also a way to resist the particular violence that kinship identifications might entail.

The poems that follow continue to circle, or "revolve" around Eros—referencing the "heat" that bodies give off, females with flowers, a man holding a woman's knees, monogamy, bathroom luxuries, the endearments "darling" and "my love." And then, toward the end of the sequence, perhaps with tongue in cheek, Niedecker references one of our culture's foundational romantic scenes, one that thereby introduces the violence that is perhaps lurking behind these poems all along:

> Balcony scene in
> Romeo and Juliet—
> a white kerchief
> comes into a
> pocket shirred
> onto a blue silk
> gown.
>
> Or from Row
> L in the balcony? (*Lorine Niedecker*, 63)

Focusing on just the final two lines of this poem (though much could be said about the variously arranged objects in lines 3–7), we find interesting confusions. Elizabeth Robinson notes that "from Row / L in the balcony" positions the speaker (or someone) in the audience, perhaps watching *Romeo and Juliet* unfold.[18] This is convincing, but given that "Row" could easily be short for "Romeo," there are other ways to read these lines as well. Perhaps they wonder whether the kerchief (the only noun that could readily take the place of direct object here) has been dropped *from* the balcony above, but in that case "Row" would be in the balcony, rather than in the courtyard as we expect him to be. If "L" is an initial (rather than a row designation), then we begin to wonder if "L" stands for Lorine, in which case Lorine is "in the balcony," standing in for Juliet. But "L" could as easily stand for Louis, the lover to whom so many of these poems are addressed. This leaves us nowhere, or more readily, anywhere. "L" could be a row name, or it could be Row's name. Either L, Lorine or Louis, could be in the balcony; either could be below.

It does seem that Niedecker is playing with the lovers' shared initial here, for "What's in a name?" as Juliet says. If "I'll be no one," why must I bear a name at all ("Romeo, doff thy name")? Indeed, the violence of belonging to a name, the violence that clinging to kinship can generate, is Shakespeare's theme: "'Tis but thy name that is my enemy"; "The orchard walls are high and hard to climb, / And the place death, considering who thou art, / If any of my kinsmen find thee here."[19] The play's true battle is not between Montagues and Capulets but between the enforced boundaries of family, name, and property and the freedom and anonymity of erotic love and desire. Reading back now to the second poem discussed above, perhaps we can understand better the stakes in being "no one." To be *no one* is to resist the violence of kinship pacts, of names, property, and patriarchal family.[20] That *I FLY MY ROUNDS*, despite its Surrealist tendencies, is in some way a poem of protest becomes even clearer when Niedecker writes "I don't hum / the least of my resistance, / I give it fly."[21]

Indeed, flight is a recurring metaphor in these poems, as it is in Shakespeare's play, signaling in both works the liberty of love as against the rigidity and violence of the patriarchal family. Recall that when Juliet asks Romeo how he arrived in the Capulet's orchard, he answers, "With love's light wings did I o'er-perch these walls; / For stony limits cannot hold love out, / And what love can do that dares love attempt; / Therefore thy kinsmen are no let to me." This rejection of walls is echoed throughout Niedecker's poem too, perhaps most simply in the final poem, in which she writes, "Jesus, I'm / going out / and throw / my arms / around" (*Lorine Niedecker*, 67). "I would I were thy bird," says Romeo to Juliet; says Niedecker to Zukofsky: "I like a / loved one to / be apt in / the wing." The small, intimate gesture—the gift, be it the poem or the ring that Juliet passes to Romeo—is also birdlike, a frail and free thing, momentarily escaping, even as it points to, the violence of the surrounding culture.

Thirty years later, as Lyndon Johnson waged all-out war in Vietnam, Niedecker created her *Homemade Poems* for Cid Corman. (Thanks to the Lost and Found project at CUNY, directed by Ammiel Alcalay, *Homemade Poems* is now available in facsimile form). Along with this gift, she included the following letter:

> Dear Cid,
> I somehow feel compelled to send you the product of the last year, just to keep in touch. I know you're not printing [*Origin*]. I even brave school kid's paints to show where we live! It's been _____
> *a year*! I wish you and Louie and Celia and I could sit around a table. Otherwise, poetry has to do it.
> Please don't mind my 'metaphysical' in my last letter. I meant it but evidently didn't use the right word. Your work and Louie's, there's no use—for me—to look farther.
> These then with love—
> Lorine[22]

The poems stand in for the physical proximity of one's friends. They are made with love, with love in mind, on a small pad bound with cardboard and covered in wrapping paper, which includes a watercolor by Niedecker of her house on Black Hawk Island. Much less obscure than the poems of *I FLY MY ROUNDS*, these handwritten lyrics discuss love and friendship directly, such as in "Laundromat": "Casual, sudsy // social love // at the tubs," and in the following untitled poem: "If only my friend / would return / and remove the leaves / from my eaves / troughs" (*Lorine Niedecker*, 202, 203). There are poems for or about Ian Finlay, Zukofsky, and Niedecker's husband, Albert Millen ("He's / the one for me"); about important nineteenth-century radicals Margaret Fuller, Mary Shelley, and Ruskin; and about weather and the seasons. A gesture of friendship and a poetics, the book opens in the midst of a debate: "Consider at the outset: / to be thin for thought / or thick cream blossomy" (200). Corman's work, which Niedecker loved ("Sun Rock Man is so *good*," she exclaims in 1963) (35) is famous for being "thin" on the page, comparable to Robert Creeley's narrow verses; his poems are dense, nonetheless, with thought. Niedecker ends this poem with a teasing admonishment—"don't be afraid / to pour wine over

cabbage"—but from this moment of play, she deepens the terms of friendship: "Ah your face / but it's whether / you can keep me warm." Here, in just
three lines, we discover the vulnerabilities, the differences, the need, and the
doubt that real friendships encompass.

References to war and violence are here too, more overtly than in *I FLY
MY ROUNDS*:

Spring
  stood there
    all body

Head
  blown off
    (war)

  showed up
    downstream

October
  in the head
    of spring

  Birch, sumac
  before
    the blast (*Lorine Niedecker*, 211)

Spring is a headless body, its head floating downstream with October inside:
a surreal image for sure, but not inexplicable. On the one hand, it speaks of
springtime's ability to blast us out of thought into sensation, which is the
theme of another poem just a few pages later in which Niedecker writes,
"As you know mind / aint what attracts me / [. . .] but what was sensed /
by them guys" (206). On the other hand, the poem points away from the
immediacy and pleasures of spring to something much darker. With war in
mind and in memory, the birch and sumac at the end of the poem take on a
nostalgic feel, as if the poem longs for a previous time of peace and pleasure,
a time "before the blast."

And yet, a yearning toward the sensual is itself not at all trivial. It is, I
think, what ties all the poems in this volume together. It's the dare with
which the book opens ("don't be afraid / to pour wine over cabbage") and
with which it ends. "Wild strawberries," the final poem begins, "Ruskin's
consolation // His grey diaries / instanced with Rose."[23] The pleasures of
body, tongue, and nose, of the meal with friends she imagines in her ac-

companying letter—it's the work of poetry to remind us of these things, to take us out of our heads, the "Metaphysical Club," and return us to the body with its longings, pleasures, vulnerabilities, and loves. And, of course, the handmade book is not only an immediate vehicle for these ideas, it's also an instantiation of them. Bearing the mark of the hand, it becomes an emissary of the body, an instance of what Niedecker calls "Life's dance," in which "social love" draws us near.

How this "labor of love" functions in opposition to violence and war becomes evident four months later. In February 1965 Niedecker writes to Corman again, this time proposing an anthology of short poems, "just the essence of poetry," in which she imagines including two of Sappho's poems, translated by Mary Barnard. The second of these I quote in full:

Some say a cavalry corps,
some infantry, some again,
will maintain that the swift ones
of our fleet are the finest
sight on dark earth; but I say
that whatever one loves, is.[24]

The poem speaks for itself, but one item deserves to be pointed out, and that is the comma in the final line. I don't know how Barnard justified this comma, knowing nothing of Sappho's Greek, but in English the choice is striking. The comma allows the poem's obvious assertion (that the finest sight on earth, rather than being the institutions and tools of war, is whatever one loves) to open into a far more radical claim: that love is generative, that if we love something we bring it *thereby* into being. Certainly this is true of poetry, for poets anyway. But it's also true of friendship—a *thing* that doesn't exist without our love. And it's this belief that abides in the handmade object, and that allows these fragile, seemingly ephemeral things to function as instances of resistance to love's opponents: violence and war.

I would now like to turn briefly to three poet/artists from our time: Linda Norton, Jill Magi, and Maria Damon. My desire to write about some of the work by these women has less to do with their being directly influenced by Niedecker (though with Norton, that is certainly the case)[25] than with the specific qualities of their work. For each of these women, the handmade poem/object is in direct response to war—specifically to the wars on terror we are now, and seemingly forevermore, engaged in. More broadly understood, their works are a response to violence in its many forms and institutions. I will begin with Norton, focusing not on her writing here (though it is also engaged with questions of violence, especially in relation to poverty and race) but on her collage work, for it's in this discipline that I find her closest to Niedecker.

In a series of collages she titled "Dark White," images of World War II and Vietnam soldiers, taken from a waterlogged book on the history of photography and a guide to Vietnam collectibles, are positioned in diagonal relationship to images of mostly domestic objects, clipped from magazines. In one case, a large cooking pot hangs over the head of a soldier seated cross-legged on the ground eating a meal. In another, a drawer containing folded clothes or linens hovers near a soldier's helmeted head. A third shows three soldiers bent over, stalking with rifles out, while above their heads a lush bath towel, or perhaps the corner of a sheet, seems to hang suspended.

That these modest collages are works of protest seems to me obvious, but exactly what they protest is not so simple to discern. On the one hand, we might see the domestic objects as providing the soldiers with some kind of comfort, as if existing in their dreams, or as if signaling homes and families that await them. On the other hand, Norton, very much like Niedecker, is acutely aware of the close relationship between war and capitalism. These commodities, then, far from being the antidote to war and its discomforts, are in fact its motive/cause. They hover above the heads of these soldiers less like angels and more like dictating gods—threatening and demanding, pressing the soldiers into violent action. These contrasting readings are what make the collages so haunting, and what make them most like Niedecker's poems too, for Niedecker also holds a very ambivalent relationship to domestic space, at once valuing its privacy and quiet, and at the same time reviling the ownership and commodification that domestic space tends to insist upon.[26]

Jill Magi, like Norton, works in a variety of disciplines: poetry, prose, book making, embroidery, and other textile work. Her website's list of works includes "Book Works," "Stitched Works," "Remnants," "Threads," and "Small Books," which range from large-scale installation and durational performance to ephemeral and immediate objects (under the category "Small Books" Magi has written: "Written quickly, typed up, stapled, and given away"). Her newest book, a work of fiction titled *LABOR*, explores the hierarchization of academic labor—contrasting the lives of characters (an archivist, an activist, an adjunct professor, and a tenured professor) engaged in various levels of institutional labor. *LABOR* has another life too, as a performance/installation. Describing the making of this version of *LABOR*, Magi writes:

Linda Norton, untitled collages from the series "Dark White," 2014. Reproduced with permission from the artist.

LABOR began with my virtual, screen-based encounter with the Wagner Labor Archive finding guide. At that time, in 2008, it was all on-line. On election-day, while some felt hopeful about Obama and "change," I felt depressed and became engrossed with entry after entry of "radical" US history and labor activism. Electronically, I high-lighted, copied, and pasted the entire finding guide, chunk by chunk, into a word document, printed it out and slapped a title page on it: *LABOR*. But I knew I needed to mediate the language. So I went to the archive itself, and called up random files so that I could just sit there and touch the pages. I didn't know what I would do with any of it. Before the book came out, I took this printed-out finding guide and attempted to recopy all of its entries by hand on large sheets of news-print. I filmed this. I only got about 10% in. My hand was cramping and the work was excruciating—I also had a sequence of nightmares featuring dead people who were very unhappy. I had to stop.[27]

Clearly, Magi's work is concerned with capital, addressing the problems of commodity culture and labor inequities in a variety of strategies involv-ing the handmade. Here I would like to focus on her 2011 book *SLOT*. *SLOT* is concerned with the memorial, especially the war memorial, as a failed site of public grieving and accountability. Poems draw text from the websites and pamphlets of public memorials, often war memorials, but also civil rights memorials, and others. We are given a sense of the futility or pre-sumption of these sites in passages such as the following:

Dear Theater:
By climbing aboard the actual bus on which Rosa Parks' protest began, we can sit down and become the subject to a recording of the driver's voice demanding that we, positioned as Rosa Parks, move or leave.
[. . .]
Hall of Commitment
Here they sign a statement of personal commitment to the cause, their portrait is taken, and their faces are added to a video-mosaic of faces that merge and rise up the tower in an iconic representation of the community of Human Rights constantly replenishing itself.[28]

Or in the following perverse instance:

At the Colonial Williamsburg Escaped Slave Program, begun in 2000, guests are approached by a runaway slave. Visitors know that they

are surrounded by slave catchers and so the park's guests must re-
act instinctively to the situation. "This has turned out to be a really
intense visitor experience and is one of its most popular programs."
(*SLOT*, 44)

A few pages later, Magi highlights the distancing effect of the war memorial
in particular: "In the elevator, a recording of a soldier's voice describes the
scene and concludes by asking: / 'How could it happen?' / Purchase a guide-
book. Walk through the notorious gate" (57). The memorial-as-spectacle
becomes in these pages yet another form of violence by granting its visitors
a false sense of empathy, or an easily earned (the price of a ticket) representation of their own participation in the "community of Human Rights," or
by offering them a "way out"—a way to avoid, rather than answer, the soldier's fundamental question.

But *SLOT* also includes photographs, and it's in these images that Magi
seems to suggest alternate forms of engagement. One series of images show
us Magi's own hands, engaged in some sort of struggle with knotted thread.
During the time she was writing *SLOT*, Magi was also working on an installation she called "Wall Piece," in which she pierced her studio's walls
with hundreds of tiny holes into which she glued strings. She then played
the strings like a harp, producing a tangled mess of knots. In this series of
images, her hands are shown tangling and untangling these knots, as if indicating the complexity of the problems that her text explores. Magi also
includes photographs of her hands holding swatches of cloth over the museum maps and brochures. In this sequence, the gentle touch of the hand
suggests a covering, as one might cover a baby, or a shrouding, as one might
shroud the dead. The brochures have been speaking to us all along with
their institutional voice, their failed attempts to heal. In these sets of images,
the hand interrupts with its own language—a language of struggle and difficulty, a language of touch, intimacy, and care.

By way of conclusion, I'll turn finally to the needlepoint poetry of poet,
textile artist, and critic Maria Damon.[29] Most of Damon's handmade works
are originally gifts for friends, such as the piece titled "Mark's Now," made
for her friend the poet Mark Nowak when he "came out as a Marxist,"
which simply displays the word "Red"; or the piece titled "EM" in memory
of Emma Bernstein, made as a gift to her parents and brother, in which a
highly decorative "E" is surrounded by the names of the family members. The
piece I would like to discuss here is titled "Poetry 1 and 2." It includes two
rectangular cloths embroidered with the word *Poetry* in elaborate font and

multiple colors.[30] In a short introduction to this work, Damon explains that the project arose after her friend Stephen Vincent posted a comment about a dream on a poetry listserv: "Quite literally I had a dream last night in which the garment industry in league with the poets in opposition to the advent of war started sewing 'poetry' tags on to pants, shirts, blouses, etc. Similar to the old—or maybe it still goes on—little red Levi's tag on jeans." Vincent was writing in February 2003, as the war on terror entered its second year. "I won't spend my Sunday morning," he continues, "deducing all the implications, possibilities, down or upsides of a populace whether domestically, in school work or on the street with 'poetry' as both an intimate and public banner—with 'peace' or 'anti-war gesture' by implication."[31]

Of course, this is just a quick note, casually posted, not a carefully worked-through statement, but what I find most interesting and most moving is the assumption Vincent lets slide (even as he claims to skirt it)— that "peace" or "anti-war gesture" would be implied by the simple word "poetry." Evidently, Damon found it moving too, for she carried his dream into material presence. As Vincent and Damon both know, a gesture as small as this can do nothing to stop a war. Even if thousands of people were to wear the "poetry" armbands (as I think of them), there would certainly be no effect on the war itself. But poetry is almost always an intimate gesture, and it affects change at the level of the individual. The implications of "Poetry 1 and 2"—a work that includes Vincent's dream, his communication of the dream, the reception of the dream, the sewing and photographing of the pieces, and the free publication of the pieces as part of Damon's online book *Meshwards*—is that poetry matters in the face of war. It matters not because it will save lives (though it can) but because it is a labor of love, a labor for love—and as such it is a refusal of war and all the institutions that support war. And perhaps when the hand of the maker is most evident, felt in the very fibers of the object, the intimacy and urgency of the labor is all the more potent.

And so, I end this essay where I began, in a dream, the dream in which love counters war. It's a vital dream, a necessary dream, but it will inevitably feel futile, even despairing, to its dreamers. Let me return, then, to William Morris. In the final passage of *News from Nowhere*, his protagonist, William Guest, having concluded his visit to the utopian future, is awakening in present-day London:

> I lay in my bed in my house at dingy Hammersmith thinking about it all; and trying to consider if I was overwhelmed with despair at find-

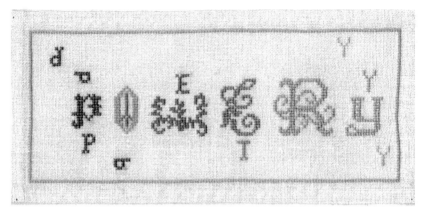

Maria Damon, "Poetry 1" (linen and cotton).
Reproduced with permission from the artist.

ing I had been dreaming a dream; and strange to say, I found that I was not so despairing.

Or indeed was it a dream? If so, why was I so conscious all along that I was really seeing all that new life from the outside, still wrapped up in the prejudices, the anxieties, the distrust of this time of doubt and struggle?

All along, though those friends were so real to me, I had been feeling as if I had no business amongst them: as though the time would come when they would reject me, and say, as Ellen's last mournful look seemed to say, "No, it will not do; you cannot be of us; you belong so entirely to the unhappiness of the past that our happiness even would weary you. Go back again, now you have seen us, and your outward eyes have learned that in spite of all the infallible maxims of your day there is yet a time of rest in store for the world, when mastery has changed into fellowship—but not before. Go back again, then, and while you live you will see all round you people engaged in making others live lives which are not their own, while they themselves care nothing for their own real lives—men who hate life though they fear death. Go back and be the happier for having seen us, for having added a little hope to your struggle. Go on living while you may, striving, with whatsoever pain and labour needs must be, to build up little by little the new day of fellowship, and rest, and happiness."

Yes, surely! And if others can see it as I have seen it, then it may be called a vision rather than a dream.[32]

9

THE LONG MOMENT OF OBJECTIVISM

REZNIKOFF, BÄCKER, FITTERMAN, AND

HOLOCAUST REPRESENTATION

STEVE MCCAFFERY

Nach Auschwitz ein Gedicht zu schrieben ist barbarisch.
—Theodor Adorno

It is customary to terminate Objectivism with the death of its final practitioner, Carl Rakosi, in 2004. However, the significance of Charles Reznikoff's 1975 work *Holocaust* to recent poetics and conceptual practice is noteworthy and suggests the legitimate extension of Objectivism to such recent work. To frame Objectivism's "long moment" (a phrase taken from Jeff Derksen's book *Annihilated Time*), this essay moves to link two contemporary works that engage the Shoah through meta-mediation: Heimrad Bäcker's 1986 *transcript*, and Robert Fitterman's 2011 *Holocaust Museum* (in response to Reznikoff's earlier text). This troika of texts underscores a commonality of theme (the attempted extermination of European Jewry) handled in a similarity of method (appropriation and retranscription).

I am in broad agreement with Berel Lang's contention that "all Holocaust literature aspires to the condition of history" and in so doing challenges its own governing literary conventions and presuppositions, and I will attempt to show how Reznikoff's, Bäcker's, and Fitterman's texts all ascribe to this aspiration.[1] We might note in them not necessarily a common search for a poetic form adequate to the Holocaust but rather a strident abnegation of any aesthetic. The horrors of the Shoah are frequently held to be indescribable and unspeakable, and this inability to find words is a common trope of antiquity.[2] However, such rhetorical turns to ineffability find a new use in establishing the ahistorical status of "Auschwitz" as a transcendental limit event rendered unspeakable.

In ruminating on the latter, Hilda Schiff poses a representational crux that is germane to any consideration of Holocaust representation: "What could the ontological status of a poem be after Auschwitz? How could poetic language itself be anything but superficial, irrelevant, marginal in a world of such horror since language was incommensurate to express it?"[3]

Following Lang, I wish to claim that all three texts situate 'poetic literature' within the limits of history and ethics and in so doing modify what *poetic literature* is; they are counterpreterite in a strictly mediated sense in that they speak not directly but rather through extracted material evidence and facts that are reorganized in a different discursive context from that of their sources. At the same time, the 'style' of these three texts situates not in literary inscription but in the selection and orchestration of available linguistic data. There are no imaginary itineraries or fictitious adumbrations along the vectors of lyrical lament or narrative adornment. Whether Reznikoff, Fitterman, and Bäcker can, or should, be considered 'Holocaust writers' remains a moot point, but the ethical and historical imperative entailed in their choice of subject is binding. All three texts are generically translocated: a feature that lends support to Lang's thesis that "the genres of Holocaust writing may be blurred under the moral and historical weight of its subject." I argue that they are of a metageneric order relative to the broad genre of Holocaust writing.[4] In distinction from diaries and memoirs and such poems as Plath's "Daddy," which exploits Holocaust imagery for personal lyric purposes, the three works engaged here negotiate variant institutional mediations and historical constraints. In so doing they largely avoid the implications in Hayden White's imputation to historiography that it utilizes the very tropes and constructions of the literary.[5] These three texts address neither the contingency nor the necessity of the Nazi genocide but rather serve to repurpose Holocaust data while additionally questioning their own status as literary texts identifiable by poetic style. All three works moreover involve an unavoidable deferral in that they are composed after the fact as gatherings from preexisting documents. The temporal deferral of the subject matter by several decades would seem to require, or at least petition, imaginative reconstruction in its attempted resuscitation of events from the past; however, this is not the case, and all three writers resist such blandishment. Their texts are less *about* the Holocaust (as it is portrayed through imaginative reconstitution or fictional confection) than they concern its mediating machinery and its archives. Rather than represent, these three texts *re-present* the language of that historical moment.

Mediation of this kind introduces an obliqueness into residual representation. Lists (Bäcker), captions (Fitterman), and court transcriptions (Reznikoff) act as historical anchors to a past, yet none introduces an imaginative or judgmental dimension. It is as if the *symplegma* of facts with their historical, moral, and ethical burdens produce a claustrophobic space sufficient for aesthetic and imaginative intervention to be impossible. Indeed, in all three works, there is as much a moral burden not to imaginatively portray such a subject. The extraliterary is treated as the materially literal. Considered together they can be read as a trilogy whose common subject is the ineluctable mediation of both immediacy and fact (by labels, titles, captions, testimonies, and transcriptions). There is a common dispassionate tone conveyed in the language of these formats, a metadata enacted upon transcription. All three works eschew legal terminology that would call for justice being done and judgment passed—the rhetoric of justice and outrage, for instance—and propose instead a neo-rhetoric governed by the single mandate to retranscribe, recontextualize, and thoroughly exorcise the aesthetic.

Reznikoff's Holocaust

In his 1931 essay "Sincerity and Objectification with Special Reference to the Work of Charles Reznikoff," Louis Zukofsky draws attention to "the clarity of image and word tone" in Reznikoff's work, earned by the poet's methodological adherence to two criteria: sincerity and objectification.[6] Sincerity breeds a poetry that manifests "the detail, not mirage, of seeing, of thinking [attaining] a rested totality," that is, an objectification. Words carry ideation into structure by "the arrangement, into one apprehended unit, of minor units of sincerity." Zukofsky proceeds to assess the ratio of articulated facts to that "rested totality [. . .] designated an art form."[7] Norman Finkelstein rightly calls *Holocaust* "the endpoint of Objectivism's testimonial strain [. . .] a *confrontation* with history set at the limit of Reznikoff's art," and I intend to add little or nothing to the body of criticism now extant on Reznikoff's extended poem, but rather to situate it as an inaugural text of a series of works that deal with the same broad subject of testimonial and mediation.[8]

Reznikoff had first addressed the issue of the Jewish genocide in a 1959 poem, "Inscriptions 1944–1956," where a short passage occurs that reads as the epitome of *Holocaust*:

One man
escapes for the ghetto of Warsaw
where thousands have been killed

or led away in tens of thousands, hundreds of thousands
to die in concentration camps,
to be put in trucks, in railway cars, in gullies of the woods,
in gas chambers[9]

As Lang reminds us, "Reflection on the Holocaust [. . .] forces the viewer
into history."[10] With this in mind, it is easy to comprehend how the poem
marks a departure from Enlightenment faith in universality (which would
elevate the necessity of historical particularities) to such discrete evidences
of history. Reznikoff's text, moreover, brings Objectivist poetics into the
sphere of Holocaust literature at the same time as it confronts literature
with a historical and also an ethical burden. *Holocaust* also situates, within
a continuing preoccupation in the poet's writing, the themes and events
of Jewish history. Reznikoff once harbored aspirations to become a professional historian, and this historical proclivity is evident in such poems
as "The Synagogue Defeated, Anno 1096," "Jews in Babylonia," and "The
Fifth Book of the Maccabees."[11] Thus contextualized, *Holocaust* attests to
Reznikoff's continuing preoccupation with Jewish history.

The appearance of the book in the mid-1970s is timely if we hold Lang's
assessment of the cultural memory among contemporary American Jews
of that decade to be true. "By the 1970s," he claims, "historical evidence
had accumulated of the muted response within the American-Jewish community as a whole during the years of the Nazi genocide."[12] Unlike in his
Testimony, Reznikoff chose not to include an opening epigraph—and fittingly so—for the book consists entirely of the transcribed voices of nameless proximate witnesses in which Reznikoff's own voice (and judgment) is
withheld. This tactic of erasure, silence, and authorial withholding is most
important to a full understanding of the poem, for, in essence, *Holocaust*,
unlike its sources, is a text of anonymity. First published in its entirety in
book form in 1975, a short section of ten or so pages (dated 1973) was included in Reznikoff's 1974 new and selected poems, *By the Well of Living
and Seeing*. This limited section is important in revealing the poet's earlier
plan of vocalizing the poem through a narrator and a witness. Reznikoff
obviously abandoned that format, as both "THE NARRATOR" and "THE
WITNESS" (as they appear in 1973) are expunged from the final version in
favor of presenting raw information grouped into numbered stanzas and
sections; the 'character' of "the narrator" disappears (in 1975) except as an
unnamed function, while "the witness" gives way to a voiceless text of re-
transcribed testimony. Reznikoff is at no pains to hide his sources, as the

small note on the first half title states: "All that follows is based on a United States government publication, *Trials of the Criminals before the Nuremberg Military Tribunal*, and the records of the Adolf Eichmann trial in Jerusalem."[13] Reznikoff first experimented with this method of regurgitated court transcription forty or so years earlier in his planned multivolume *Testimony*, part I, which appeared through the Objectivist Press in 1934 and later in 1965, with a second volume appearing in 1979, after *Holocaust*.[14]

In both of these volumes, he names his method "recitative." Reznikoff was on familiar terrain, being himself a trained attorney, and the seeds of his mining of court transcripts go back to his early work during the Depression in the offices of a law publishing company where his job was to read through and summarize law cases for *Corpus Juris*. He describes his job as one of reading, sifting, and selecting for a written summarization. "I might go through a volume of a thousand pages and find just one case from which to take the facts and rearrange them so as to be interesting." He admits to being attracted to trial case documents because of their ecumenical availability; a case, he writes, "is in the public domain. No one has a right to it, but everyone can use it."[15] Rather than a radical breakthrough in Objectivist poetics, Reznikoff's method of modified retranscription seems a natural outcome of his nonpoetic employment. Moreover, Reznikoff grounded his own sense of "objectivism" explicitly in court testimonial:

> Evidence to be admissible in a trial *cannot state conclusions of fact: it must state the facts themselves.* For example, a witness in an action for negligence cannot say: the man injured was negligent in crossing the street. He must limit himself to a description of how the man crossed: did he stop before crossing? Did he look? Did he listen? *The conclusions of fact are for the jury — and, let us add in our case, for the reader.*[16]

In discussing *Testimony*, Reznikoff speaks of the psychological (if not the ethical) imperative to transcribe with a minimum of intervention — an obligation with equal, if not more, applicability to *Holocaust*, which confronts "a reality that [he] felt as a reader and could not portray adequately in any other way."[17] That said, feeling is not absent but mediated, and manifests in the process of selection, as Reznikoff himself makes clear in a 1969 interview with L. S. Dembo: "The feeling is there in the selection of the material; you pick certain things that are significant — that's your feeling."[18]

It is important to comprehend the extent of Reznikoff's willful alterations of his source material. The organization clearly reveals a narrative and chronological intention. There are twelve sections, beginning with "Deportation" and moving through "Invasion," "Research," "Ghettoes," "Massacres," "Gas Chambers and Gas Trucks," "Work Camps," "Children," "Entertainment," "Mass Graves," "Marches," and concluding with "Escapes." The text's final short section reads: "About six thousand Danish Jews were rescued / and only a few hundred captured by the Germans."[19] This is by no means a poetic ending, nor at variance with the recitative method of the rest of the work, but this sequencing does register a positive implication: escape, liberation, a new life. Janet Sutherland's painstaking analysis of a passage from *Holocaust* against its source in *The Eichmann Trial in Jerusalem* adduces the extent of Reznikoff's alteration and "attentive reshaping" of his source material: temporal sequence is altered, repetitions removed, phrasing altered, and information removed.[20] The alterations and omissions she cites certainly disprove Sidra DeKoven Ezrahi's claim that Reznikoff's poem shows "the absence of any visible editorial hand."[21] The extent of exclusion in his process of selection is indeed enormous: all testifiers' names, all material ancillary to the affidavits, all racial and social groups other than Jews (e.g., Poles, Gypsies, POWs) are expunged.

The removal of names especially has a powerful metonymic effect. A name particularizes, and the act of genocide obliterates initially all individuality before it implements death on a large scale. Reznikoff himself is aware of this suppression. "The names become of very little importance. [. . .] What is important is the said."[22] Let us clarify: transcribed testimony is not a performative utterance, is not per se an act of either writing (diary) or speaking (testimonial). Indeed, one of the enduring significances of *Holocaust* (one most important to the legacy of Conceptual Writing) is the replacement of the act of writing by the *archontic* act of organization and selection.[23] I disagree with Linda Simon's claim that Reznikoff takes a definite moral stand.[24] Indeed, it is the absence of judgment and authorial comment that is most compelling in the work.

> He was taken out of the camp he was in
> for "road building."
> But it was not for road building:
> it was to hide traces of the Nazi murders during the past three
>   years.[25]

Schiff remarks on the "spare yet vivid immediacy" of *Holocaust*, but I wish to stress its status as mediation.[26] *Holocaust* is not a descriptive poem, nor a narrative text, at least not in any direct sense; by selective recycling of court transcripts it adduces the inevitable mediation of all affect—especially that of the institution of the law. The voice in the passage above is not an omniscient narrative voice but rather the mediated (i.e., transcribed) voice of a single, nameless person's testimony. The total effect is one of testimony on testimony: from camp guards to inmates distanced from immediacy by mediation.

There is no direct proximity to the *feel* of events in *Holocaust*. Reznikoff eschews lyric rhetoric and the biblical tradition of lamentation alike, opting for the dispassionate, transcribed testimonials of court witnesses. The detached tone of Reznikoff's piece can be usefully compared to the factual prose renditions in Raul Hilberg's *The Destruction of the European Jews*:

> The Jews deported to the Ostland were shot in Kaunas, Riga and Minsk.
>
> Those who were routed to occupied Poland died there in the death camps at Kulmhof, Auschwitz, Belzec, Sobibor, Treblinka, and Lublin (Majdanek). Most of the Theresienstadt Jews who did not succumb in the ghetto were ultimately gassed in Auschwitz.[27]

So why did Reznikoff not choose prose? For Janet Sutherland, the line breaks and variant line lengths that Reznikoff introduces into his recitative method constitute "an *indirect* emotional content."[28] Formally speaking, retranscription is exemplary of the genre of treated or found poetry that includes, in its ancestral series, Yeats's notorious lineation of a prose passage of Pater's, which starts the 1935 *Oxford Book of Modern Verse*, itself reminiscent of Duchamp's treated readymades. The modified lineation (from prose to verse) registers Reznikoff's deliberate minimizing of poetic control and lyric presence in the poem.

Fitterman's Holocaust Museum

Robert Fitterman is generally considered one of the foremost practitioners of Conceptual Writing, but rather than this obvious and natural identification, I wish to address *Holocaust Museum* as a metageneric example of Holocaust literature. As such, the work stands in stark contrast to such cultural productions as Holocaust films and documentaries that install and presuppose imagery. Indeed, Fitterman's *Holocaust Museum* successfully realizes in writing Laura Mulvey's exhortation to remove all visual pleasure from cinema.[29] There is, of course, an eerie affiliation between the artistic technique of appropriation and the historical decades of the 1930s and 1940s, for Fitterman's method of appropriation (like Reznikoff's) inflects the defining kinetics of National Socialism (annexation, relocation, selection). Is *Holocaust Museum* then another instance of Marx's famous claim, in *The Eighteenth Brumaire*, that history repeats itself first as tragedy, then as farce—with Fitterman's book supplying the farcical return? Fitterman is certainly mindful of his two literary exemplars, quoting passages from both Reznikoff's and Bäcker's books in a page of epigraphs. Like both predecessors, the language in Fitterman's work is found and reorganized. The book consists of a collection of captions to absent photographs culled from the vast photographic archives of the United States Holocaust Memorial Museum in Washington, DC.

The conspicuous gesture in the composition is the omission of all photographs, an act that provokes the broader cultural question of the relation of word to image. Like Reznikoff, Fitterman chooses to group his material into discrete sections, many of which articulate to form the hint of a narrative progression: from propaganda through book burnings, deportation, concentration camps, gas chambers, mass graves, to Liberation. Other sections enumerate aspects of daily, material appearance and (dis)possessions: uniforms, shoes, jewelry, hair. The trope of naming absence is not original and is central to at least two contemporary works. Stanislas Lem's 1971 *Doskonala próznía* (*A Perfect Vacuum*) comprises reviews of nonexistent books, texts reviewed but never capable of being read. My own group of poems, "Pictures at an Exhibition," presents a number of empty rectangles above which appears the title of a painting (partly real, partly imaginary) and beneath which appears a poem by way of comment.[30] There is also a 2011 piece by Spanish artist Rogelio López Cuenca (relevant to this cluster of works) that comprises a white rectangle with the following text placed in the center: "For copyright reasons image is not available."

Both Lem's book and McCaffery's texts pose the same problem as *Holocaust Museum*—namely, how to look at what is unseen. But there are important differences beyond the issue of representation. Lem's and my work were conceived in the spirit of 'pataphysics playfully aimed at offering imaginary solutions to the problem posed by nonexistence (in Lem's case) and by things both existent and nonexistent (in mine). The copyright prohibition in Cuenca's piece, however, takes the form of the biblical proscription against images when mediated through the legal discourse of property and ownership. Obviously, Fittermanian 'absence' is of a different order from these other absences. For one, the photographs exist at a known institutional location; second, the burden of the historical content cannot be handled through the science of imaginary solutions. *Holocaust Museum* is in part an intervention into the question of how we handle the past, and specifically the Holocaust archive. Fitterman's work also raises issues (to be addressed shortly) of the curatorial function and of the ethics of Holocaust representation (in fiction, documentary, photographs, and so forth).

Another comparable art piece is Christian Boltanski's 1990 "The Missing House" in Berlin. Boltanski frames and labels an absence, namely the site of an apartment house in central Berlin tenanted by Jewish residents that was destroyed by Allied bombing in 1945. Boltanski memorialized the space by placing signs within it indicating the names of the residents and the approximate sites of where they lived. If not original or alone, Fitterman's text stands as by far the most caustically relentless in that the work is an unbroken list, in appearance reminiscent of short prose stanzas. In contrast to Boltanski's choice of a preexisting void, Fitterman's void is an induced absence willed by the poet himself. The reader is deprived of photic gratification but not linguistic signs. Indeed, the labels and their content suffocate. A page of entries in *Holocaust Museum* reads like a curatorial inventory. The blunt lack of sophistication, the absence of judgment, interpretation, and stylistic intrusion, and the unrelenting factuality of the language render the transfer from museum to literature of an emphatically passive order:

> Close-up of Ustasa victims lying in a mass grave.
> [Photograph # 46461]

The passivity is more obvious in the following successive pair of entries:

> The bodies of former inmates are laid out in a mass grave in the Mauthausen concentration camp.
> [Photograph #15675]
>
> The bodies of former inmates are laid out in a mass grave in the Mauthausen concentration camp.
> [Photograph #15674][31]

These last two passages are not of the order of repetition but of sequencing, and the question immediately arises why Fitterman chooses to reverse the order of the photographic numbering. This liquid shifting of data, modified by selection and idiosyncratic orchestration, renders Fitterman's role as more of a meta-curator acting upon the curatorial role of selection and presentation than of a poet.

> Bales of the hair of female prisoners found in the warehouses of Auschwitz at the liberation.
> [Photograph #85742]

Bales of the hair from female prisoners, numbered for shipment to Germany, found at the liberation of Auschwitz.
[Photograph #14220]

Nadia Cohen (with short hair) with the children that she is taking care of in the camp.
[Photograph #44542]

Nadia Cohen with a group in Israel that came on Aliyah. Nadia is on the right (with short black hair) behind three kids.
[Photograph #44537] (85)

As is evident from these quotations, each entry terminates with a photographic catalogue number, the sequence of which does not always follow a sequential order. In places the numbering seems counter to the chronology. For example, one entry (dated to the liberation of the camp) is numbered #85742, while another postwar photograph taken in Israel is numbered #44537. How do we read this numbering and its seeming illogicality? The stubborn presence of these numbers underscores the fact that these are statistics of a photographic archive that classify in a way that does not relate to the chronological events of the histories they record. These asynchronous numbers further emphasize that the text is metadata, selected from a vaster archive and, as such, render *Holocaust Museum* antiabsorbent (in Charles Bernstein's sense), calling attention to the fact that these numbers are pointers to photographic objects withheld (in the context of the book) from the reader's gaze. As a reiteration via transcription, *Holocaust Museum* does not replicate the people and objects the replicated texts refer to. Indeed, in a radical separation of image from word; a fundamental 'belonging' is severed. One of the successes of Fitterman's book, then, is the reenvisioning of a museum of artifacts as a museum of words. The shifting of textual material from the institutional context of the museum to that of literature reduces both the museum and the 'poem' to unworkability.

The problematic voyeurism of Holocaust photography (and Holocaust representation in general) is ably stated by Charles Bernstein:

Every scene depicted, including the documentary photos at the Holocaust Memorial Museum, strikes, like a blow to the mind, as fundamentally incommensurable, the surface of a surface. You have heard it before: the familiar, in some ways comforting, lament that many Hollywood films — and many journalistic and novelistic works — have engaged in a voyeurism bordering on Nazi porn.[32]

Friedrich Achtleitner echoes Bernstein's assessment, warning of the corruptibility and seduction of the photographic image as a descriptive medium. Speaking specifically of the Holocaust, he avers that "description of any kind stands in the way of reality, covers it over. Photographs showing piles of naked, dead, human beings, starved to the point of becoming skeletons, turn into ornamentation: captured in the horrible reality of an image, these have little to do with the dimensions of actual horror and suffering."[33] One might argue, in light of these comments, that *Holocaust Museum* marks doubly a paradigm shift from image to text (addressing the degenerated status of the former in our ethos precisely by emancipating the caption from its predetermined function) and also a radical shift in the ethics of representation.

Is *Holocaust Museum* to be read, then, as an antidote to such voyeuristic proclivities as Bernstein and Achtleitner isolate? A purification of textual record from the potential blandishments proffered by photographic images? Lily Duffy writes perceptively on this issue in her "Conceptual Failure as Several Kinds of Success in Robert Fitterman's Holocaust Museum":

> When a piece demonstrates the discrepancy between idea and execution—when what works in concept (for example, the written word *being* the visual image, rather than just referencing/conjuring it) reveals its artifice and deficiency in execution (the reader not experiencing the written word as, or in the same way as, the visual image)—it has been successful. In other words, the written word can, in highly mimetic writing, "be" (mimic, represent) the visual image *within* the writing (its conceptual framework), but it cannot literally recreate the experience of *seeing* (with one's eyes) the visual image it is referencing. This is one of the reasons why Fitterman's conceptual project, *Holocaust Museum*, is successful at what it does.[34]

Rather than reiterate Duffy's approach through conceptualism, I want to inflect her claims into another dimension to argue that Fitterman's book ranks as a successful example of *subtraction*, in Alain Badiou's precise sense of that term. Badiou poses two orientations that he considers central to our era. The first is toward the destruction of semblance to arrive at the real by way of a purification; the second is subtractive—that is, designed to measure an unavoidable negativity.[35] If Badiou's postulate is true ("That the century does not hesitate to sacrifice the image so that the real may finally arise in the artistic gesture"), then Fitterman's method is neither a destructive nor a liberating text, but rather a minimalization to a zero point (131).

Holocaust Museum effectively cleanses deictic language by subtracting (but not destroying) the objects it was designed to point to. Rather than an antinomy of word and image and the play of signs and absences, there remains the caption understood as a minimal image. Considered this way, Fitterman's book is an arrangement that places the image "at the edge of the void, in a network of cuts and appearances" (132). To support this claim requires concurrence with the assertion that the captions are still controlled by a corresponding image, an assertion strengthened in its truth by the persistent presence of the photographic reference numbers at the end of each entry. Indeed, the textual excess that comprises *Holocaust Museum* adduces the persistence of the image rather than its obliteration. To translate *Holocaust Museum* into a destructive text would require the removal of all captions to offer the reader (apart from any chosen paratext) a blank book.

There is another dimension to this work other than that of history and image. As a subtractive text, *Holocaust Museum* approximates a secular version of a central tenet of negative theology, namely, the phenomenon of the absent God. As Ilse Bulhof and Laurens ten Kate explain: "In the expanding modern life there is no place for a limit, for an 'exterior' to which people relate and that plays an active, if mysterious and often frightening, role in daily experience. [. . .] This exterior becomes empty, and as a result God can be spoken of only in purely negative, empty words."[36]

The architectural fabric of the museum and the contents housed therein function in this thetic proposition precisely as this empty exterior addressed, but still potent, in its absence.

Fitterman's subtractive poetics are perhaps best contrasted with visual artist Shimon Attie's 1991–1992 project "The Writing on the Wall," which comprises a restoration of retinal affect by way of slide projections. Utilizing a similar projective technique to that employed by Krysztof Wodiczko, Attie projected onto the facades of buildings, in what was the Jewish Scheunen Quarter of Berlin, the photographic images of signs, people, and activities, thus obtaining an arresting diachronic superimposition of the past and present, simultaneously provoking reflections on memory and its loss and change. There is also an added value, here, of symbolic action, a restitution of an ethnic, urban space through a manufactured flight back through time. At the same time, Attie's piece makes us pause and consider the illusory states induced by images, a phantasmatic conjuration of the simulacrum from which optic blandishments Fitterman's text is totally expunged. In addition, *Holocaust Museum* provokes a further questioning as to where *the real* resides in a museum of photographs. Fitterman short-circuits the duplication of title and image. In this sense, it can be considered an antirepresentational work. However, the indication of an absence is itself both a theological inflection and an institutional critique. The situational complexities of *Holocaust Museum* are evident: as both Conceptual Writing and Holocaust literature, it can be read equally as a critique of the museum and curatorial role, as well as a broad cultural comment on the hegemony of text over image in the information age.

Bäcker's transcript

Holocaust and *Holocaust Museum* are linked not only by a common historical subject but by a racial commonality in their respective authors. Both Fitterman and Reznikoff are Jewish, placing them in a similar proximity to the appropriated material as a conjugate cultural memory. In the case of Bäcker's *transcript*, we have a text constructed on and out of the same theme of the mediated Shoah by a noted Austrian avant-garde writer, concrete poet, and former member of the Hitler Youth. First published in Germany in 1986, and in its English translation more than two decades later in 2010, *transcript* is not a testimonial text but is primarily a re-presentation of historically specific language: the documentary, bureaucratic, and propagandistic lingo of the Third Reich; it especially exposes the basic and banal mediation of bureaucratic mechanisms that made possible the attempted Nazi final solution. As Bäcker himself explains, "Every part of *transcript* is a quotation; anything that might seem invented or fantastic is a verifiable document."[37] As a veritable Bartleby of the Third Reich, Bäcker constructs and arranges according to a quotational poetics designed to expose the bureaucratic underpinnings of the process of deportation, incarceration, and extermination. He *confronts* the Holocaust in its bureaucratic appurtenances, a veritable archive of stuff, a statistical sublime. *transcript* places persistent emphasis on the bureaucratic language of National Socialism, a language Bäcker himself describes as "a deadly gibberish" (131).

It will be useful at the outset of this examination to point out some of the significant differences between *transcript* and Reznikoff's and Fitterman's texts. First and foremost, unlike the other two texts, Bäcker's title makes no reference to the Holocaust; and indeed the scope of its subject is broader: the entire bureaucratic language of National Socialism. Next is the relative range of material from which Bäcker draws his quotations. The repeated nature of the material in Reznikoff and Fitterman takes a different form in *transcript*, for these are novel lists and entries or at least novel in their range. Where Reznikoff draws on two sources and Fitterman relies on just one,

Bäcker draws on forty-six titles and from a wide assortment of materials: timetables, telephone numbers, criminal charges, arrest reports, statistics of various kinds, letters, marginalia. A third difference locates in the visual appearance of the pages. Reznikoff divides prose testimonial into purposeful line breaks that create the appearance of poetic lines; there are stanza divisions but on an irregular patterning, and sections of *Holocaust* are clearly demarcated by their full-page half titles. In the case of Fitterman's *Holocaust Museum*, the visual appearance seems deliberately uninviting. Although the numerical labeling that closes each entry evokes an institutional rhythm (excepting the sectional divisions in larger type and on individual half titles), the pages themselves are densely packed, uniform, and aesthetically unpleasing. By contrast, *transcript's* pages are redolent with typographical variety and formal patterning, from full-page lists to one-line entries. Moreover, some pages are handwritten and others photo-facsimiles of autograph documents (including a note in Hitler's hand), the combined effect of which is to introduce a gestural component into the readerly experience.

A fourth difference among these three works lies in their respective paratextual apparatuses. The cover of the first edition of *Holocaust* is printed on laminated stock in black and red with a black double-rule border enclosing an oval image of flames; the red-black contrast carries forward into the crimson endpapers and the rubricated title page; the lower cover is plain laminated white. The cover of the second edition of *Holocaust Museum* replaces a purely typographic cover with a large black square that dominates the front cover and divides the letterpress. The English translation of *transcript* is purely typographic, comprising a background text on which is superimposed both author name and title. It additionally supplements the main text with both an afterword (by fellow Austrian poet Fredrich Achtleitner) and an afterword to the English edition by Patrick Greaney—both of which offer interpretations and explanations of Bäcker's project. Most significant, however, is the lack of endnotes in both Reznikoff's and Fitterman's texts. Sources are acknowledged in both works, but the exhaustive referencing of each page of *transcript* and the accompanying bibliography are conspicuously absent from Reznikoff's and Fitterman's texts. It is the presence of these notes and bibliography (named by Bäcker "MONUMENTA GERMANIAE HISTORICA [q.v.]") that propel *transcript* into a gestural, performative text, involving the reader as an active, physical participant in effecting the offered interreferences from front to back, text to apparatus. Indeed, one of the distinct codicological values of *transcript* lies in its elevation of paratextual supportive material to the level of first-order attention.

When first encountering the pages of *transcript*, the reader is confronted with decontextualized language arranged in a decidedly poetic way; there is an unmistakable formal patterning to each page. Many passages have the superficial appearance of short lyric texts or prose poems characterized by their lack of identifiable context, for instance the following:

16 storage space for sawdust
17 storage space for straw
18 bodies piled here
19 drainpipe for blood
20 cesspool (87)

and

it was a heavy russian benzene engine, presumably a tank engine or a tractor with at least 200 h.p. (V-8 engine, water cooled). we switched from "open valve" to "cell." (57)

Others are self-explanatory:

as a rule hitler's breakfast consisted of a glass of warmed (but never boiled) milk, a slice of oldenburg black bread (a whole-grain rye-bread), a piece of zwieback or danish crisp bread as well as an apple. (99)

Some titles explain the text at the outset, perhaps the most chillingly ironic of which is:

auschwitz telephones
no. 18
no. 45
no. 17
no. 33
no. 21

no. 41
no. 76
no. 16
no. 74
no. 1

no. F III/2

no. 32

no. 62

no. 315

no. 55 (29)

Bäcker admits his debt and inspiration to Raul Hilberg, who first exposed the everyday details of the complex Nazi bureaucracy in his 1961 work *The Destruction of the European Jews*. Like Hilberg, Bäcker illumines certain details occluded in the major narratives, contributing to the *petite histoire* of the Reich's bureaucracy. Bäcker describes his method of quotation as a positive practice of transportation between two isolations. "If a document is torn out of its own isolation and forced into the isolation of a formal principle, it achieves a new efficacy. [. . .] Documents are literature that writes itself and is recognized as literature" (149). However, much of this 'literature' gains the gibberish that Bäcker himself calls into question:

expedite fully here!
1) along with enclosure of documents as herewith designated below
2) in re report list 19/43
3) after one month 4/27
4) this is re working file
right to a pardon
state insurance commission, berlin
(L. S.)
(seal)
identical signature
by pneumatic post!
personal! (107)

The passage is representative of many of the entries, the forms, lists, and memos enigmatic to a reader in the fixed isolation of the page, but which become charged with significance when their source is revealed. The above passage, for instance, Bäcker takes from Günther Weisenborn's 1953 book *The Silent Uprising: A Report on the Resistance Movement of the German People from 1939 to 1945*. Or, for example, consider the following poignant passage: "i probably won't see you again, won't hear your voice, won't kiss you. but how i want to see you, if only once!"—which is chosen from Piero Malvezzi and Giovanni Pirelli's 1955 documentary gathering, *And the Fires Shall Not Consume You—Last Letters from Fighters in the European Resis-*

tance Condemned to Death (71). As well as its irony and tonal variety (absent in Reznikoff's and Fitterman's texts), *transcript* offers itself to a reader as a gestural work, a text allowing the reader's active participation in a tripartite rhythm from entry to endnote to bibliography and back to entry again.

We can read Bäcker's method of selection, separation, and recontextualization as metonymic of the political period it reflects: the selection and deportation of Jews that constitutes a large part of the poem's 'subject.' Similarly, the white space surrounding the texts evokes not an aesthetic purity à la Mallarmé but an absence understood as a disappearance. For instance, the following, taken from Reinhard Kühnl's *German Fascism in Sources and Document* (1977), gains its force not only from its stark factuality, but also from being suspended as a single line above a page of otherwise blank space:

> the card file on the dead was larger by far than the one on the living. (127)

It may be a point of literary curiosity that the Shoah and its consequences should be the strange attractor for three divergent poetic scrutinies. From the perspective of history and ethics, however, it is clear that its attendant atrocities compelled of creative practice an ethical burden, a burden that manifests obedience not as expressive proactivity, an emotive assertiveness, nor as a negative dialectic, but as a willful reticence, a self-silencing that challenges the very *telos* of Romantic and modernist poetics. Reznikoff remains silent so others may speak, or what they said be reiterated. Fitterman reduces a photographic archive to a minimal image. Bäcker exhumes to rearrange in formal patterns the infrastructural bureaucratic gibberish behind the deeds of the Third Reich. All three works fall within the heterodoxical genre of written readings; all three present the stark factuality of data, refuse judgment, and remain obdurately inconclusive, for conclusions, as Reznikoff reminds, are for the reader. Curiously, the license to practice quotation can be found in Zukofsky's 1931 essay: "It is more important for the communal good that individual authors should spend their time recording and objectifying good writing wherever it is found [. . .] than that a plenum of authors should fund their fame on all sort of personal vagueness—often called 'sophistication.'"[38]

Holocaust, transcript, and *Holocaust Museum* exemplify such objectification taken to *extremis.*

If we accept Heidegger's contention that poetry (understood as the essence of art) is the founding of truth in its three senses (of bestowing, grounding, and beginning), then *Holocaust, transcript,* and *Holocaust Mu-*

seum show that the truth of a past lies in its experience as mediating data.[39] Moreover, a poetics of total quotation and appropriation is a poethics of alterity in which the other/subject becomes paramount and the poet removes into something more than Eliotian impersonality. We know the popular argument that poetry should not be accountable to history. The fact that Keats erroneously introduces Cortés into his famous sonnet "On First Looking into Chapman's Homer," gazing from a peak in Darien out into the Pacific, rather than the historically accurate figure of Balboa, surely does not depreciate the poem's value as great poetry. But in the instance of the Jewish extermination, that we eponymously name "Auschwitz," such a historical event is of a different order (even after factoring in that it was Cortés who initiated the earlier extermination of the Aztec people). There are *limit events* that register an ethical force that commands historical integrity. In their variant ways, *Holocaust, transcript,* and *Holocaust Museum* obey that command. This is Objectivist sincerity as it must be "after Auschwitz."

CODA

POETICS AND PRAXIS 'AFTER' OBJECTIVISM:

ROUNDTABLE DISCUSSION

RAE ARMANTROUT, JEANNE HEUVING,

RUTH JENNISON, DAVID LAU, MARK MCMORRIS,

AND CHRIS NEALON

*In what ways are Objectivist values (of sincerity and
objectification, contingency, socialization and documentation, etc.)
useful or not useful in writing, reading, and teaching contemporary
poetry, especially from social and political perspectives?
How do Objectivist modalities of assemblage and collage, broadly
considered, resonate in contemporary praxis? And how might these
and other Objectivist social or political considerations of form figure
in the years ahead?*

Rae Armantrout: I've always been struck by the tension in George Oppen's
poetry between his Marxian commitments to community and his emphasis on the "singular." It may be the "shipwreck of the singular" he returns to, but this disaster, replayed so often, seems inevitable. When we
confront "The absolute singular // The unearthly bonds / Of the singular" we're not simply dealing, it appears, with a mistaken egoistic view
that might be corrected, but with something deeper. I think this standing
within the stubborn singular is Oppen's version of "sincerity." There is
never the easy absorption of—or unification with—others that we find in
many poets, from Walt Whitman to, more recently, James Wright.

I mention Wright strategically because I want to contrast Wright's
well-known poem "A Blessing" with Oppen's poem "Psalm." "Psalm,"
like many of Oppen's poems, I would argue, is a poem of encounter, in
this case, an encounter with wild deer. When the speaker comes upon

them suddenly, their very existence startles him: "That they are there!" Oppen makes the reader sense the otherness of the deer by using unusual adjectives to describe them. Their eyes are "effortless," their teeth are "alien." It's clear, though, that they are the natives in this place, that they have nibbled paths through the woods. In the third stanza Oppen replaces such exclamations of surprise. Now it is "They who are there." In the end the perspective reverses. It is the deer who are now startled and stare. Note that he doesn't assert anything about them more than what can be observed. He has little truck with metaphor or personification.

Now, by contrast, let's look at what happens in "A Blessing" by James Wright. In this poem, the speaker and an unnamed companion stop beside a pasture where two "Indian" ponies are grazing. One wonders why Wright bothered to bring in the word *Indian*. I know it refers to a certain breed of horse, related to a mustang, often marked with white spots. Is he just being specific, or is there something else at work here? In any case, Wright's speaker and his friend feel no hesitation about entering the ponies' territory, probably by stepping over a fence. How do the horses feel about this? Wright is happy to provide us with that information. "Their eyes darken with kindness." In fact, "they can hardly contain their happiness." So Wright has no qualms about entering another's space, nor about reading another's mind. He is as welcome as he wants to be. How does he know about the interior lives of the horses? He doesn't tell us. They approach him. He immediately sexualizes the "slenderer one" and grasps her in an embrace. Any campus bulletin might have warned him about silence and consent! Wright's poem may (or may not) seem a little naive to us now, but poems of this tendency are still circulating. Of the two approaches, I prefer Oppen's. Oppen will never stop being a white, male, Western individual—but in this poem I sense him trying to get at what a world of equality and respect would look like. He's miming it, if you will.

Jeanne Heuving: An Objectivist value that enters into my teaching is the importance of experiential truth or existential truth. In the wake of the turn to language and poststructuralism more generally, just what might comprise these truths is indeed much more complicated than in preceding times. In Charles Altieri's afterword to *The Objectivist Nexus*, he suggests that certain poets not identified with Objectivism further objectivist values and discusses at some length how Lyn Hejinian's and Charles Bernstein's works achieve Zukofsky's values, respectively, of "sincerity" and "objectification." And yet Altieri suggests they fall short or outside of Objectivist values because there is insufficient sense of a tested existence in their work, or as he puts it: "Objectivism insists on clear connections between the effort to establish [a writing] and the exemplifying of existential commitments to pursue lives self-reflexively worth living."[1] In short, I see his call for a writing that measures itself in relationship to existence clearly evident in Oppen and Niedecker, but hovering, without conscious validation or exploration, in much current innovative poetry or discussion thereof—no doubt because of the difficulty of conceiving such clearly demarcated realms as experience and existence in our languaged world, and because the demand to do so all too easily tends to collapse into mainstream lyricism without sufficient attention to the conditions of meaning making (or wordsmithing). In what ways do Objectivist values demand that we return to or create a new understanding of existence and its measure in our language acts? And how would these values be registered in a time radically changed by 'new' and social media—for instance, might the impulse for some conceptual poetry evince such values?

Chris Nealon: I agree with Rae's comparative readings of the poems from Oppen and Wright. Oppen is thinking less about himself, keeping his ego out of the poem (or so it can seem), whereas Wright seems all caught up in projecting himself onto the animals he's observing. And it's natural enough to prefer the poem that doesn't spend its time going "I-I-I-I-I," as Heather McHugh once wrote. It may even be natural to associate reduction of ego in poetry to a left-wing politics, though of course a critic like Altieri is at pains to keep the politics of the Objectivists at arm's reach, since for him (and for others writing in this vein), the moment when self-reflexivity leads to a choice or a decision, to a taking of sides, all the 'poetry' in a poem is fatally compromised. Poetry, in this vein of criticism, is all about 'value' as potentiality. So to find even implicitly that we sense or desire a link between minimalist technique, or collage, and a politics—say, a radical politics of communality, possibly even communism—this desire feels like a nice corrective to the depoliticization of Oppen especially.

Even so, I'm reluctant to link good politics to keeping your ego in check, and I'm reluctant to champion 'singularity' as the basis for a politics. Not that anyone here is doing that. But there are discourses outside our roundtable in which a politics of humility, for instance, and a championing of singularity eventually loop around to become anti-Marxist. This is evident in the rejection of Marxist thought in the environmental movement, which champions a critique of humanity (more than, say, rich people or rich nations) as the problem for the environment. And in the postwar history of continental thought, a key word like *singularity*, whatever the beautiful and fragile particulars it describes in literal terms, drifts into being a counterterm to words like *collectivity*. This has to do with a significant left-wing, anti-Hegelian tradition in Europe, which tends to read the championing of a *dialectic* as a way of imagining iron-clad laws of history (a Prussian Hegel, you could say), or as a ruthless in-strumentalization of 'the workers' as the only agents of historical change (the Stalinist Hegel, in essence). Liberal individualist traditions on both side of the Atlantic are quick, therefore, to seize on anything that seems like a counterweight to a bad 'communism' that sees no difference, only classes, and that gets caught up in the ego worship of leaders.

Heuving: I appreciate Rae's calling our attention to not only a difference in poetics, but also to a difference in ways of being in the world. Her care-ful description contrasts with current hubris within the university itself in which students are being compelled to act as a 'we' who help 'others,' whether in college applications or classrooms, without much thought of the nominations of *we* and *others*.

In my classes I often introduce the idea of the singular through Agam-ben's discussion of it in *The Coming of Community* as a concept that me-diates the binary between particularity and universality, torquing our concept of the individual in useful ways and therefore changing the bi-nary between individualism and the community. I suggest (with little or no recourse to Oppen) that singularity is an improved way of think-ing about our place and importance in the world. In my undergraduate classes, and sometimes in graduate courses as well, I produce this evi-dence for singularity: all faces, voices, plant life, and other organisms in the world are similar to and different from one another. Humans (and crows) have an amazing capacity to recognize singular entities. I also bring up this idea when MFA students despair the question, What need is there for individual writers in a world of so many commonly held, press-ing problems? With the idea of singularity, we move somewhat apace of a set of limited and despairing ideas. With respect to Objectivist poetics, is singularity similar to or different from Zukofsky's emphasis on the "detail" and "thinking with the things as they exist," or is singularity a necessary prelude to these?

Mark McMorris: In Zukofsky's "speech framed to be heard," the reader is thrown back upon the hearing of speech instead of toward a welcoming meaning, and what keeps you in the hearing ministers to the openness of the serial form. Rather than writing the lyric whole, contemporary poets bend toward more ruminant language, the building of chains, the assembly of fields of thinking—a dispersal of attention over many particulars. The framing of speech to be heard, though (very audible, in different rhetorical modes, in Bunting as in Taggart)—I don't know whether this approach to heighten the material form of the syllable fits with the contemporary interest in series and assemblage, so far as one would also say that the Objectivist legacy is a force in the work in question.

In his critical writings, Zukofsky is still under the influence of the poetics of speech that I can trace through Eliot, Pound, and Williams, but I can also find the valorization of speech, as idiom, in John Ciardi's introduction to the *Mid-century American Poets* anthology.[2] At mid-century, speech is a wide-ranging idea. Only one of its emphases concerns the American identity of the poetry that employs idioms peculiar to American speech. Zukofsky's "plain speech" performs this function of localizing the poem in a place; but to him speech has lots of other implications, ranging from its correspondence, rendered in the vocal cords, with dance, to promoting through syllables an awareness and semblance of *order*, common to all humanity.

Heuving: Mid-century American poetics introduce into the later twentieth and twenty-first century two seemingly opposite concepts, or concepts that emphasize very different poetic dispensations, namely Objectivist and Projectivist. While both aim to be interventionist, their implications for how one should go about writing a poem, the actual process of poetic composition, is quite different. I will hazard some sense of distinction here, in the recounted legacies of these poetics, if not in the poets, poems, or their fully rendered poetics. Objectivist poetics find support in William Carlos Williams's "No ideas but in things," in his notion that a poem is a "machine made of words," and in Zukofsky's "thinking with things," whereas Projectivist poetics find definition in Olson's "ONE PERCEPTION MUST DIRECTLY [. . .] LEAD TO A FURTHER PERCEPTION" and "a poem is energy transferred from where the poet got it [. . .] by way of the poem itself, all the way over to, the reader." Although Olson's prowess, especially given his Maximus figure, is implicated in stances available to him as a white male, his poetics have been important to women and nonwhite poets, including Kathleen Fraser, Susan Howe, and Nathaniel Mackey, among others. Are these poets Objectivist or Projectivist? I would say both. While Mackey in *Discrepant Engagement* allies himself with Projectivist and open field poetics, his very concept of "discrepant engagement" shares a great deal with Oppen, and his intense engagement with language at the level of the syllable, with Zukofsky. Both Projectivist and Objectivist poetics are important for these poets because, indeed, they need to register their own sense of the objective realities that pertain as well as address discrimination and oppression through a projective poetics that encourages libidinized or irrational leaps in perception, and perhaps ultimately judgment.

I think what comprises a 'politics' as written as poetry as well as the question of politics itself is complex, given the multiplicity of political situations we are in, including institutional, national elections, Occupy Wall Street, the immigrant crises, Black Lives Matter, et cetera. I began with questions I find germane to institutional politics that we share and may see differently. I find an ethos that does not inquire into *my* or *your* subjectivity in relationship to *others* troubling. I do put considerable stock in the historical-psychological subject, whoever she may be, but not so much as an "ego," but as a situated existence. And I find certain poetic practices or formal choices, if you will, access and produce this situated existence differently.

Nealon: And yet the critique of poetic ego is at root a critique of the Romantics that, in every version I've ever seen, underestimates and caricatures the Romantics themselves! Such readings don't take into account the history of Romantic *curiosity* about nature, and curiosity about the ego. It's easy to forget that that curiosity was itself more often than not linked to left-wing (if not communist) views about politics, and that the high point, in poetic history at least, of the critique of the Romantics came to us from Pound, whose highly masculinist pursuit of objectivity shapes the Objectivists' concerns. I'm curious about the fact and history and problem and possibility of humans having egos, which are survival mechanisms; but I'm not in a rush to critique the ego per se. And I love singularity: I'm deeply moved by the lowercase-*s singularity* born of the flux of the world, the singularity of faces and flowers and lives and places. And I like Oppen and Niedecker (I'm not much for Zukofsky). But I've been trying for some time now to identify the sources of the pleasure their poetry gives me without making immediate recourse to the idea of 'Objectivist values' or even 'Objectivist technique.' Whatever Pound's animus against Romantic and especially Victorian sentimentality, the critique of poetic ego is ancient—so I'm not sure whether the un-egoic practice of these poets is unique to them.

And as for collage and juxtaposition—here's Maurice Valency, writing about troubadour poetry in 1958: "In general the Provençal love-song has not, in the Aristotelian sense of the term, an end nor, strictly speaking, a beginning [. . .] what the chanson illustrates is a method of composition which involves the juxtaposition, not the subordination of units."[3] There's nothing about collage, or about humility, unique to the Objectivists, though they may have shaken and stirred those things especially well. What this leads me to do, in recent years, is to practice a kind of agnosticism about the relationship between technique and ethics, or technique and politics; there may be one, but trying to name it leads me into mazes. Instead, I find myself wanting to think through the loose but interesting mesh of genre and poetic history when I read a poet like, say, Oppen.

McMorris: One common formal interest of Zukofsky, Oppen of the 1960s, Niedecker, and Reznikoff is in what Zukofsky called "speech," and, once, "plain speech." In Bunting I don't know that I would call it 'plain,' but the language sounds like speech, with a heightening of syllabic accent and hiatus. The serial poem and the method of assemblage are compatible with this interest in speech, though obviously the personality does not assemble into an ostensible whole, in the manner of discrete lyric poems. In "A" Zuk appears to distinguish between the material form of syllables capable of sustaining interest in their own right, on the one hand, and on the other, the meaning of words, which he denigrates with a parenthetical particle:

Why
not 'speech
framed to
be heard

for its
own sake
even over

its interest
of' (de)
'meaning'[4]

This double gesture questions speech as phonological form, which allows him to translate Catullus based upon phonemic resemblance, and puts him quite close to vanguard movements, like sound poetry or language writing, in the effort to pry open the sign and displace the interior bond—to disturb or demean the usual cultural logic of American poems.

One way that I think about seriality (in Oppen as in Taggart, in Elizabeth Robinson as in Ann-Marie Albiach, say) is that the signified remains incomplete at any point; meaning accumulates, but is errant; not only is there more to say, the serial isn't structured to bring you any closer to the end. I have the sense that this turn away from endings is attractive to many poets writing today: that, compared to the assembly of a field, the making of a lyric whole seems precious, demeaning of experience, or false—not particular enough. Zukofsky, of course, saw the "Objective" in the movement of "historic and contemporary particulars." Connected to perception, his "particulars," like Oppen's, refer to the philosophical tradition he absorbed. And it is in relation to phenomenology that I would, naturally, inquire into the legacy of the serial particular in contemporary poetry after Objectivism.

Ruth Jennison: Chris observes the difficulty and perhaps nonutility of developing some kind of metric for the relationship between 'technique and politics.' Objectivism ratifies this position in at least one important sense; while Objectivist forms mediate various left orientations to questions of, for example, consciousness and totality, those politics cannot be said to inhere in the forms themselves. Indeed, these forms are portable to poets of whom it cannot be said to possess a full-throated anticapitalist politics (Rae's example below of Flarf is perfect). By contrast, Objectivists marry specific contents to their forms; talking about Objectivist techniques, or forms, without reference to those contents risks positing a metric against which Nealon cautions. Objectivist parataxis is hardly unique, but when adjacencies, as they do very often in early "A," insist on connection between, for example, revolutionary developments in the rural United States and the revolutionary upheavals in the Soviet Union or China, the form is invested with a set of verifiable left politics. Objectivism possesses a very wide formal range among its practitioners; to list them all is to list almost every possible formal quality of poetry.

I want to suggest here that the ecumenical nature of the grouping indexes a profoundly nonsectarian moment on the left in both poetics and politics. Where we might expect formal imperatives from a manifesto like the "Program," instead we find encouragements toward principles of composition, underwritten by a fidelity to the historically situated data of the world. This might suggest to the contemporary reader a transhistorical portability of an Objectivist method, but it is important, I think, to see the ways in which Objectivist formal diversity is connected to a precise moment in which there was a significant measure of political unity—riven though it was by divisions of race and gender. So, there's a sense in which political commitment and ideological homogeneity provides the condition of possibility for a set of open, diverse formal approaches.

Armantrout: I agree with Chris that Objectivism can't be defined by certain formal techniques, even in conjunction with certain attitudes, such as a desire to restrain egoistic interventions. Poetic movements are difficult to corral and define. Some of the techniques associated with Objectivism in this forum—juxtaposition, collage, and a tendency (or at least a desire) to restrain ego—can be found across the spectrum of contemporary 'experimental' poetry. The Flarf poets, for example, work entirely with found texts in a way that precludes direct personal expression, but I don't think anyone would call them Objectivist poets. Of course, it's difficult to truly banish ego. I can imagine viewing Oppen's speaker (with a jaundiced eye) as a self-dramatizing truth teller. What's particularly moving to me in Oppen's "Of Being Numerous" is the way both the "singular" and the collective are sites of great trouble. Oppen can't be comfortable with either; in fact, the whole poem is really his anguished vacillation between the two poles—as in sections 18–20, which deal with the war in Vietnam. Those lines are unfortunately as appropriate to our present moment as to the time in which they were written. The insane fly in the bottle is, I think, an emblem of the singular (often associated in Oppen with shipwreck). The president, however "ordinary," and the helicopter pilot alone in his cockpit are alone—singular in their power, and "insane." But the populace at home, waiting to be excited by the nightly war footage, is clearly no better. Perhaps then the poet positions himself as alone in his objection and anguish. But that can't be quite right either. There was an antiwar movement, after all, though Oppen doesn't choose to mention it.

David Lau: As someone who was born the year Zukofsky died, I'm part of a generation of poets who encountered the finished tomes of "A" and Niedecker's and Oppen's *Collected Poems*, as well as Zukofsky's prose studies and essays, which were not widely known in his own life. I can recall going into Prairie Lights in Iowa City as a graduate student and seeing all these Zukofsky prose volumes. It was quite a time to engage these works because of the spadework-essays that had been done already by Michael Palmer, Michael Davidson, DuPlessis, Jenny Penberthy, Barrett Watten, et cetera; the generation after the Objectivists shaped my understanding of the Objectivists.

In the period since the great financial crisis of 2008, the Objectivists' Great Depression–era work appears in a new, semianalogous historical light, an immediate context for a younger anticapitalist generation. It is a rich tradition at this point. Their status as a 'school' is also a dialectical problem, one that taught me how to think of other schools as possessing shared affinities within sharp aesthetic differences.

I found it enormously emboldening to encounter their work in the late '90s. I was becoming much more historically minded and thinking through the changes I lived through in California at the end of the Cold War. I knew and had been taught the works of the first generation of modernists. Outside of courses, in volumes from New Directions, Cal, Gnomon, and Johns Hopkins—here, instead, were left poets, with extraordinary poetic gifts and forthright political commitments, making complex use of syntax, lineation, and an array of understated music and specific, unobtrusive anticapitalist references. These were poetic means through which urban conditions and historical and personal changes became palpable with a braided and multifaceted intensity.

Armantrout: Is membership in a poetic *school* defined by historical factors such as where a poet published and with whom they associated, or is it determined by aesthetic factors such as similarity of style? Certainly this has been an issue among the Language Writers. Does one need to have been part of a certain social circle, or does one need to write in a certain way instead? And what way would that be? The works of, say, Lyn Hejinian and Charles Bernstein could never be confused with one another. One can make the same case about the Objectivist poets. Oppen's philosophical tug-of-war between the claims of the many and the singular, Reznikoff's documentary poetics, and Niedecker's wry, precisely tuned observations of (circumscribed) place may not seem all that similar in retrospect. Reznikoff's work seems more like Claudia Rankine's than like Niedecker's, and Niedecker seems (to me) more like contemporary poet Joseph Massey than like Oppen.

Lau: The Objectivists can't be wholly separated from the context of the '20s and '30s, the interwar period of crisis and class struggles in which they were formed as writers and poets, even if they wrote poetry that was partially at odds with the socialist realist mandates of the left during those times. In an uncollected poem, Oppen writes: "I am a man of

The Thirties." He and Mary would join the Communist Party USA in the Popular Front era, perhaps the most significant time in the CPUSA's history. But it was also a time of contradictions and deplorable developments on the left, with thoroughgoing Stalinization, the defeats of the Popular Front governments in Spain and France, and the "compromises" with Roosevelt's Democrats.

But the Objectivists' work certainly resonates with anticapitalist poetry in the present, of which there's a certain tendency. The serial forms and long poems—whose quasi-musical architecture is covertly detectable—by Nathaniel Mackey, Michael Palmer, Rachel Blau DuPlessis, and others are informed by their work, though assemblage and collage forms both predate the Objectivists and have parallel exemplars during their moment. Some contemporary examples of poetry derived from textual appropriation can also claim affinities with some of the Objectivists, Reznikoff most notably. The impersonal, intellectual lyricism of Niedecker and Oppen have continuing influence on Language and post-Language poets. Zukofsky's innovative approach to translation has informed so many translators. Children of immigrants in several cases, the Objectivists' works will perhaps begin to speak to a younger generation of immigrant and first-generation poets with political and poetic ambitions. But from another vantage point—that of the world of creative writing programs—Objectivism is still mostly unread or else barely known. While the Objectivists have had and continue to have a particularly strong influence on a certain sector of contemporary poets and schools (some of whom are contributing to this roundtable), their legacy still needs to be upheld as contemporary. And it needs to be communicated to a younger, digital generation.

Jennison: I want to begin by appreciating David's historical contextualization of Objectivism. "Objectivism" is a nexus, or constellation, braided together with the processes of the first mass radicalizations in twentieth-century America. Although never officially aligned with the Communist Party, Objectivist works and political alignments are illuminated in richer detail when examined in the context of widespread militant organization against a capitalism in crisis, a capitalism whose legitimacy was no longer ratified by any kind of national consensus. The accompanying efflorescence of left letters, of anticapitalist print organs, performances, films, and poetics provides Objectivism with its rich ambient intertextuality. I don't wish to retread ground already richly sown with historical accounts of the Objectivist moment, but beginning with the punctuality of their intervention seems to me to be a way in to speaking to some key points of intersection in this conversation: the stakes or even possibility of identifying an enduring set of Objectivist values, or even ethics and the alignment of form with political commitment. In some ways and not in others, the present is also host to a renovation of anticapitalist action and theory (occupation/the movement of the squares/communization/ revolts against white supremacy), and correspondingly we find a vibrant new layer of poets united not by form but by politics.

Some things are gained and many lost in the transubstantiation of formal imperatives and political alignments into, respectively, poetic comportments and systems of ethics. I speak here rather sheepishly as a critic among poets and poet critics; and the practice of poetry isn't always enlarged by the negation of the question of ethics. However thusly hobbled, I want to remark on the historical parallax that structures the shift to reading Objectivism through the lens of ethics, whether of egoic dilation or subtraction, or 'sincerity' or 'objectivity.' Certainly no one would want to claim that Objectivists did not have ethics, and it is more than possible that they had many shared ethics. That said, for Objectivists concepts like objectivity were arguably less decisionist than they were the coordinates of the relationship of poetry (not necessarily the poet) to the material world. The beginning of the "Program" helps to illustrate this:

> *An Objective: (Optics)—The lens bringing the rays from an object to a focus. (Military use)—That which is aimed at. (Use extended to poetry)—Desire for what is objectively perfect, inextricably the direction of historic and contemporary particulars.*[5]

There is much to say about this excerpt; one could comment on the debt to Marx's figurations of lenses when describing the workings of the commodity fetish, or the ways that poetry here aligns with militancy. But I want to point out that an objective is not an ethics around which history flows but rather a desire to orient properly to the "direction" in which the data of history moves. Here poetry involves a dual project that cannot be unlinked from corollary tasks of revolutionary politics: both to diagnose the directional movement of history and its actors, and to move in that direction. Alongside? Lost within? At the front? These are question that Objectivism does not ask or answer, and this silence is in itself interesting.

Armantrout: Ruth asks how poetry can both diagnose and move with the direction of history. This question was posed with urgency in the '30s and again in the '60s. We've talked more about the '30s than the '60s— but Oppen, though he declares himself a "man of the '30s," is dealing with the "insanity" of the war in Vietnam in *Of Being Numerous*. His critique of the warriors is direct; his critique of the new left antiwar movement is oblique yet palpable. It's their very communalism that makes him uncomfortable, one senses, despite his Marxist affiliations. Maybe their styles of communal life didn't suit him? Does it come down to that? He no longer felt himself at home in the moving current of the present. Perhaps a better-known and more dramatic working out of the issue Ruth raises can be found in the antiwar poems of Denise Levertov and in Robert Duncan's response to them in their correspondence. Levertov wanted to not only diagnose (as Oppen does) but to move with the currents of protest. Most later readers now agree with Duncan that the polemical cast this gave her poetry diminished it. One question would be: *Can* one be caught up in the events of a moment, carried by the current, and also write lasting poetry? I hope so.

NOTES

INTRODUCTION

1. Lorine Niedecker, "Hand Crocheted Rug," in *Lorine Niedecker: Collected Works*, ed. Jenny Penberthy (Berkeley: University of California Press, 2002), 103.

2. William Carlos Williams, *Paterson (Book One)* (New York: New Directions, 1946), unpaginated.

3. Louis Zukofsky, "Sincerity and Objectification: With Special Reference to the Work of Charles Reznikoff," *Poetry* 37.5 (1931): 273.

4. Our italicized language here echoes Louis Zukofsky's foundational essay, "An Objective" (1967).

5. *Poetry* 37.5 (1931). The table of contents includes, in the following order: poems by Carl Rakosi, Louis Zukofsky, Howard Weeks, Robert McAlmon, Joyce Hopkins, Charles Reznikoff, Norman Macleod, Kenneth Rexroth, S. Theodore Hecht, George Oppen, Harry Roskolenkier, Whittaker Chambers, Henry Zolinsky, Basil Bunting, and Jesse Loewenthal; two poems from Arthur Rimbaud translated by Emanuel Carnevali; poems by John Wheelwright, Richard Johns, Martha Champion, and William Carlos Williams; and Zukofsky's two statements on Objectivist poetics, "Program: 'Objectivists' 1931" and "Sincerity and Objectification: With Special Reference to the Work of Charles Reznikoff." The collection then presents a multifaceted *Symposium*—a dialogic assemblage of paratexts—concluding with a discussion of André Salmon's poetry translated and cowritten by René Taupin and Zukofsky.

6. Ruth Jennison, *The Zukofsky Era: Modernity, Margins, and the Avant-Garde* (Baltimore: Johns Hopkins University Press, 2012), 9.

7. Mark Scroggins, *Intricate Thicket: Reading Late Modernist Poetries* (Tuscaloosa: University of Alabama Press, 2015), 234; and Hugh Kenner, *A Homemade World: The American Modernist Writers* (1975; repr., Baltimore: Johns Hopkins University Press, 1989), 187.

8. Zukovsky, "Sincerity and Objectification," 273.

9. Peter Quartermain, *Disjunctive Poetics: From Gertrude Stein and Louis Zukofsky to Susan Howe* (Cambridge: Cambridge University Press, 1992), 2.

10. Charles Altieri, "The Objectivist Tradition," in *The Objectivist Nexus: Essays in Cultural Poetics*, ed. Rachel Blau DuPlessis and Peter Quartermain (Tuscaloosa: University of Alabama Press, 1999), 29.

11. Henry Weinfield, *The Music of Thought in the Poetry of George Oppen and William Bronk* (Iowa City: University of Iowa Press, 2009), 28.

12. The "Objectivists" volume of *Poetry* 37.5 (1931) famously frustrates the proposition that there could be such a poetics. The diversity of aesthetics, modes and methods, poetics and politics represented therein emphasizes a variety of practices. Zukofsky elaborated and revised his own statements on the movement between 1931 and 1967. The discourse gathered new significance in 1968, when L. S. Dembo invited Louis Zukofsky, Charles Reznikoff, George Oppen, and Carl Rakosi (but unfortunately not Lorine Niedecker, although she was living only a few miles away) to the University of Wisconsin for a series of interviews connected to a course on modern poetry he was teaching. The publication of those interviews in 1969 marks the opening of critical debate in the United States about Objectivism and the Objectivists. See L. S. Dembo, "The 'Objectivist' Poet: Four Interviews," *Contemporary Literature* 10 (1969): 155–219. See also Norman Finkelstein, "What Was Objectivism?," in *The Utopian Moment in Contemporary American Poetry* (Lewisburg: Bucknell University Press, 1988), 35–46; Burton Hatlen, "Objectivism," in *Encyclopedia of American Poetry*, ed. Eric L. Haralson (Chicago: Fitzroy Dearborn, 2001), 517–20; and Burt Kimmelman, "Objectivist Poetics since 1970," in *The World in Time and Space: Towards a History of Innovative American Poetry in Our Time*, ed. Edward Foster and Joseph Donahue (Jersey City, NJ: Talisman House, 2002), 161–84.

13. Despite the heterogeneity of artists, writers, and schools collected in Zukofsky's February 1931 "Objectivists" volume of *Poetry*, the field of scholarship and criticism since Dembo's interviews has been dominated by reductive narratives concerning the development and legacy of Objectivism and Objectivist writing. See, for example, Michael Heller, *Conviction's Net of Branches: Essays on the Objectivist Poets and Poetry* (Carbondale: Southern Illinois University Press, 1985). Heller's brisk and influential volume positions the Objectivists, "in their preference for the clear physical eye over 'the erring brain,' [as] the direct inheritors of that aspect of Whitman"; and posits Objectivism as "a truly prophetic art" (15), grounding his argument in close readings of the works of Oppen, Rakosi, Reznikoff, and Zukofsky. Heller also considers Lorine Niedecker's writing, but only insofar as her "poems most clearly correspond to Zukofsky's theorizing concerning sound" (49). Dembo's and Heller's shaping of the field complements the willingness of the few poets (Reznikoff, Oppen, and Rakosi) who accepted the movement's provisional identity. Dembo's and Heller's works also dovetailed with the macro-narrative established by Hugh Kenner's *The Pound Era* (Berkeley: University of California Press, 1971), which continues to inform more recent studies of the Objectivists vis-à-vis high modernism and late modernism. See, respectively, Stephen Voyce, *Poetic Community: Avant-Garde Activism and Cold War Culture* (Toronto: University of Toronto Press, 2013); and Jan Schreiber, *Sparring with the Sun: Poets and the Way We Think about Poetry in the Late Days of Modernism* (Champaign, IL: Antilever Press, 2013). For a vital critique of these paradigms, see Rachel Blau DuPlessis, *Purple Passages: Pound, Eliot, Zukofsky, Olson, Creeley and the Ends of Patriarchal Poetry* (Iowa City: University of Iowa Press, 2012).

14. Compared with Dembo's and Heller's configurations, Andrew McAllister builds his anthology around the works of Zukofsky, Oppen, Reznikoff, Rakosi, and also Niedecker, Rexroth, Muriel Rukeyser, and Bunting. See *The Objectivists*, ed. Andrew McAllister (Hexham, UK: Bloodaxe, 1996). DuPlessis and Quartermain complement these frameworks by shaping *The Objectivist Nexus* (hereafter referred to as *Nexus*) around their foundational six poets—Bunting, Niedecker, Oppen, Rakosi, Reznikoff, and Zukofsky—within a diversified field of modernist and post-modernist aesthetics, poetics, and praxis from Europe to the United States, United Kingdom, and Canada.

15. Charles Altieri, "The Transformations of Objectivism: An Afterword," *Nexus*, 302.

16. Louis Zukofsky, "An Objective," in *Prepositions +: The Collected Critical Essays*, ed. Mark Scroggins (Hanover, NH: Wesleyan University Press, 2000), 13, 18.

17. We recognize the claims advanced by DuPlessis and Quartermain for the organizational methodology of *Nexus*: "Objectivist writing [is] aware of its own historical contingency and situatedness, and Objectivist poetics [is] a site of complexity, contestation, interrogation, and disagreement" (6). However, their formulation of *historical contingency* receives no further development within the scope of their collection beyond this single mention. In this regard, our volume elaborates upon the foundational work in *Nexus*, celebrating as well as critiquing that volume's sequentialist and genealogical paradigm.

18. Here, and in dialogue with *Nexus*, we would emphasize the diversity of writers and artistic practices as integral to the legacy of Objectivism and Objectivist principles. On the notion of disruptive innovation as a challenge to literary history, canon and field formations, and the politics of academia, see Charles Bernstein, *Attack of the Difficult Poems* (Chicago: University of Chicago Press, 2011).

19. Harriet Monroe, "The Arrogance of Youth," *Poetry* 37.6 (1931): 333. See also Marjorie Perloff, "'Barbed-Wire Entanglements': The 'New American Poetry,' 1930–32," *Modernism/Modernity* 2.1 (1995): 145–75.

20. Louis Zukofsky, "Program: 'Objectivists' 1931," *Poetry* 37.5 (1931): 268.

21. For explications of this epigraph, see, for example, Burton Hatlen, "A Poetics of Marginality and Resistance: The Objectivist Poets in Context," *Nexus*, 38–39; and Ming-Qian Ma, "Be Aware of 'the Medusa's Glance': The Objectivist Lens and Carl Rakosi's Poetics of Strabismal Seeing," *Nexus*, 56–59. For extended readings of the trope of optics in Objectivist poetics, see Heller, *Conviction's Net of Branches*; and Monique Vescia, *Depression Glass: Documentary Photography and the Medium of the Camera-Eye in Charles Reznikoff, George Oppen, and William Carlos Williams* (New York: Routledge, 2006).

22. Charles Bernstein, "Foreword," *Prepositions +*, viii–ix.

23. Vescia, *Depression Glass*, 100. See Louis Zukofsky, "American Poetry 1920–1930," *Prepositions +*, 137–51.

24. This essay emerged from *5 Statements for Poetry* (San Francisco: San Francisco State College, 1958). "An Objective" first appeared in the first edition of *Prepositions: The Collected Critical Essays of Louis Zukofsky* (London: Rapp and Carroll,

1967). As Bernstein notes, "An Objective" is "based on three essays Zukofsky wrote in 1930 and 1931 [. . .] two of which were published in the breakthrough 'Objectivists' issue of *Poetry*" (vii).

25. Lionel Trilling, *Sincerity and Authenticity* (Cambridge, MA: Harvard University Press, 1972), 8.

26. *The Philosophy of Marx*, trans. Chris Turner, 2nd ed. (New York: Verso, 2007), 37–38.

27. John Stuart Mill, "Thoughts on Poetry and Its Varieties," *Crayon* 7.4 (1860): 93–97.

28. Lyn Hejinian, *The Logic of Inquiry* (Berkeley: University of California Press, 2000), 202.

29. These omissions include Zukofsky's reflections on the contexts and occasions that shaped his decisions in assembling the February 1931 issue of *Poetry*.

30. Louis Zukofsky, "Foreword," *Prepositions +*, 187.

31. In the preface to *An "Objectivists" Anthology* (New York: TO Press, 1931), Zukofsky discusses poetry as a constructivist process comparable to that of cabinet-making.

32. In this regard, we would also echo Rorty's resilient belief in poetry: "To see one's language, one's conscience, one's morality, and one's highest hopes as contingent products, as literalizations of what once were accidentally produced metaphors, is to adopt a self-identity which suits one for citizenship in such an ideally liberal state." Richard Rorty, *Contingency, Irony, and Solidarity* (Cambridge: Cambridge University Press, 1989), 61.

33. And also Oppen's rebuke: "We said / *Objectivist* [not Objectivism]" (c. 1972). See , respectively, George Oppen, "Morality Play," cited in *Nexus* (1); and "Untitled: '[. . .] will,'" in *Selected Prose, Daybooks, and Papers*, ed. Stephen Cope (Berkeley: University of California Press, 2007), 45.

34. Kenneth Rexroth, *American Poetry in the Twentieth Century* (New York: Herder and Herder, 1971), 111.

35. Carl Rakosi, *Collected Prose* (Orono, ME: National Poetry Foundation, 1983), 79.

36. Louis Zukofsky, "About the Gas Age," *Prepositions +*, 170–71. In his note on this statement, Zukofsky reflects that this "answer to a question from the audience following my reading at the American Embassy, London, May 21, 1969 [. . .] was not intended for publication, but an unauthorized mangled transcription of what I said was published in Newcastle upon Tyne that year without my knowledge" (169). Zukofsky offered a similar (yet more contextually nuanced) statement in his interview with L. S. Dembo on May 16, 1968. See "Interview," *Prepositions +*, 229–30.

37. Rachel Blau DuPlessis and Peter Quartermain, "Introduction," *Nexus*, 4.

38. An insightful and relevant discussion may be found in Michael Davidson's *Ghostlier Demarcations*, which traces Objectivism back to Marx's notion of the commodity fetish via George Lukács's key concept of *reification*. Lukács, Davidson reminds us, claimed that the commodity structure encompasses social relations be-

tween individuals and "takes on the character of a thing and thus acquires a 'phantom objectivity,' an autonomy that seems so strictly rational and all-embracing as to conceal every trace of its fundamental nature: the relation between people." In personal correspondence, the Zukofsky scholar Mark Scroggins writes that there is "no record of LZ [*sic*] having read Lukács or any other 'Western Marxists.' He knew his Marx and Engels, and he'd read Lenin and some Trotsky—and I imagine he kept up to some degree with stuff in *New Masses* and such—but no Lukács as far as I can tell." However, Zukofsky had no need for access to Lukács's essay (first published in 1923, when Zukofsky was a college student) to understand social relations as an objective condition, as a fact. The notion has been central to the social sciences, and to the field of sociology (and of anthropology) specifically, since its inauguration as an academic discipline by Emile Durkheim, who, as the esteemed anthropologist Michael Taussig puts it, belabored "the invisible presence, the intangibility, the literally unspeakable but begging to be spoken nature of 'society' [. . .] to the degree of fanaticism." See, respectively, Michael Davidson, "Dismantling 'Mantis': Reification, Louis Zukofsky, and Objectivist Poetics," in *Ghostlier Demarcations: Modern Poetry and the Material World* (Berkeley: University of California Press, 1997), 116–34; George Lukács, "Reification and the Consciousness of the Proletariat," *History and Class Consciousness: Studies in Marxist Dialectics*, trans. Rodney Livingstone (Cambridge, MA: MIT Press, 1976), 83; and Michael Taussig, *The Nervous System* (Abingdon, UK: Routledge, 1991), 121. On this point, DuPlessis and Quartermain ("Introduction," 3–4) note the resonance of Ernst Bloch's 1935 essay, "Marxism and Poetry," in *The Utopian Function of Art and Literature*, trans. Jack Zipes and Frank Mecklenburg (Cambridge, MA: MIT Press, 1988), 156–62.

39. This concept, which adapts theoretical arguments from (among others) Stephen Greenblatt, Jerome McGann, and Michel Foucault, inherits unresolved binary antitheses and chiastic formulations:

> When we say we want to study Objectivist poets via a cultural poetics, we are, at one and the same time, trying to present culturalist readings—that is, readings alert to the material world, politics, society, and history, and readings concerned with the production, dissemination, and reception of poetic texts—and, as well, readings analyzing the poetic assumptions and textual choices that animate a set of practitioners. (21)

40. See especially Ron Silliman, "Third Phase Objectivism," *Paideuma* 10.1 (1981): 85–89. Silliman's influential model articulates a capacious formulation for literary reception that includes a third, or "renaissance phase" (late 1950s and after), distinguished by a "resurgence of interest in existing texts with the production of new writings" (85).

41. *On the Anarchy of Poetry: A Guide for the Unruly* (New York: Fordham University Press, 2008), 99–101.

42. Gilles Deleuze and Félix Guattari, *A Thousand Plateaus: Capitalism and Schizophrenia*, trans. Brian Massumi (Minneapolis: University of Minnesota Press, 1987), 23.

43. "Embracing the Verb of It: Black Experimental Writers, Innovative or Innovating?," Panel, AWP, Boston, 2013.

44. William Carlos Williams, *The Autobiography of William Carlos Williams* (New York: New Directions, 1951), 264.

45. Gertrude Stein, *Composition as Explanation* (London: Hogarth Press, 1926), 17; Marianne Moore, *Idiosyncrasy and Technique: Two Lectures* (Berkeley and Los Angeles: University of California Press, 1958); Marianne Moore, *Twentieth-Century American Poetics: Poets on the Art of Poetry*, ed. Dana Gioia, David Mason, and Meg Schoerke (Boston: McGraw Hill, 2004), 95.

46. Charles Olson, "Projective Verse," in *Poetry New York* (New York, 1950), unpaginated.

47. Denise Levertov, "Some Notes on Organic Form," *Poetry* 106.6 (1965): 424.

48. Altieri, "Objectivist Tradition," 32.

49. *Surge: Drafts 96–114* (Cromer, UK: Salt, 2013), 13, 10, 1–19.

50. DuPlessis and Quartermain, "Introduction," 17.

51. Burton Hatlen, "Marginality and Resistance," *Nexus*, 53.

52. Charles Bernstein, "Reznikoff's Nearness," *Nexus*, 237.

53. Ma, "Be Aware of 'the Medusa's Glance,'" 69.

54. Altieri, "Objectivist Tradition," 30.

55. *Music of Thought*, 201–4.

56. Burton Hatlen is—to the best of our knowledge—the only critic in the field (and the only contributor to *Nexus*) who considers Tyler's and Ford's contributions to the *Symposium*. However, Hatlen dismisses their significance and overlooks the matters we address here because he does not question Zukofsky's distrust of Surrealism and of these two precocious teenage "American surrealists" ("Marginality and Resistance," 40).

57. Parker Tyler and Charles Henri Ford, "Symposium," *Poetry* 37.5 (1931): 287.

58. Louis Zukofsky and René Taupin, "Symposium," *Poetry* 37.5 (1931): 290.

59. Those who contribute to, or who are discussed in, these dialogues are Parker Tyler, Charles Henri Ford, Samuel Putnam, Zukofsky, André Salmon, Apollinaire, Baudelaire, Mallarmé, and René Taupin.

60. Although Jennison provides rich discussions of Objectivism vis-à-vis linguistic remediation and historical materialism (20–22, 75), *The Zukofsky Era* does not address this key formulation from Tyler and Ford concerning contingent disruption.

61. Hatlen, "Marginality and Resistance," 40.

62. Louis Zukofsky, "Sincerity and Objectification: With Special Reference to the Work of Charles Reznikoff," *Poetry* 37.5 (1931): 279.

63. Louis Zukofsky, "Symposium," *Poetry* 37.5 (1931): 288 (emphasis added).

64. See Andrew Crozier, "Zukofsky's List," *Nexus*, 275–85. Crozier's essay is the only one in *Nexus* to acknowledge the relevance of René Taupin's *L'Influence du symbolisme français sur la poésie américaine (de 1910 à 1920)* for Zukofsky's emerging counterargument for the contingent contemporaneity of the first generation of modernists (Pound, Williams, Eliot, Moore, H. D.), who continued to develop their

poetics beyond 1920 and *after* Imagism (280). However, Crozier does not consider the essay on André Salmon's poetry that concludes the *Symposium*.

65. René Taupin and Louis Zukofsky, "Three Poems by André Salmon," *Poetry* 37.5 (1931): 289.

66. "An Objective," *Prepositions +*, 13, 18.

67. Indeed, this aspect of Zukofsky's attunement to a poetics of contingent contemporaneity follows lines of flight kindred with rhizomatic networks. See also Zukofsky, "American Poetry 1920–1930," *Prepositions +*, 137–51. After Deleuze and Guattari, we would transpose their notion of the rhizome as "composed not of units but of dimensions, or rather directions in motion [having] neither beginning nor end, but always a middle (*milieu*) from which it grows and which it overspills" (*A Thousand Plateaus*, 21) to our work here. In our tracings *after Objectivism*, we would advocate a "Nomadology, the opposite of a history" (23) attuned to the underground network of contingent disruption signaled *between* Zukofsky's contrasting concerns for *historic and contemporary particulars*—that is, between "a thing or things as well as an event or chain of events" and also "no literary production" for "nine reigns" ("An Objective," 12). In "An Objective" (and his companion statements) Zukofsky travels horizontally and sporadically across time, drawing asynchronous examples from a heterogeneous range of works, topics, and figures, including "an Egyptian pulled-glass bottle in the shape of a fish or oak leaves," Bach's *Matthew Passion*, "and the rise of metallurgical plants in Siberia" (12); Homer's "*the wet waves* not our *the wet waves*"(15); "the meaning of science in modern civilization as pointed out in Thorstein Veblen" (16); poems by Donne, Shakespeare, Dante, and Byron. In fact, his threefold notion of *complexity* in contemporary poetry combines Renaissance and early modern theories of polysemous signification, the metaphysical conceit, and epic-parodic capaciousness with particular attention to "the matter of [the] poetic object and its simple entirety" (18). See also Bernstein, "Reznikoff's Nearness," 210–39. Bernstein finds a Nomadology at work in Reznikoff's poetics (219).

68. Lyn Heijinian, "The Rejection of Closure," in *The Language of Inquiry* (Berkeley: University of California Press, 2000), 41–58.

69. "Assemblages are passional, they are compositions of desire. Desire has nothing to do with a natural or spontaneous determination; there is no desire but assembling, assembled, desire" (*A Thousand Plateaus*, 399).

70. This rendering of symbolic value echoes Althusser's subversion and containment dialectic characteristic of Ideological State Apparatuses. See Louis Althusser, "Ideology and Ideological State Apparatuses," in *Lenin and Philosophy and Other Essays*, trans. Ben Brewster (London: New Left Books, 1971), 121–73.

71. Friedrich Engels, quoted in Roberto J. Antonio, "Karl Marx," in *The Blackwell Companion to Major Social Theorists*, ed. George Ritzer (Malden, MA: Blackwell, 2000), 108.

72. In *Nexus*, see Alan Golding, "George Oppen's Serial Poems," 84–103; and Peter Nicholls, "Of Being Ethical: Reflections on George Oppen," 240–53. See also, for example, Joseph M. Conte, *Unending Design: The Forms of Postmodern Poetry*

(Ithaca, NY: Cornell University Press, 1991); Linda Reinfeld, *Language Poetry: Writing as Rescue* (Baton Rouge: Louisiana State University Press, 1992); Barrett Watten, *The Constructivist Moment: From Material Text to Cultural Poetics* (Middletown, CT: Wesleyan University Press, 2003); and G. Matthew Jenkins, *Poetic Obligation: Ethics in Experimental American Poetry after 1945* (Iowa City: University of Iowa Press, 2008). Reconsiderations of Objectivist poetics and praxis vis-à-vis contingent disruption would suggest new readings of kindred articulations, such as "dislocation[s] of perspective" (210) and "defamiliarization technique[s]" (238). See, respectively, Susan Howe, "Rae Armantrout, *Extremities*," and Rae Armantrout, "Carla Harryman, *Under the Bridge*," both in *The L=A=N=G=U=A=G=E Book*, ed. Bruce Andrews and Charles Bernstein (Carbondale: Southern Illinois University Press, 1984).

73. We organized two panels concerning our general theme, 'After' Objectivism, for two events: the first in 2012 for the Rocky Mountain Modern Language Association conference (Boulder); and the second in 2015 for the Louisville Conference on Literature and Culture since 1900.

74. See, for example, Arjun Appadurai, *The Social Life of Things: Commodities in Cultural Perspective* (Cambridge: Cambridge University Press, 1986); Bill Brown, *A Sense of Things: The Object Matter of American Literature* (Chicago: University of Chicago Press, 2003); Graham Harman, *Tool-Being: Heidegger and the Metaphysics of Objects* (Peru, IL: Open Court, 2002); Evan Selinger, ed., *Postphenomenology: A Critical Companion to Ihde* (Albany: State University of New York Press, 2006); Levi Bryant, Graham Harman, and Nick Srnicek, eds., *The Speculative Turn: Continental Materialism and Realism* (Melbourne: re.press, 2011); Ian Bogost, *Alien Phenomenology* (Ann Arbor: Open Humanities Press, 2012); and Robert Ranisch and Stefan Lorenz Sorgner, eds., *Post- and Transhumanism: An Introduction* (Frankfurt: Peter Lang, 2014).

75. See, for example, Claudia Rankine and Juliana Spahr, eds., *American Women Poets in the 21st Century: Where Lyric Meets Language* (Middletown, CT: Wesleyan University Press, 2002); Eric Haralson, ed., *Reading the Middle Generation Anew: Culture, Community, and Form in Twentieth-Century American Poetry* (Iowa City: University of Iowa Press, 2006); Mutlu Konuk Blasing, *Lyric Poetry: The Pain and the Pleasure of Words* (Princeton, NJ: Princeton University Press, 2007); and Maria Damon and Ira Livingston, eds., *Poetry and Cultural Studies: A Reader* (Urbana: University of Illinois Press, 2009). The 2012 *Shape of the I* poetics conference at the University of Colorado, Boulder—coordinated by Julie Carr, one of the contributors to this collection—offered another step in these directions.

76. Aldon Nielsen, *Reading Race: White American Poets and the Racial Discourse in the Twentieth Century* (Athens: University of Georgia Press, 1988), 93–97, 100.

77. Aldon Nielsen, *Integral Music: Languages of African American Innovation* (Tuscaloosa: University of Alabama Press, 2004), 80.

78. Nathaniel Mackey, *Paracritical Hinge: Essays, Talks, Notes, Interviews* (Madison: University of Wisconsin Press, 2005), 253, 308, 335.

79. Aldon Neilsen, *Black Chant: Languages of African-American Postmodernism* (Cambridge: Cambridge University Press, 1997).

80. See W. Scott Howard, "Limits, Lacunae and Liminality: New and Recent Poetry by William Bronk, Ed Roberson, and Gustaf Sobin," *Denver Quarterly* 34.4 (2000): 107–23; "Sapphire [Ramona Lofton]," in *The Greenwood Encyclopedia of African American Literature*, vol. 4, ed. Hans Ostrom and J. David Macey (Westport, CT: Greenwood Press, 2005), 1432–33; and W. Scott Howard, "'Fire harvest: harvest fire': Resistance, Sacrifice and Historicity in the Elegies of Robert Hayden," in Haralson, *Reading the Middle Generation Anew*, 133–52.

81. Joshua Clover, *The Lyric Theory Reader: A Critical Anthology* (Baltimore: Johns Hopkins University Press, 2013), dust jacket.

82. Jenny Penberthy, "Life and Writing," in *Lorine Niedecker: Collected Works*, ed. Jenny Penberthy (Berkeley: University of California Press, 2002), 3.

83. Simone du Beauvoir, *The Ethics of Ambiguity*, trans. Bernard Frechtman (New York: Kensington Press, 1976), 45–46.

84. Bill Brown, "Thing Theory," *Critical Inquiry* 28.1 (2001): 1–22.

85. Fred Moten, *In the Break: The Aesthetics of the Black Radical Tradition* (Minneapolis: University of Minnesota Press, 2003), 1, 255–57.

86. John T. Hamilton, *Soliciting Darkness: Pindar, Obscurity, and the Classical Tradition* (Cambridge, MA: Harvard University Press, 2004), 5–12.

87. See, for example, Maria Sabina, *Selections*, ed. Jerome Rothenberg (Berkeley: University of California Press, 2003).

88. Davidson, *Ghostlier Demarcations*, 118.

89. This discussion (which took place during the summer and fall months of 2016) was facilitated and moderated digitally through a wiki, then collaboratively edited for inclusion in this volume.

CHAPTER ONE

1. Rachel Blau DuPlessis and Peter Quartermain, *The Objectivist Nexus: Essays in Cultural Poetics* (Tuscaloosa: University of Alabama Press, 1999), 17–22.

2. This essay is one example of negotiating the junctures and slippages between personnel and poetics. Another would be a Jeffrey Twichell-Waas article that could be read as a pre-critique of the position I take here. As a beautifully articulate Zukofsky critic, whose work is always useful, he nonetheless has chosen to shake Zukofsky loose from any "objectivist" moorings ("What Were the 'Objectivist' Poets?," *Modernism/Modernity* 22.2 [April 2015]: 315–41). Here is another: Celia Thaew Zukofsky published, in 1979 (one year after LZ's death), a compendium called *American Friends* (New York: C.Z. Publications, 1979, www.z-site.net/american-friends), pairing selected citations from a full historical range of US authors (from the earliest period) with selected citations from Zukofsky (a work now available via Z-site). A full range, that is, with the *exception* of any objectivist denizen and any author beyond modernism. In his own historical terms, echoed by this very deliberate/motivated selection, Zukofsky was a US author and a modernist author. In the early to mid-twentieth century, the authors selected include Dreiser, Stephen Crane, Mencken, William Carlos Williams, Stevens, Stein, Pound, Moore, Eliot, Barnes, cummings, Faulkner, Fitzgerald, and Hemingway, as well as design theorists and ar-

chitects like Buckminster Fuller and Frank Lloyd Wright. Notably missing are Reznikoff, Bunting, Oppen, and Niedecker, as well as H. D., Hart Crane, and Langston Hughes. They are not "friends" for purposes of *American Friends*.

3. However, see the recovery of unknown Oppen poems from the time that *Discrete Series* was taking final shape; David Brandon Hobbs found (at the Beinecke Library) a cache of Oppen poems that Zukofsky had sent to Pound in 1930. They are filled with observation of sensations, affects, and physical bodies, and only some are tonally spare. This remarkable manuscript necessitates a rereading of Oppen's early work. David B. Hobbs, "A Brief Introduction to 21 Poems by George Oppen with Appendix: *21 Poems by George Oppen*," *Journal of Modern Literature* 40.1 (Fall 2016): 1–22.

4. Perhaps some of their early poems were written in tandem or in dialogue. Louis Zukofsky, *Complete Short Poetry* (Baltimore: Johns Hopkins University Press, 1991), 58–61 [for Karl Marx], 28; George Oppen, *New Collected Poems*, ed. Michael Davidson (New York: New Directions, 2002), 34.

5. Mary Oppen, *Meaning a Life: An Autobiography* (Santa Barbara: Black Sparrow Press, 1978), 91.

6. Barry Ahearn, ed., *The Selected Letters of Louis Zukofsky*, http://www.z-site .net/selected-letters-of-louis-zukofsky. Letter to Rexroth from 1941, 188.

7. Ibid., 138. TO Press with Zukofsky as the editor was actualized by Oppen's inheritance (which he accessed at age twenty-one in 1929). In 1931 Oppen offered Zukofsky a salary of $100 a month to serve as editor. Calculated on the basis of the US inflation rate (1,454.6 percent from 1931 to 2014), this would have been around $1,450 per month now (a low-end living wage for the time), but in a year or two (by 1933), after publishing work by Williams, Pound, and *An "Objectivists" Anthology* (ed. Zukofsky), the Oppens decided, influenced by the Depression, that the press had to contract, so they withdrew from this financial arrangement. Pound's increasingly fascist enthusiasms probably played a role (there had been plans to publish his collected prose). Perhaps there were other implications of keeping a friend on a salary, as well as other choices by Oppen for the uses of his income. This is one source of Zukofsky's sense of betrayal.

8. An underacknowledged spur to Oppen's return to writing was his reading, ca. 1956, of the City Lights *Howl*, brought down to Mexico by a young visitor (this noted by Linda Oppen during the Oppen panel at the Woodberry Poetry Room, Harvard University, October 2011). Allen Ginsberg's is a work of leftist sentiments, passionate rage, personal sincerity, and a social catalogue with critique—all terms also idiomatic to Oppen.

9. This trope alludes to Zukofsky's beloved "horse" metaphor. See Michele J. Leggott, *Reading Zukofsky's "80 Flowers"* (Baltimore: Johns Hopkins University Press, 1989), 84–85; Mark Scroggins, *The Poem of a Life: A Biography of Louis Zukofsky* (Emeryville, CA: Shoemaker and Hoard, 2007), 194–98.

10. In telling this "story" focused on the relationship between Oppen and Zukofsky, I have here left out discussions of Niedecker and Reznikoff in the long-term

nexus and as writers of long serially constructed poems, and the role of Cid Corman in bringing Zukofsky's work to print.

11. Scroggins, *Poem of a Life*, 133–34, 329, 207; the letters on Z-site, 516, n32, and letter 46 to Laughlin in 1940.

12. The back-and-forth may be read in Oppen's *Selected Letters*, 68–70, and in Scroggins, *Poem of a Life*, 335–38. The *Selected Letters* reveals much fussing and arranging and disagreeing over the scope of the collection, while never quite acknowledging the larger meanings of a "selected" versus a "collected." The collected format was, from Zukofsky's side, necessary and nonnegotiable. Hence Zukofsky would not negotiate, which rankled Oppen; for his part Oppen would not understand that this prospective publication was, for Zukofsky, a test of Oppen's fundamental loyalty to Zukofsky's career. This situation became a complete stalemate that saw both Oppen trying every which way to get Zukofsky to allow for some selection to be made and Zukofsky desiring inclusion in the general publication plan but on his terms only.

13. *ALL: The Collected Short Poems 1923–1958* (1965) and *ALL: The Collected Short Poems 1956–1964* (1966); both are W. W. Norton (New York).

14. These remarks are based on DuPlessis, *Purple Passages: Pound, Eliot, Zukofsky, Olson, Creeley and the Ends of Patriarchal Poetry* (Iowa City: University of Iowa Press, 2012), 59–75.

15. "'The Philosophy of the Astonished,'" ed. Rachel Blau DuPlessis, *Sulfur* 27 (Fall 1990): 203.

16. Charles Tomlinson, "Objectivists: Zukofsky and Oppen," in *Some Americans: A Personal Record* (Berkeley: University of California Press, 1981): 45–73. The salient passage is on 64–66.

17. In contrast, Oppen hardly appears in Zukofsky's letters (those in print and online) nor at all in his essays; however, there appears an Oppen wartime anecdote in "A-13" (written in 1960), 291. In contrast, Zukofsky appears a good deal in Oppen's "daybook" writings. Oppen also dedicates "The Lighthouses," a late poem, to Zukofsky.

18. Respectively, *Selected Letters* 151–52, 194, and *Selected Prose, Daybooks, and Papers*, ed. Stephen Cope (Berkeley: University of California Press, 2007), 99; and *Selected Letters*, 152.

19. "An Adequate Vision: A George Oppen Daybook," ed. Michael Davidson, *Ironwood* 26 (Fall 1985): 30.

20. George Oppen, "The Anthropologist of Myself: A Selection from Working Papers," ed. Rachel Blau DuPlessis, *Sulfur* 26 (Spring 1990): 149.

21. "The Circumstances: A Selection from George Oppen's Uncollected Writing," ed. Rachel Blau DuPlessis, *Sulfur* 25 (Fall 1989): 19–20.

22. My thanks as always to Peter Quartermain's precise comments and for this point—it's his.

23. *Sulfur* 25: 19; *Selected Letters*, 37.

24. "'Meaning Is to Be Here': A Selection from the Daybook," ed. Cynthia

Anderson, *Conjunctions* 10 (1987): 200. Inclusive pagination, 186–208. A comment by Jeffrey Twitchell-Waas verifies Oppen's comments: Zukofsky "primarily composed by self-consciously reworking prior textual materials" by others; www.z-site .net/lz-notes-on-the-bible.

25. *Contemporary Literature* 10.2 (Spring 1969): 203.

26. Dembo missed the fifth necessary poet—Lorine Niedecker, who lived only about thirty miles from the Madison campus of the University of Wisconsin, where the interviews were conducted.

27. Make whatever adjustments you'd like for all these "men."

28. I hesitate to state the obvious—one could reverse these and propose ways in which Zukofsky's allegiance was to the world, and Oppen's to the word. Overgeneralization works that way.

29. The minor prophets are counted as "one" book in Hebrew tradition.

30. Zukofsky's comment on the inner back jacket flap of *"A"* (Berkeley: University of California Press, 1978).

31. All the people are cited with their permission and with thanks for their enormous generosity in answering my query.

32. I also see Zukofsky's work as having two endings; see DuPlessis, *Purple Passages*, 80–85.

33. My evocation of these women writers is motivated by several things—Dahlen's own literary feminist cultural attitude, parallel to mine, her critique of other writers—including Oppen—for ignoring the work of modernist women, and the strong influence of the recovery work on behalf of modernist women writers, e.g., in the *HOW(ever)* formation. This work for the (often belated) reception of women writers (in which I participated) demanded and worked to forward a gender-inclusive vision of modernist writing.

34. Ron Silliman, "Preface," in *The Age of Huts (Compleat)* (Berkeley: University of California Press, 2007), ix; this work is 311 pages long to add to *The Alphabet*'s length.

35. An important in-depth literary history/memoir is Barrett Watten, *Questions of Poetics: Language Writing and Consequences* (Iowa City: University of Iowa Press, 2016).

36. In what follows I am extracting statements from her two emails, August 2014 and October 2014.

37. Roman Jakobson, "Linguistics and Poetics," in *Language in Literature*, ed. Krystyna Pomorska and Stephen Rudy (Cambridge, MA: Harvard University Press, 1987), 71.

CHAPTER TWO

1. Bertolt Brecht, *Bertolt Brecht Poems 1913–1956*, ed. John Willet and Ralph Mannheim (New York: Methuen, 1976), 318.

2. George Oppen, "The Mind's Own Place," in *Selected Prose, Daybooks, and Papers*, ed. Stephen Cope (Berkeley: University of California Press, 2007), 36.

3. George Oppen, *Selected Letters of George Oppen*, ed. Rachel Blau DuPlessis (Durham, NC: Duke University Press), 22.

4. Oppen, "A Letter," *Selected Prose*, 44.

5. L. S. Dembo, "Oppen on His Poems: A Discussion," in *George Oppen: Man and Poet*, ed. Burton Hatlen (Orono, ME: National Poetry Foundation, 1981), 213.

6. Oppen, "Statement on Poetics," *Selected Prose*, 48.

7. Louise Glück, "The Education of the Poet," in *Proofs and Theories: Essays on Poetry* (Hopewell, NJ: Ecco Press, 1994), 7. While it may well be the case that suffering is "recognizable," it goes without saying that the same can't be said about any given solution to it. "The undecidable *is* the political. There is politics precisely because there is undecidability" (Barbara Johnson, "Apostrophe, Animation, and Abortion," *Diacritics* 16.1 [1986], 35).

8. Oppen, "Statement on Poetics," 47.

9. George Oppen, *New Collected Poems* (New York: New Directions, 2002), 33.

10. Oppen, *Selected Letters*, 131.

11. Oppen, *New Collected Poems*, 93.

12. "The Joy of Writing," in *Essay on Literature, Written by the Third Century Poet, Lu Chi*, trans. Shih-hsing Chen (Portland, ME: Anthoesen Press, 1953), quoted in Richard Swigg, "The Test of Belief; or, Why George Oppen Quarreled with Denise Levertov," *Jacket2* (October 25, 2012), 7.

13. Dembo, "Oppen on His Poems," 209.

14. Louise Glück, *The Wild Iris* (Hopewell, NJ: Ecco Press, 1992), 27.

15. Michael Palmer, "On Objectivism," in *Active Boundaries: Selected Essays and Talks* (New York: New Directions, 2008), 232. The Oppen passage on which Palmer is commenting is from "The Mind's Own Place," 31–32: "It is possible to find a metaphor for anything, an analogue: but the image is encountered, not found; it is an account of the poet's perception, the act of perception; it is a test of sincerity, a test of conviction, the rare poetic quality of truthfulness."

16. Oppen, *New Collected Poems*, 163.

17. See "On George Oppen" and "Disruption, Hesitation, Silence," in *Proofs and Theories: Essays on Poetry* (Hopewell, NJ: Ecco Press, 1994), and "Our Life in Six Lyrical Poems: George Oppen," available in podcast, video, and transcript formats at http://www.philoctetes.org/calendar/our_life_in_six_lyrical_poems_george_oppen.

18. Charles Reznikoff, *Poems 1918-1975: The Complete Poems of Charles Reznikoff* (Santa Rosa, CA: Black Sparrow Press, 1989), 121. Among other places, Oppen's misquoting can be found in his foreword to Reznikoff's *Poems 1937-1975*.

19. William Carlos Williams, *The Collected Poems of William Carlos Williams* (New York: New Directions, 1988), 55.

20. Joshua Clover, "Words Pithy and Plain," *New York Times Book Review* (January 22, 2006), 13.

21. Reznikoff, *Poems 1918-1975*, 116.

22. Dembo, "Oppen on His Poems," 203.

23. Tony Hoagland, "Three Tenors: Glück, Hass, Pinsky, and the Deployment

of Talent," in *Real Sofistikashun: Essays on Poetry and Craft* (Saint Paul: Graywolf Press, 2006), 58.

24. Oppen, *New Collected Poems*, 41.

25. Burton Hatlen, "'Not Altogether Lone in a Lone Universe': George Oppen's *The Materials*," in *George Oppen: Man and Poet*, ed. Burton Hatlen (Orono, ME: National Poetry Foundation, 1981), 347.

26. Dembo, "Oppen on His Poems," 205–6.

27. Glück, *Wild Iris*, 29.

28. William Carlos Williams, *Selected Essays of William Carlos Williams* (New York: Random House, 1954), 256. It's worth noting that Oppen disapproved of this definition of poetry: "And the poem is not built out of words, one cannot make a poem by sticking words into it, it is the poem which makes the words and contains their meaning. One cannot reach out for *roses* and *elephants* and *essences* and put them in a poem" (*Selected Letters*, 123).

29. Glück, *Wild Iris*, 39.

30. Allen Grossman, "Nuclear Violence, Institutions of Holiness, and the Structures of Poetry," in *The Long Schoolroom: Lessons in the Bitter Logic of the Poetic Principle* (Ann Arbor: University of Michigan Press, 1997), 174.

31. Louise Glück, "The Idea of Courage," in *Proofs and Theories: Essays on Poetry* (Hopewell, NJ: Ecco Press, 1994), 25.

32. Oppen, "The Mind's Own Place," 35.

33. Oppen, *Selected Letters*, 21.

34. Rachel Blau DuPlessis, ed., "The Circumstances: A Selection from George Oppen's Uncollected Writing," *Sulfur* 25 (Fall 1989): 14.

35. Oppen, *New Collected Poems*, 35.

36. Cynthia Anderson, "'Meaning Is to Be Here': A Selection from the Daybook," *Conjunctions* 10 (1987): 198.

CHAPTER THREE

1. *Lorine Niedecker: Collected Works*, ed. Jenny Penberthy (Berkeley: University of California Press, 2002). Cited throughout as *CW*.

2. *XEclogue* (Vancouver: Tsunami, 1993).

3. *The Apothecary* (Vancouver: Tsunami, 1991).

4. *Debbie: An Epic* (Vancouver: New Star, 1997).

5. *The Weather* (Vancouver: New Star, 2002).

6. See Robertson's discussion of the recording in "'In Phonographic Deep Song': Sounding Niedecker," in *Radical Vernacular: Lorine Niedecker and the Poetics of Place*, ed. Elizabeth Willis (Iowa City: University of Iowa Press, 2008), 89.

7. *The Granite Pail: The Selected Poems of Lorine Niedecker*, ed. Cid Corman (San Francisco: North Point, 1985).

8. Catriona Strang, fellow student and poet, and close intellectual companion, recalls, "We both tried to find all the Niedecker we could get our hands on." In Vancouver they would have had easy access to my articles on Niedecker published in Roy Miki's *Line* magazine: in 1985, "Poems from Letters: The Lorine Niedecker–

Louis Zukofsky Correspondence"; and in spring 1987 my review of *The Granite Pail*. Subsequently, they would have seen "'The Revolutionary Word': Lorine Niedecker's Early Writings 1928–1946," *West Coast Line* 7, 26.1 (Spring 1992): 75–98. The same issue included "The 'New Goose' Manuscript," 99–110.

9. *From This Condensery: The Complete Writing of Lorine Niedecker*, ed. Robert Bertholf (Highlands, NC: Jargon Society, 1985).

10. Email to author, 2015.

11. Named by the previous owner and Olson scholar, the late Ralph Maud. Robertson owned and ran Proprioception Books from 1990 to 1994.

12. Jenny Penberthy, *Niedecker and the Correspondence with Zukofsky 1931–1970* (New York: Cambridge University Press, 1993).

13. The calendar poem appeared in *Sulfur* 41 (Fall 1997): 42–71.

14. *Moving Borders: Three Decades of Innovative Writing by Women*, ed. Mary Margaret Sloan (Jersey City, NJ: Talisman House, 1998), 10–15. The anthology also included two poems from Robertson's *XEclogue*.

15. My talk was a version of the George Oppen Memorial Lecture I had given at the Poetry Center, San Francisco, on December 4, 1997: "A Little Too Little: Re-reading Lorine Niedecker." Other events in the series were a panel discussion on Objectivism, including Peter Quartermain and myself, and films on Reznikoff, Rakosi, Zukofsky and Bunting, and the Oppens.

16. "'In Phonographic Deep Song,'" 83–90.

17. *From This Condensery* (hereafter referred to as *FTC*) omits the triptych poems "Canvass" and "Beyond What" and also "Synamism." It treats "Stage Directions" as "Creative Prose." Two other important early works, "Progression" and "Next Year or I Fly My Rounds, Tempestuous," were recovered after the publication of *FTC*.

18. In fact, "Domestic & Unavoidable," "The President of the Holding Company," and "Fancy Another Day Gone" (*FTC*, 233–41) were written not as radio plays but as poems. See *CW*, 68–78, 371.

19. Robertson's notebooks are among her papers in the Contemporary Literature Collection, Simon Fraser University Special Collections and Rare Books, Burnaby, BC.

20. Niedecker, "Fancy Another Day Gone," *CW*, 77–78.

21. Email to the author, 2015.

22. *The Weather*, 70–78.

23. Rachel Blau DuPlessis and Peter Quartermain, "Introduction," in *The Objectivist Nexus: Essays in Cultural Poetics*, ed. Rachel Blau DuPlessis and Peter Quartermain (Tuscaloosa: University of Alabama Press, 1999), 5 (*The Objectivist Nexus* hereafter referred to as *Nexus*).

24. Niedecker told Clayton Eshleman, "I went to school to Objectivism" (November 18, 1967). Robertson recalls writers she encountered as a student: "bp Nichol, Pound, Mallarmé, McCaffery, Beckett, the Objectivists" (interview with Michael Nardone, "Lisa Robertson," *Dialogues*, November 2010), http://sound object.net/texts/robertson.

25. Ron Silliman, "Third Phase Objectivism," *Paideuma* 10.1 (Spring 1981):

85–89; Charles Bernstein, *Content's Dream: Essays 1975-1984* (Los Angeles: Sun and Moon, 1986). In the late 1980s Robertson attended KSW workshops given by Lyn Hejinian and Charles Bernstein.

26. Email to the author, 2015.

27. Email from Robertson to the author, 2015. *Sulfur* was edited by Clayton Eshleman from 1981 to 2000.

28. *Nexus*, 3.

29. Robertson, Strang, Nancy Shaw, Christine Stewart, Susan Clark.

30. They would have been aware of multiple errors in the editing of *From This Condensery*, detailed in my reviews in *Sagetrieb* 5.2 (Fall 1986): 139–51, in *HOW(ever)* 4.1 (April 1987): 14–15, and in the *Times Literary Supplement* 4,408 (September 25-October 1, 1987): 1,043.

31. This work was later published in *The Birth-Mark: Unsettling the Wilderness in American Literary History* (Middletown, CT: Wesleyan University Press, 1993).

32. "Note" at the end of *XEclogue* (Vancouver: Tsunami, 1993), n.p. In Robertson's 2000 KSW talk on Sitwell, she outlined the F. R. Leavis–engineered ostracism of Sitwell on the grounds of her too technical attention to sound and rhythm—a "flaw," Robertson noted, that was often attributed to women's poetry by male critics.

33. Andrew Klobucar and Michael Barnholden, eds., "Introduction," in *Writing Class: The Kootenay School of Writing Anthology* (Vancouver: New Star, 1999), 43.

34. Burton Hatlen, "A Poetics of Marginality and Resistance: The Objectivist Poets in Context," *Nexus*, 47–48.

35. We know very little about Niedecker in the 1930s. She was never interviewed aside from the thirty-second truncated interview following the reading recorded by Corman in November 1970. The forceful articulations in her 1930s letters to Harriet Monroe, Ezra Pound, and Mary Hoard leave one all too aware of the lost content of her letters to Zukofsky from the same period.

36. "Sub-entries" is the title of a missing series of which "Stage Directions" and "Synamism" were parts.

37. Interview with Michael Nardone, "Lisa Robertson," *Dialogues*, November 2010, http://soundobject.net/texts/robertson.

38. Ted Byrne and Lisa Robertson, "This Animal, the Pronoun: An Interview," *The Capilano Review* 3.15 (Fall 2011): 37.

39. "Andy Fitch with Lisa Robertson," *The Conversant* 2012, http://theconversant.org/?p=4100.

40. *Giantess: The Organ of the New Abjectionists* was edited by Robertson, Strang, Christine Stewart, and Susan Clark and published only one issue, in June 1995.

41. "Lorine Niedecker: Letters to *Poetry* Magazine 1931-1937," in *Lorine Niedecker: Woman and Poet*, ed. Jenny Penberthy (Orono, ME: National Poetry Foundation, 1996), 181.

42. "Letter to Mary Hoard," in Penberthy, *Lorine Niedecker: Woman and Poet*, 87.

43. "Andy Fitch with Lisa Robertson."

44. Robertson and Carina Elisabeth Beddari, *The Present Is Unfinished: a Con-*

versation, Audiatur 2013, 12, https://audiaturbok.no/forlag/audiatur/the-present-is-unfinished.

45. Byrne and Robertson, "This Animal, the Pronoun," 34.

46. For example, Mina Loy's essay, "Modern Poetry" (c. 1925): "It is the direct response of the poet's mind to the modern world of varieties in which he finds himself. In each one we can discover his particular inheritance of that world's beauty." In *The Lost Lunar Baedeker,* ed. Roger Conover (New York: Farrar, Straus and Giroux, 1996), 158.

47. Byrne and Robertson, "This Animal, the Pronoun," 34–35.

48. Niedecker and Robertson continue to engage strategies for avoiding a centralized subject, Niedecker with the conceit of anonymous authorship in her *New Goose* poems and her use of personae. She and Robertson make frequent use of citation. A poet's anonymity is, of course, what Niedecker literally seeks within her community. I refer to her desire to suppress authorship in *Niedecker and the Correspondence with Zukofsky,* 73. Rachel Blau DuPlessis takes these points further in her brilliant and seminal essay, "Lorine Niedecker, the Anonymous: Gender, Class, Genre and Resistances," in Penberthy, *Lorine Niedecker: Woman and Poet,* 113–38.

49. Unpublished letter from Kenneth Cox to August Kleinzahler, December 20, 1996, The Poetry Collection, SUNY Buffalo.

50. Sina Queyras, "All Sides Now: A Correspondence with Lisa Robertson," *Poetry: Harriet Blog,* March 2010, http://www.poetryfoundation.org/harriet/2010/03/on-rs-boat-correspondence-with-lisa-robertson.

51. Niedecker to Mary Hoard, in Penberthy, *Lorine Niedecker: Woman and Poet,* 87.

52. In his *Nexus* essay, "Lorine Niedecker's Folk Base and Her Challenge to the American Avant-Garde," Peter Middleton makes a strong argument for Niedecker's complex deployment of intersubjective relations within the context of her folk poetry (*Nexus,* 172–77).

53. Niedecker to Harriet Monroe, in Penberthy, *Lorine Niedecker: Woman and Poet,* 177, and to Mary Hoard (ibid., 87). The poems were rejected by Harriet Monroe as "Utter mystification" (ibid., 184), dismissed by Pound, and questioned by Zukofsky: "Says he: is it logic? Which he *would* say" (letter to Mary Hoard, 88).

54. Niedecker to Monroe, in Penberthy, *Lorine Niedecker: Woman and Poet,* 181; Niedecker to Hoard (ibid., 88).

55. Niedecker to Corman, February 14, 1968, in *Between Your House and Mine: The Letters of Lorine Niedecker to Cid Corman, 1960 to 1970,* ed. Lisa Pater Faranda (Durham, NC: Duke University Press, 1986), 153.

56. Byrne and Robertson, "This Animal, the Pronoun," 34.

57. Referring to pronoun use in *The Weather.* Byrne and Robertson, "This Animal, the Pronoun," 34.

58. Louis Zukofsky, "An Objective," in *Prepositions: The Collected Critical Essays of Louis Zukofsky* (New York: Horizon, 1967), 24.

59. Charles Altieri, "The Objectivist Tradition," *Nexus,* 31.

60. Jay Smith, "Interview: Lisa Robertson," *Danforth Review* (Winter 2007).

61. A sequence of "Mother Goose" poems went to Harriet Monroe in February 1936. See *CW*, 85–91.

62. Robertson and Carina Elisabeth Beddari, *The Present Is Unfinished: A Conversation*, Audiatur 2013, 12, https://audiaturbok.no/forlag/audiatur/the-present -is-unfinished.

63. Robertson in Brecken Hancock's "An Interview with Lisa Robertson," *Canadian Women in the Literary Arts* (2013), http://cwila.com/an-interview-with-lisa -robertson/.

64. "Wasted Energy" (*CW*, 368), her high school poem, documents phatic language used—and clearly relished by Niedecker—in her school community.

65. Lisa Robertson, *Nilling* (Toronto: Bookthug, 2012), 55.

66. There are two toasts in Robertson's *Debbie: An Epic* (1997). Both are delivered in footnotes—lines 115 and 384.

67. Evident also in another poem, "Van Gogh could see / twenty-seven varieties / of black / in cap- / italism" (*CW*, 183).

68. "The Weather: A Report on Sincerity," *Chicago Review* 51/52.4/1 (Spring 2006): 28–29. The essay was completed in 1999.

69. "The Weather: A Report on Sincerity," *Chicago Review* 51/52.4/1 (Spring 2006): 28. Robertson recognized exchanges about the weather as a community discourse during her 1998–99 residency at Cambridge University.

70. In the final "Note" in *XEclogue* (n.p.), Robertson asserts the "necessity for women's tactical intervention in official genres."

71. Dating back to Spenser's *The Shepheardes Calender* (1597).

72. We know Niedecker read Lawrence's *Fantasia on the Unconscious* in 1933. We also know that Zukofsky thought highly of Lawrence's *Studies in Classic American Literature*, which he read in the late 1920s (see "Letters between Zukofsky and Ezra Pound," ed. Barry Ahearn, *Montemora* 8 [1981]: 158–65). Niedecker would surely have read Lawrence's *Studies*, with its hilarious tirade against Franklin's almanacs. Her early poems suggest a sustained critique. She contrasts Pound as the "best of all Almanac Makers," whose *XXX Cantos* provide information based in the senses.

73. One recalls Robertson's satirical horoscope column written between 2001 and 2003 for *Nest* magazine and published under the pen name Swann.

74. "Sometime soon I hope to add a section to 'Year Before Last' or set up anyhow a 'Year After Next' to discredit all journal method everywhere" (to Monroe, May 31, 1934) (Penberthy, *Lorine Niedecker: Woman and Poet*, 186). These poems along with "Eleven Month Stare" and "Almanac Maker" are likely part of the same large critical project. None has survived.

75. Thanks to Andy Oler for providing this pasted-over text drawn from an original copy of *The Sunlit Calendar*.

76. Louis Zukofsky, "Influence," *Prepositions: The Collected Critical Essays of Louis Zukofsky* (Berkeley: University of California Press, 1981), 127.

77. Among the Lisa Robertson Papers, Simon Fraser University, Burnaby, BC.

78. Email to the author, 2015. Additionally, "Aha, yes—for LN, automatic writing and dream—for me, back then—cut-up. I would type out detailed but fairly nor-

mative descriptions of things—my garden, say, looked at very closely, and described daily—then cut up and scramble these descriptions to achieve odd associations, then re-smooth the grammar."

79. There is no explicit mention of cut-up techniques in the small body of remaining prose; however, the poetry itself suggests such experiment: the triptych poems, for example, "Canvass" and "Beyond What" (*CW*, 33–34).

80. "Program: 'Objectivists': 1931," *Poetry* (February 1931): 269. (Strabismus is a condition that prevents both eyes from aligning simultaneously with an object.) Curiously, the strong statement of Zukofsky's does not appear in Ming-Qian Ma's argument for Rakosi's strabismal vision in his essay "Be Aware of 'the Medusa's Glance': The Objectivist Lens and Carl Rakosi's Poetics of Strabismal Seeing," *Nexus*, 56–83. It's worth noting that Charles Altieri's essay in *Nexus*, "The Objectivist Tradition," makes a compelling argument for collage as a defining form for Objectivism giving credence to Niedecker's intuition of compatibility between Surrealism and Objectivism (31).

81. In *Radical Vernacular*, 83–90.

82. Robertson began her Atget recording project in 2003. Her essay "Disquiet" in *Nilling* (55–70) addresses the project and ideas of silence, noise, and listening.

83. Kai Fierle-Hedrick with Lisa Robertson, "Lifted: An Interview with Lisa Robertson," *Chicago Review* 51/52.4/1 (Spring 2006): 49. In the same interview she acknowledges learning about the syllable from Niedecker, among others (50).

84. "'In Phonographic Deep Song,'" 86.

85. "Fall" (*CW*, 206): "Early morning corn / shock quick river / edge ice crack duck / talk // Grasses' dry / membranous / breaks tick-tack tiny / wind strips[.]"

86. "'In Phonographic Deep Song,'" 87.

87. Comments such as these abound in Niedecker's letters; for example, she writes to Corman about Eshleman's poetry: "[. . .] there is such a thing as silence. [. . .] Art is cooler than he thinks" (unpublished letter, February 14, 1968).

88. Steve Goodman, *Sonic Warfare: Sound, Affect, and the Ecology of Fear* (Cambridge, MA: MIT Press, 2010), 191.

89. Sina Queyras, "All Sides Now: A Correspondence with Lisa Robertson."

90. Robertson credits sound artist Pauline Oliveros's listening practice; I add Salomé Voegelin as another exemplary commentator on listening. *Sonic Possible Worlds: Hearing the Continuum of Sound* (London: Bloomsbury, 2014), 84.

91. Voegelin, *Sonic Possible Worlds*, 84.

92. Unpublished, undated letter to Kenneth Cox.

93. Mark Cochrane, "Stuttering Continuity (or, Like It's 1999): An Interview with Lisa Robertson at Cambridge," *Open Letter* 13.6 (Summer 2008): 85.

94. Voegelin, *Sonic Possible Worlds*, 169.

95. To Zukofsky, February 7, 1964, "I'm trembling on the verge of something, a form of poetic thinking. [. . .] I don't know if it's called metaphysical or not, not necessarily, I guess, but anyhow this has been in me from the beginning." Penberthy, *Niedecker and the Correspondence with Zukofsky*, 343.

96. "Andy Fitch with Lisa Robertson."

CHAPTER FOUR

1. A shorter version of this essay appeared in *Blackbox Manifold* 16 (2016), http://www.manifold.group.shef.ac.uk/issue16/AlanGoldingEssayBM16.pdf. Rachel Blau DuPlessis, *Pitch: Drafts 77–95* (London: Salt, 2010), 42 (hereafter referred to as *Pitch*). "Hard Copy" is a crucial document in DuPlessis's career-long conversation with the work of George Oppen. Specifically, this serial poem *within* the larger serial project of *Drafts* is in dialogue with Oppen's "Of Being Numerous," including (to note only surface features) the forty-section structure that mirrors Oppen's own and the direct echo of Oppen's conclusion (itself cited from Whitman), the phrase "quite curious." For sustained commentary, see Libbie Rifkin, "'That We Can Somehow Add Each to Each Other?': George Oppen between Denise Levertov and Rachel Blau DuPlessis," *Contemporary Literature* 51.4 (Winter 2010): 703–35, and especially 723–31.

2. Louis Zukofsky, *Prepositions +: The Collected Critical Essays*, ed. Mark Scroggins (Middletown, CT: Wesleyan University Press, 2001), 214, 189.

3. Zukofsky, *Prepositions*, 194.

4. For DuPlessis on the "thing," see her essay "The Topos of the 'Thing': Some Thoughts on 'Objectivist' Poetics," in *The Idea and the Thing in Modernist American Poetry*, ed. Cristina Giorcelli (Palermo, Italy: ILA Palma, 2001), 31–51.

5. George Oppen, *Selected Prose, Daybooks, and Papers* (Berkeley: University of California Press, 2007).

6. Rachel Blau DuPlessis and Peter Quartermain, "Introduction," in *The Objectivist Nexus: Essays in Cultural Poetics*, ed. Rachel Blau DuPlessis and Peter Quartermain (Tuscaloosa: University of Alabama Press, 1999), 3 (*The Objectivist Nexus* hereafter referred to as *Nexus*.

7. DuPlessis and Quartermain, "Introduction," 4. See also Rachel Blau DuPlessis, "The Blazes of Poetry: Remarks on Segmentivity and Seriality with Special Reference to Blaser and Oppen," in *The Recovery of the Public World: Essays on Poetics in Honour of Robin Blaser*, ed. Charles Watts and Edward Byrne (Burnaby, BC: Talon Books, 1999), 287–99.

8. DuPlessis and Quartermain, "Introduction," 7, 3. Cf. DuPlessis's recent and even stronger claim that "perhaps the most distinctive contribution of objectivist poetics is the mid-length to very long serial poem," in her essay "Objectivist Poetry and Poetics," in *The Cambridge Companion to Modern American Poetry*, ed. Walter Kalaidjian (New York: Cambridge University Press, 2015), 95. On the connection of Objectivist seriality to "thought, cognition, investigation," see Alan Golding, "George Oppen's Serial Poems," *Nexus*, 84–103, and Burton Hatlen, "Opening Up the Text: George Oppen's 'Of Being Numerous,'" *Ironwood* 13.2 (Fall 1985): 263–95.

9. Rachel Blau DuPlessis, "Lorine Niedecker's 'Paean to Place' and Its Reflective Fusions," in *Radical Vernacular: Lorine Niedecker and the Poetics of Place*, ed. Elizabeth Willis (Iowa City: University of Iowa Press, 2008), 162.

10. DuPlessis, "Lorine Niedecker's 'Paean,'" 163.

11. Charles Bernstein writes of Reznikoff that "with his first book, he introduced cubo-seriality into American poetry: serial poems that have a modular, rather than a sequential, relation to one another." Bernstein, "Brooklyn Boy Makes Good: Charles Reznikoff, the Poet of New York," *Brooklyn Rail*, March 5, 2006, http://www.brooklynrail.org/2006/03/books/brooklyn-boy-makes-good-charles -reznikoff-the-poet-of-new-york. One would also want to take into account DuPlessis's offhand but historically persuasive reference to "the invention of the serial poem in early modernism (possibly by Loy)" in her *Genders, Races, and Religious Cultures in Modern American Poetry, 1908–1934* (New York: Cambridge University Press, 2001), 55. Mina Loy's "Songs to Joannes" was first published as "Love Songs I–IV" in the experimental little magazine *Others* 1.1 (July 1915), 6–8; and the revised "Songs to Joannes," now in thirty-four sections, was published in *Others* 3.6 (April 1917): 3–20, taking up the whole issue.

12. Ezra Pound, *Gaudier-Brzeska: A Memoir* (New York: New Directions, 1970), 94.

13. DuPlessis and Quartermain, "Introduction," 22.

14. "Objectivist Poetry," 99.

15. For DuPlessis's most recent comments on the idea of writing "after," see her "After the Long Poem," *Dibur Literary Journal* 4 (Spring 2017): 5–13.

16. Rachel Blau DuPlessis, *Blue Studios: Poetry and Its Cultural Work* (Tuscaloosa: University of Alabama Press, 2006), 210. DuPlessis's frequent use of the phrase "jot and tittle" may well have encoded into it her awareness of Pound's anti-Semitism. She quotes, for instance, his assertion that "not a jot or tittle of the Hebraic alphabet can pass into the text without danger of contaminating it" (250).

17. Rachel Blau DuPlessis, *Surge: Drafts 96–114* (Cromer, UK: Salt, 2013), 11 (hereafter referred to as *Surge*).

18. *Surge*, 3. For recent observations on "IT IS," see DuPlessis's 2017 essay "Autobiography of a Practice," *Thresholds* 1 (www.openthresholds.org/issue/1): *Drafts* "manifests its commitment to seriality on a very large scale—you might say that the sections all point outward and inward as a series of explorations into the world and thus into IT. Into the two oddities of all oddities: IT and IS. These words indicate *being* itself (thus *Drafts* is an ontological poem). They also address being *itself*, within this cosmological and ecological poem, at times meditating on actual scientific findings as told by journalism, at times speculating on the universe" (n.p.).

19. George Oppen, *Selected Prose*, 32; George Oppen, *New Collected Poems*, ed. Michael Davidson (New York: New Directions, 2008), 99.

20. *Surge*, 12. DuPlessis seems to be invoking two relevant intertexts here, from Whitman's "Song of Myself" (another candidate for the first serial poem)—"I and this mystery here we stand" (Walt Whitman, *Leaves of Grass and Other Writings*, ed. Michael Moon [New York: W. W. Norton, 2002], 28); and from Oppen—"The self is no mystery, the mystery is / That there is something for us to stand on" (Oppen, *New Collected Poems*, 159).

21. *Drafts 1–38, Toll* (Middletown, CT: Wesleyan University Press, 2001), 225

(hereafter referred to as *Toll*). As one form of post-Objectivist deixis, we might consider the title of Barrett Watten's important magazine of early Language writing, *This*.

22. DuPlessis quotes Zukofsky's words in *Toll*, 225–26.

23. *Toll*, 180. The letter *a* recurs as beginning, invitation, or "incipience": "Ask the letter A / and it may tell you // to continue," for instance, in Rachel Blau Du-Plessis, *The Collage Poems of Drafts* (London: Salt, 2011), 6.

24. Rachel DuPlessis, *The Pink Guitar: Writing as Feminist Practice* (New York: Routledge, 1990), 147.

25. For a valuable prior analysis of the "little words," including "it," in *Toll*, see Libbie Rifkin, "Little Words and Redemptive Criticism: Some Points on *Drafts*," *HOW2* 1.8 (2002), https://www.asu.edu/pipercwcenter/how2journal/archive/on line_archive/v1_8_2002/current/forum/rifkin.htm. Regarding "the line of one," and the related terms *fold* and *grid*, for readers unfamiliar with the structure of *Drafts*: between the writing of Draft 19 and Draft 20, DuPlessis writes, "I decided to repeat some version of these themes or materials in the same general order every nineteen poems, folding one group over another, making new works but works evoking motifs and themes in the former one—and also [. . .] generating new images, materials and themes as I went" in "a recurrent but free structure," a procedure but not a plan (*Surge*, 7). Thus, with a "fold" every nineteen poems, the "line of one" would include Drafts 1, 20, 39, 58, 77, and 96, all in some degree of conversation with each other; the "line of two" would include Drafts 2, 21, 40, 59, 78, and 97; and so on. Starting with *Drafts 39-57, Pledge, with Draft, Unnumbered: Précis* (Cambridge: Salt, 2004), DuPlessis included a diagrammatic grid laying out the structure of the lines and folds as it expanded with every volume.

26. The epigraphs appear in *Drafts* (Elmwood, CT: Potes & Poets Press, 1991), which includes Drafts 3–14 in the first book-length gathering of the project. When DuPlessis reprints these poems as part of *Drafts 1-38*, she replaces the Coolidge epigraph with one from Keats.

27. Robert Creeley, *The Collected Poems of Robert Creeley 1945-1975* (Berkeley: University of California Press, 1982), 391, 294. A variation entirely apposite for *Drafts* would be "as soon as / I speak, it / speaks," and indeed we find something close to that in "Draft 76: Work Table with Scale Models": "It / (still / speaking) / is still, speaking." Rachel Blau DuPlessis, *Torques: Drafts 58-76* (Cambridge, UK: Salt, 2007), 132 (hereafter referred to as *Torques*).

28. *Toll*, 5, 4. DuPlessis's use of "CANO"/"I sing" invokes a canonical epic beginning, that of Virgil's *Aeneid*, as she notes in *Blue Studios*, 234.

29. *Toll*, 2. A different sort of essay from this one would discuss how the material page in *Drafts* is not just thematized but insistently foregrounded through drawings, handwriting, double columns, typographic marks, boldface and italics, shifts in font size, capitals, obtrusive typos, blacked-out text, mail art, visual collage, and generous use of interlineal and intralineal white space, both an acknowledgment and an extension of the materiality of prior Objectivist texts. In these ways *Drafts* has

a deep kinship with the visually exploratory work of Susan Howe. DuPlessis wrote some of the earliest commentary on this aspect of Howe's work (even connecting it to Oppen) in the chapter "'Whowe': On Susan Howe" (*Pink Guitar*, 123–39). For an important treatment of Objectivist and post-Objectivist materiality, see Michael Davidson, *Ghostlier Demarcations: Modern Poetry and the Material Word* (Berkeley: University of California Press, 1997), 64–93. On visual materiality specifically in DuPlessis, see Ron Silliman, "Un-scene, Ur-new: The History of the Longpoem and 'The Collage Poems of Drafts,'" http://jacket2.org/article/un-scene-ur-new.

30. Charles Reznikoff, *The Poems of Charles Reznikoff 1918–1975*, ed. Seamus Cooney (Boston: David R. Godine, 2005), 107.

31. *Toll*, 9. For the "darker, antecedent sea," see *Toll*, 10.

32. Louis Zukofsky, *"A"* (Berkeley: University of California Press, 1978), 1.

33. William Carlos Williams, *Spring and All* (New York: New Directions, 2011), 13.

34. *Toll*, 267. Note the foregrounding of "work" in the title of poems on the line of nineteen, the last numbered poem in each volume: "Draft 19: Working Conditions," "Draft 38: Georgics & Shadow," "Draft 57: Workplace, Nekuia," "Draft 76: Work Table with Scale Models," "Draft 95: Erg."

35. *Torques*, 136. For the idea of the "infinite series," see Joseph M. Conte, *Unending Design: The Forms of Postmodern Poetry* (Ithaca, NY: Cornell University Press, 1991). Actually, Conte places the Objectivist work that he discusses (Oppen's *Discrete Series*, Zukofsky's *Anew*, Niedecker's "Lake Superior") in the category of the "finite series"—though one source for the phrase "infinite series" is the first section of Oppen's "Of Being Numerous."

36. Quotations in this and the previous sentence come from DuPlessis, *Pitch*, 172. It is notable that DuPlessis turns to a perfectly regular iambic pentameter to "start it up again," as if the continuing work depends both on a repeated return to the history of Anglophone poetry (encoded in the iambic meter) and on doing that history just enough violence to jog it into renewed life but not destroy it ("I knock it hard").

37. Rachel Blau DuPlessis, "An Interview with Rachel Blau DuPlessis," with Jeanne Heuving, *Contemporary Literature* 45.3 (Fall 2004), 403.

38. Naomi Schor, *Reading in Detail: Aesthetics and the Feminine* (New York: Methuen, 1987), 4.

39. Schor, *Reading*, 3–4. In the preface to *Surge*, DuPlessis writes, "I don't want to say too much about scale and gender, because any stereotypical observation—however situationally true—risks restating (re-instantiating) patterns we want to reject" (9). One can assent without finding the comment disabling for considerations of scale and gender, especially when she moves immediately into a long paragraph on the history of female authorship.

40. Susan Stanford Friedman, "When a 'Long' Poem Is a 'Big' Poem: Self-Authorizing Strategies in Women's Twentieth-Century 'Long Poems,'" in *Feminisms: An Anthology of Literary Theory and Criticism*, ed. Robyn R. Warhol and Diane Price Herndl (New Brunswick, NJ: Rutgers University Press, 1997), 721. The definitive book-length study of the female-authored long poem remains Lynn Keller, *Forms*

of Expansion: Recent Long Poems by Women (Chicago: University of Chicago Press, 1997), which contains one of the earliest sustained discussions of *Drafts* as a "feminist serial long poem" (276).

41. *Surge*, preface, 2.

42. *Toll*, 9. We can take "not hero" as "not Ezra Pound" (not Pound's sequence of heroic males in *The Cantos*) and, even more explicitly, "not polis" as "not Charles Olson" (whose *Maximus Poems* takes "polis" as a central term).

43. Friedman, "When a 'Long' Poem," 724, 733.

44. "Not so much the world in a grain of sand / but the grain of sand in the world / defines trace": *Pitch*, 91. "Micro-moment": *Toll*, 115.

45. Daniel Bouchard has captured the macro-micro dynamic of *Drafts* nicely in his essay "A Little Yod and a Rocking Enormity: Reading *Drafts*," *Jacket2* (December 2011), http://jacket2.org/article/little-yod-and-rocking-enormity, where he lists images of smallness and uses of the word "enormous" (and its variants) side by side.

46. Cf. Patrick Pritchett's comment that "the scale of *Drafts* is monumental; its focus anti-monumental," in his review, "*Drafts 1–38, Toll*, by Rachel Blau DuPlessis," *Jacket2* (May 2003), http://jacketmagazine.com/22/prit-dupless.html, and DuPlessis's own description of *Drafts* as "a monumental task suspicious of the monumental" (*Blue Studios*, 241).

47. Rachel Blau DuPlessis, "Lyric and Experimental Long Poems: Intersections," in *Time in Time: Short Poems, Long Poems, and the Rhetoric of North American Avant-Gardism, 1963–2008*, ed. J. Mark Smith (Toronto: McGill–Queens University Press, 2013), 37. DuPlessis's comment on "how to indicate one's volume without squatting hibernations of mass" (*Pink Guitar*, 133) may seem contradictory until we recall that—despite the implications of the "mound" metaphor—"mass" for her must also be mobile, labile, porous, and hardly a matter of "squatting hibernations."

48. DuPlessis, "Lyric and Experimental Poems," 39.

49. *Torques*, 133; *Toll*, 266.

50. Ezra Pound, *The Cantos* (London: Faber and Faber, 1975), 796; on DuPlessis and Pound, see Alan Golding, "*Drafts* and Fragments: Rachel Blau DuPlessis' (Counter)-Poundian Project," *Jacket2* (December 2011), https://jacket2.org/article/drafts-and-fragments; and Bob Perelman, *Modernism the Morning After* (Tuscaloosa: University of Alabama Press, 2017), 53–68.

51. "Lyric and Experimental Poems," 50.

52. Both this and the previous quotation come from DuPlessis, *Pledge*, 121. For Zukofsky, the form for "thoughts' torsion," for "the actual twisting / Of many and diverse thoughts" "is really a sestina," that strange combination of elegance and baroque ungainliness—but the sestina considered and used "as a force," not merely "as an experiment" in seeing if one can write a sestina. Louis Zukofsky, *ALL: The Collected Short Poems 1923-1964* (New York: W. W. Norton, 1971), 73–77.

53. *Pitch*, 82, 20. Elsewhere in *Pitch*, in a self-lacerating definition of poetry and a theoretical reflection on Objectivist poetics, words are "a fetish substitute for the directness / of rubble" (49). As a recurring point of reference, Reznikoff's girder becomes almost a fetish object in later Objectivist-influenced writing. See, for ex-

ample, the use by Zukofsky biographer and poet-critic Mark Scroggins of Reznikoff for the conclusion of his poem "Whiplash" (which also alludes to Oppen): "girder still itself." Scroggins, *Torture Garden: Naked City Pastorelles* (Brooklyn: Cultural Society, 2011), n.p.

54. *Pitch*, 134. With these opening *N*s, I suspect an allusion not just to Wallace Stevens's "Poem in the Shape of a Mountain" but also to Basil Bunting's observation on Pound's *Cantos*: "There are the Alps. What is there to say about them?" (Bunting, *Collected Poems* [Oxford: Oxford University Press, 1977], 110). The first Draft and page of *Pitch* returns to this image in citing a phrase from Gershom Scholem, "'letters took on / [. . .] the shape of great mountains'" (*Pitch*, 1.)

CHAPTER FIVE

1. See Eric Mottram's "The British Poetry Revival, 1960–75," in *New British Poetries*, ed. Robert Hampson and Peter Barry (Manchester: Manchester University Press, 1993), 17–50. See, in my *The Poetry of Saying: British Poetry and Its Discontents 1950–2000* (Liverpool: Liverpool University Press, 2005), chapter 1, "The Movement Poets and the Movement Orthodoxy in the 1950s and 1960s" (20–34); chapter 2, "The British Poetry Revival 1960–1978" (35–76); and chapter 6, "Linguistically Innovative Poetry 1978–2000."

2. John Seed, "Irrelevant Objects: Basil Bunting's Poetry of the 1930s," in *The Objectivist Nexus*, ed. Rachel Blau DuPlessis and Peter Quartermain (Tuscaloosa: University of Alabama Press, 1999), 126 (*The Objectivist Nexus* hereafter referred to as *Nexus*).

3. Basil Bunting, "A Note on *Briggflatts*," in *Briggflatts* (Tarset: Bloodaxe Books, 2009), 40.

4. Basil Bunting, "The Poet's Point of View," *Briggflatts*, 44.

5. John Seed, "An English Objectivist? Basil Bunting's Other England," *Chicago Review* 44.3/4 (1998): 116.

6. Charles Altieri, "The Objectivist Tradition," *Nexus*, 32.

7. John Seed, *New and Collected Poems* (Exeter: Shearsman, 2005a), 15.

8. Altieri, "Objectivist Tradition," 32.

9. Burton Hatlen, "A Poetics of Marginality and Resistance: The Objectivist Poets in Context," *Nexus*, 53.

10. Altieri, "Objectivist Tradition," 9.

11. *New and Collected Poems*, 81.

12. John Seed, *Manchester: August 16th & 17th 1819* (London: Intercapillary Space, 2013), 48–49.

13. John Seed, *Marx: A Guide for the Perplexed* (London and New York: Continuum, 2010), 68.

14. Richard Holmes, *Shelley: The Pursuit* (London: Flamingo, 1995), 531.

15. Seed, *Manchester*, 45.

16. P. B. Shelley, *Shelley's Poetry and Prose*, ed. Donald H. Reiman and Sharon B. Powers (New York and London: Norton, 1977), 301.

17. Seed, *Manchester*, 24.

18. Shelley, *Shelley's Poetry and Prose*, 309.

19. Seed, *Manchester*, 23.

20. Shelley, *Shelley's Poetry and Prose*, 301.

21. Walter Benjamin, *The Arcades Project*, trans. Howard Eiland and Kevin McLaughlin, ed. Rolf Tiedemann (Cambridge, MA: Harvard University Press, 1999), 476.

22. Seed, *Manchester*, 52–53. In chapter 7 of my *The Meaning of Form in Contemporary Innovative Poetry* (New York: Palgrave, 2016), "The Trace of Poetry and the Non-Poetic: Conceptual Writing and Appropriation in Kenneth Goldsmith, Vanessa Place and John Seed," I treat Seed's documentary poetry as a foil to the increasingly teleologically self-serving poetics of Conceptual Writing.

23. Louis Zukofsky, *Prepositions: The Collected Critical Essays* (Berkeley: University of California Press, 1981), 12, 13.

24. William Carlos Williams, "Objectivism," in *Princeton Encyclopaedia of Poetry and Poetics*, ed. Alex Preminger (Basingstoke and London: Macmillan, 1974), 582.

25. Zukofsky, *Prepositions*, 14, 12.

26. Tim Woods, *The Poetics of the Limit* (New York: Palgrave, 2002), 5.

27. Published recently, *Smoke Rising: London 1940-1* (Bristol: Shearsman, 2015) takes a similar approach to documents from the London Blitz, but it is notable for its relative eschewal of the artifice of enjambment that is crucial to the Mayhew project.

28. Seed, *Manchester*, 52–53.

29. Seed, *Manchester*, 55; also Roland Barthes, *Camera Lucida* (London: Flamingo, 1984), 27.

30. Giorgio Agamben, *The End of the Poem: Studies in Poetics* (Stanford, CA: Stanford University Press, 1999), 109, 100.

31. For more detail, see Kellow Chesney, *The Victorian Underworld* (London: Temple Smith, 1970).

32. Seed, *Marx*, 119.

33. John Seed, *Pictures from Mayhew* (Exeter: Shearsman, 2005b), 66.

34. John Seed, *That Barrikins—Pictures from Mayhew II* (Exeter: Shearsman, 2007), 155–56.

35. Hatlen, "A Poetics," 53.

36. Seed, *Manchester*, 52–53.

37. Charles Bernstein, "Reznikoff's Nearness," *Nexus*, 234.

38. Woods, *Poetics of the Limit*, 5.

CHAPTER SIX

1. Lionel Trilling, *Sincerity and Authenticity* (Cambridge, MA: Harvard University Press, 1972), 6.

2. Jane Taylor, "'Why do you tear me from myself?,'" in *The Rhetoric of Sincerity*, ed. Ernst van Alphen and Mieke Bal (Palo Alto: Stanford University Press, 2009), 25.

3. See Herbert Read, *The Cult of Sincerity* (New York: Horizon Press, 1969).

4. Jean-Jacques Rousseau, *Confessions*, trans. Angela Scholar (New York: Oxford University Press, 2000), 5.

5. Trilling, *Sincerity and Authenticity*, 25.

6. Susan B. Rossenbaum, *Professing Sincerity: Modern Lyric Poetry, Commercial Culture, and the Crisis in Reading* (Charlottesville: University of Virginia Press, 2007), 6–7.

7. Trilling, *Sincerity and Authenticity*, 12.

8. Ibid., 135. In relation to the representation of class in British novels, Trilling remarks of characters in British novels, "He will be sincere *and* authentic, sincere *because* authentic" (115). Lingering in the artistic *representation* of sincerity (rather than its co-production) is the sense that is an effect of another quality (in this case, authenticity). Turning to Hegelian categories, Trilling does propose that "the 'honest soul' has sincerity as its essence" (115).

9. Boris Groys, "The Production of Sincerity," in *Going Public* (New York: Sternberg, 2010), 42.

10. What Groys himself skirts here is the possibility of the rejection of aesthetic judgment as also a shared politics, a rejection of *judgment* as base similar to authenticity. There may be some overlap in Oppen's position toward the loss of aesthetic judgment and "new art." In *On Being Numerous*, Oppen (in the tenth section) writes, "Or in that light. New arts! Dithyrambic, audience-as-artists!" which may be a comment on the challenge by Happenings to tradition gallery shows. However, I do think that Oppen's response here is not so stuffy, as the section ends with a non-lament that "the isolated man is dead, his world around him exhausted / And he fails! He fails, that meditative man! And indeed they cannot 'bear it'" (15). "They" are "the young in the cities," so I tend not to read a nostalgia into this section.

11. Ernst van Alphen and Mieke Bal, "Introduction," *Rhetoric of Sincerity*, 6.

12. Here I am drawing on the work of Sara Ahmed, who moves Marx's general labor theory of value into the field of affect in her essay "Affective Economies" (*Social Text* 22.2 [2004]: 117–39). For Marx, social relations do "not appear as direct social relations between persons in their work, but rather as material [*dinglich*] relations between persons and social relations between things" (Marx, *Capital*, vol. 1 [New York: Penguin Books, 1990], 166). In Marx's formula, value is relational and does not reside in an object, or in the labor that made it, but is visible only when it is exchanged for another commodity. Ahmed applies it to affect. "Affect does not reside in an object or sign," Ahmed writes, but is an affect of the circulation between objects and signs ("the accumulation of affect over time" [120]). In a manner similar to Marx's classic commodity fetishism, Ahmed goes on to describe the process in which "feelings" are produced: "Feelings appear in objects, or indeed *as* objects with a life of their own only by concealment of how they are shaped by histories, including histories of production (labor and labor time), as well as circulation or exchange" (120–21).

13. Lauren Berlant, *Cruel Optimism* (Durham, NC: Duke University Press, 2011), 66; see also Christopher Nealon, "The Case of Poetry," *Critical Inquiry* 33.4 (2007): 869: "And as the meaning of the social develops ever-greater complexity, relentlessness, and intensity, this demurral from instrumentalization opens up a space of be-

wilderment about the present that is potentially critical, even as it risks valorizing uselessness as such."

14. Louis Zukofsky, "Sincerity and Objectification: With Special Reference to the Work of Charles Reznikoff," *Poetry* 37.5 (February 1931): 272–84; the quoted phrase "the arrangement, into an apprehended unit, of minor units of sincerity" can be found on p. 274. Objectivist sincerity also has troubled roots in Ezra Pound's statement "I believe in technique as the test of man's sincerity" (Rachel Blau DuPlessis, "Objectivist Poetics and Political Vision: A Study of Oppen and Pound," in *George Oppen: Man and Poet*, ed. Burton Hatlen [Orono, ME: National Poetry Foundation, 1981], 125), which likewise ties a poetics to sincerity as issued from the "psycho-historical concept" of the subject (as Trilling reads Rousseau). As DuPlessis points out, in Pound's perspective these poetics "had an ethical dimension, for it began with the person, not the word, that is, began with sincerity" (125).

15. Rachel Blau DuPlessis and Peter Quartermain, "Introduction," in *The Objectivist Nexus: Essays in Cultural Poetics*, ed. Rachel Blau DuPlessis and Peter Quartermain (Tuscaloosa: University of Alabama Press, 1999), 1–23. Louis Zukofsky, "Sincerity and Objectification: With Special Reference to the Work of Charles Reznikoff," *Poetry* 37.5 (February 1931): 274, 284; the quoted phrase "accuracy of detail" can be found on p. 280.

16. Stephen Fredman, *A Menorah for Athena: Charles Reznikoff and the Jewish Dilemmas of Objectivist Poetry* (Chicago: University of Chicago Press, 2001), 136.

17. Sincerity can also take on a materialist and social density, as Burton Hatlen suggests: "A poetic sense of language, conjoined with a Marxian materialism, leads all the Objectivists to treat words not merely as symbols that stand in for things, but as things in their own right, 'historic and contemporary particulars' that, collectively, make up the world" ("A Poetics of Marginality and Resistance: The Objectivist Poets in Context," in *Objectivist Nexus*, 43). Hatlen's perspective concisely compresses the word, the poem, and the social here, giving the poem a historical weight within the present: the relationship of sincerity is located in the social rather than the person.

18. Charles Bernstein, "Hinge Picture (On George Oppen)," in *My Way: Speeches and Poems* (Chicago: University of Chicago Press, 1999), 192–96.

19. Yahya M. Madra and Fikret Adaman, "Neoliberal Reason and Its Forms: De-Politicization through Economization," *Antipode* 46.3 (2014): 692.

20. Michael Davidson, "Introduction: 'A Man of the Thirties,'" in *George Oppen: New Collected Poems*, ed. Michael Davidson (New York: New Directions, 2002), xx.

21. Peter Nicholls, *George Oppen and the Fate of Modernism* (New York: Oxford University Press, 2007), 120.

22. Davidson reads this with great material clarity in Zukofsky's poem "Mantis." "Zukofsky used formalism not to aestheticize social tensions but to return a degree of use-value to an increasingly instrumentalized poetry. Rather than solve the problem as Oppen did—by giving up poetry altogether—Zukofsky sought to provide an immanent critique within the terms of modernism itself" (Davidson, "Introduction," 118).

23. Ruth Jennison—in her *The Zukofsky Era: Modernity, Margins, and the Avant-Garde* (Baltimore: Johns Hopkins University Press, 2012), 71—provides a concise and expansive reading of Oppen's extension beyond Imagism:

> Energized by an increasing awareness of capitalist modernity's thickening interdependencies, Oppen distends Imagism's emotional complexes into a materialist seriality. *Discrete Series* deploys a hybridized form that merges the Imagists' focus on particulars with Objectivism's aleatory capaciousness. These forms, to be examined here in detail, allow *Discrete Series* to extend the Imagists' project of creating nonfungible, luminous forms that offer provisional indemnity against the pressures of reification while at the same time arranging such forms in a dynamic system of relational meaning.

24. New Directions, 1960.

25. George Oppen, "Of Being Numerous," in *George Oppen: New Collected Poems*, ed. Michael Davidson (New York: New Directions, 2008).

26. For the definition I am using the *American Heritage Dictionary* (which I was told was Olson's dictionary of choice): https://ahdictionary.com/word/search .html?q=paroxysm&submit.x=0&submit.y=0.

27. Brian B. Massumi, "The Future Birth of the Affective Fact: The Political Ontology of Threat," in *The Affect Theory Reader*, ed. Gregory Seigworth and Melissa Gregg (Durham, NC: Duke University Press, 2010), 52–70.

28. Oren Izenberg, "Oppen's Silence, Crusoe's Silence, and the Silence of Other Minds," *Modernism/Modernity* 13.1 (January 2006): 787–811.

29. Karl Marx, *Grundrisse: Foundations of the Critique of Political Economy*, trans. Martin Nicolaus (New York: Penguin Books, 1973), 83.

30. Marx, *Grundrisse*, 84. When Marx comes to the Robinson Crusoe of the economists in *Capital*, he debunks the naturalness of this figure (with some irony) by asking us to instead "imagine, for a change, an association of free men," where "the total product of our imagined association is a social product" (171) unlike the sun-bathed island of Crusoe. "All the characteristics of Robinson's labour here are repeated," Marx continues, "but with the difference that they are social instead of individual" (171). Marx had initiated this discussion earlier in the sixth thesis on Feuerbach: "Feuerbach resolves the religious essence into the human essence. But the human essence is no abstraction inherent in each single individual. In its reality it is the ensemble of the social relations."

31. Massimilian Tomba, *Marx's Temporalities* (Chicago: Haymarket Books, 2013), 26.

32. Oren Izenberg, "Oppen's Silence, Crusoe's Silence, and the Silence of Other Minds," *Modernism/Modernity* 13.1 (January 2006): 799.

33. Nicholls, *George Oppen*, 97–98.

34. Beverley Best, *Marxism and the Dynamic of Capital Formation: An Aesthetic of Political Economy* (New York: Palgrave McMillan, 2010), 169.

35. Marx, *Grundrisse*, 83.

36. Jennison, *Zukofsky Era*, 70.

37. Monique Vescia, *Depression Glass: Documentary Photography and the Medium of the Camera-Eye in Charles Reznikoff, George Oppen, and William Carlos Williams* (London: Routledge, 2015), 36.

38. Charles Reznikoff, *Testimony: The United States 1885–1915*, vol. 1 (Santa Barbara: Black Sparrow Press, 1978), 131.

39. Reznikoff, *Testimony*, 137.

40. Charles Reznikoff, interviewed by Larry Dembo, *Contemporary Literature* 10.2 (Spring 1969): 194.

41. Hito Steyerl, "Documentarism as Politics of Truth," http://eipcp.net/transversal/1003/steyerl2/en.

42. Hito Steyerl, "The Poor Image," in *The Wretched of the Screen* (New York: Sternberg, 2012), 43.

43. Hito Steyerl, "Documentary Uncertainty," *A Priori*, no. 15 (2007): 306.

44. Berlant, *Cruel Optimism*, 53.

CHAPTER SEVEN

1. Carla Billitteri, "William Carlos Williams and the Politics of Form," *Journal of Modern Literature* 30.2 (2007): 44–6.

2. George Oppen, "Of Being Numerous," in *George Oppen: New Collected Poems*, ed. Michael Davidson (New York: New Directions, 2008), 163.

3. George Oppen, *Selected Prose, Daybooks, and Papers*, ed. Stephen Cope (Berkeley: University of California Press, 2007).

4. Rob Halpern, "Becoming a Patient of History: George Oppen's Domesticity and the Relocation of Politics," *Chicago Review* 58.1 (2013): 50–74.

5. Oppen, "Of Being Numerous," 163, 167.

6. Peter Nicholls, "Of Being Ethical: Reflections on George Oppen," in *The Objectivist Nexus: Essays in Cultural Poetics*, ed. Rachel Blau DuPlessis and Peter Quartermain (Tuscaloosa: University of Alabama Press, 1999), 251.

7. Halpern, "Becoming a Patient of History," 52.

8. Claudia Rankine, *Citizen: An American Lyric* (Minneapolis: Graywolf Press, 2014), 59.

9. Oppen, "Of Being Numerous," 170.

10. As Marjorie Perloff has provocatively noted, "A good deal has been written about Oppen's relationship to the masses, but, at least in 'Of Being Numerous,' there is no relationship." See "The Shipwreck of the Singular: George Oppen's 'Of Being Numerous,'" in *Marjorie Perloff: Modern and Postmodern Poetry and Poetics*, http://marjorieperloff.com/essays/oppen-numerous. For a detailed discussion of Oppen's abstract and metaphysical conceptualizations of humanity—as "the populace," for example—see Peter Nicholls, *George Oppen and the Fate of Modernism* (New York: Oxford University Press, 2007), especially 93–102.

11. Dorothy Wang, *Thinking Its Presence: Race, Form and Subjectivity in Contemporary Asian-American Poetry* (Stanford, CA: Stanford University Press, 2014), 37.

12. Jared Sexton, "The Social Life of Social Death: On Afro-Pessimism and Black Optimism," *InTensions* 5 (Fall/Winter 2011), 23 (http://www.yorku.ca/intent

/issue5/articles/jaredsexton.php). Sexton borrows the term "the afterlife of slavery" from Saidiya Hartman, who originally uses it in *Lose Your Mother: A Journey along the Atlantic Slave Route* (New York: Farrar, Straus and Giroux, 2007), 6.

13. Halpern, "Patient of History," 50–52.

14. Billitteri, "William Carlos Williams," 45.

15. Oppen, "Of Being Numerous," 174.

16. Nicholls, *George Oppen*, 86.

17. Fred Moten, "Blackness and Nothingness (Mysticism in the Flesh)," *South Atlantic Quarterly* 112.4 (Fall 2013): 756.

18. This phrase, from a fragmentary letter, has been paraphrased for clarity by Peter Quartermain in *Disjunctive Poetics: From Gertrude Stein and Louis Zukofsky to Susan Howe* (New York: Cambridge University Press, 1992), 64.

19. Zukofsky, "Sincerity and Objectification: With Special Reference to the Work of Charles Reznikoff," *Poetry* 37.5 (1931): 273.

20. Jennifer Moxley, *There Are Things We Live Among* (Chicago: Flood Editions, 2012), 5.

21. The best-known call to these approaches is perhaps Stephen Best and Sharon Marcus's essay "Surface Reading: An Introduction," *Representations* 108.1 (2009): 1–21. For a supple critique of surface reading, distance reading, and their relatives, see Carolyn Lesjak, "Reading Dialectically," *Criticism* 55.2 (2013): 233–77.

22. Ben Hickman, *Crisis and the UDS Avant-Garde: Poetry and Real Politics* (Edinburgh: Edinburgh University Press, 2015), 16, 18.

23. Jeff Derksen, *The Vestiges* (Vancouver: Talonbooks, 2014), 18.

24. See especially sections 3, 4, and 5 (spanning pages 18–28).

25. Rankine, *Citizen*, 13.

26. See Dawn Lundy Martin, *Life in a Box Is a Pretty Life* (Callicoon, NY: Nightwood Editions, 2015); Fred Moten, *The Feel Trio* (Tucson: Letter Machine Editions, 2014); and M. NourbeSe Philip, *Zong!* (Toronto: Mercury Press, 2008).

27. Susan Holbrook, "M. NourbeSe Philip's Unrecoverable Subjects," *Jacket2*, March 29, 2013.

28. Jack Halberstam, "The Wild Beyond," in Fred Moten and Stefano Harney, *The Undercommons: Fugitive Planning and Black Study* (Brooklyn, NY: Minor Compositions, 2013), 8.

29. Martin, *Life in a Box*, 36.

30. See Amy De'Ath, "Decolonize or Destroy: New Feminist Poetry in the US and Canada," *Women: A Cultural Review* 29.3 (2015).

31. See Fred Moten and Stefano Harney, *The Undercommons: Fugitive Planning and Black Study* (Brooklyn, NY: Minor Compositions, 2013).

32. Moten, "Case of Blackness."

33. Moten, *The Feel Trio*, 31.

34. Philip, *Zong!*, 196, 204.

35. For just a few of these discussions about naming and identity, including the naming of black studies itself, see Hortense Spillers, "Mama's Baby, Papa's Maybe: An American Grammar Book," *Diacritics* 17:2 (1987): 64–81; Anthony Neal, "The

Naming: A Conceptualization of an African American Connotative Struggle," *Journal of Black Studies* 32.1 (2001): 50–65; Sima Farshid, "The Crucial Role of Naming in Toni Morrison's *Song of Solomon*," *Journal of African American Studies* 19.3 (2015): 329–38; Ama Mazama, "Naming and Defining: A Critical Link," *Journal of Black Studies* 40.1 (2009): 65–76.

36. Tyrone Williams, "*Zong!* (review)," *African American Review* 43.4 (2009): 785–87.

37. Martin, *Life in a Box*, 17.

38. Adam Fitzgerald, "'That's Not Poetry; It's Sociology! In Defence of Claudia Rankine's *Citizen*," *Guardian*, October 23, 2015, http://www.theguardian.com/books/booksblog/2015/oct/23/claudia-rankine-citizen-poetry-defence.

39. Sexton, "Social Life," 23.

40. Frank Wilderson III, "Gramsci's Black Marx: Whither the Slave in Civil Society?," *Social Identities* 9 (2003): 230.

41. See Chris Chen, "The Limit Point of Capitalist Equality," *Endnotes* 3 (2013): 202–23, and Jodi Melamed, *Represent and Destroy: Rationalizing Violence in the New Racial Capitalism* (Minneapolis: University of Minnesota Press, 2011).

42. To recycle Fanon's oft-quoted observation: "I came into the world imbued with the will to find a meaning in things, my spirit filled with the desire to attain to the source of the world, and then I found that I was an object in the midst of other objects (*Black Skin, White Masks* [London: Picador, 77]).

43. Rankine, *Citizen*, 71.

44. Cited in Rex Butler, ed., *The Žižek Dictionary* (New York: Routledge, 2014), 143.

45. See, for example, Melamed, *Represent and Destroy*, and Glen Coulthard, *Red Skin, White Masks* (Minneapolis: University of Minnesota Press, 2014) for sustained critiques of liberal multiculturalism and the politics of recognition.

46. See Pound's famous 1918 essays, "A Retrospect" and "A Few Don'ts" (http://www.poetryfoundation.org/learning/essay/237886), and Bök's scientific-poetic experiment, *The Xenotext* (http://triplehelixblog.com/2014/01/the-xenotext-experiment).

47. Wang, *Thinking Its Presence*, 20.

48. Rankine, *Citizen*, 72.

49. Hortense Spillers, "Mama's Baby, Papa's Maybe: An American Grammar Book," *Diacritics* 17.2 (Summer 1987): 74.

50. Six black students at Jena High School in Louisiana were arrested in December 2006 after a school fight in which a white student suffered a concussion and multiple bruises. The six black students were initially charged with attempted murder and conspiracy, in a case that drew national attention.

51. Rankine, *Citizen*, 101.

52. Moten and Harney, *Undercommons*, 18, 20. Moten often reformulates this idea across his poetic and critical work, in a recent conversation with Robin Kelley, for example: "What's at stake is fugitive movement in and out of the frame, bar, or whatever externally imposed social logic—a movement of escape, the stealth of the

stolen that can be said, since it inheres in every closed circle, to break every enclosure." "Do Black Lives Matter: Robin D. G. Kelley and Fred Moten in Conversation," Vimeo video, 1:35:26, posted by Critical Resistance, January 15, 2015, https://vimeo.com/116111740.

53. Sexton, *Amalgamation Schemes* (Minneapolis: University of Minnesota Press, 2008), 40.

54. See Sianne Ngai, "Visceral Abstractions," *GLQ: A Journal of Lesbian and Gay Studies* 21.1 (January 2015): 33–63.

55. Wilderson, *Red, White and Black* (Durham, NC: Duke University Press, 2010), 11.

56. This snappy formulation is Robert Hartman's paraphrased translation of Hegel's *A General Introduction to the Philosophy of History*. See Georg Wilhelm Friedrich Hegel, *Reason in History: A General Introduction to the Philosophy of History* (New York: Library of Liberal Arts and Bobbs-Merrill, 1953), 38. For a more up-to-date (and well-received) translation, see *Lectures on the Philosophy of World History*, vol. 1: *Manuscripts of the Introduction and the Lectures of 1822-3*, ed. Robert F. Brown and Peter C. Hodgson (Oxford: Oxford University Press, 2011).

57. For a discussion of beginnings and the aporias surrounding "the role of the absolute" in Hegel's work, see Paul Ashton, "The Beginning before the Beginning: Hegel and the Activation of Philosophy," *Cosmos and History* 3.2–3 (2007): 328–56.

58. Andrew Ross, "The New Sentence and the Commodity Form: Recent American Writing," in *Marxism and the Interpretation of Culture*, ed. Cary Nelson and Lawrence Grossberg (Champaign: University of Illinois Press, 1988), 363.

59. As Wilderson has argued, "We need to apprehend the profound and irreconcilable difference between White supremacy (the *colonial utility* of the Sand Creek massacre) and anti-Blackness (the human race's necessity for violence against Black people)" ("Afropessimism and the End of Redemption," *These Occcupied Times*, March 30, 2016). To put the point rather bluntly: Objectivist poets are not white supremacists, but they are part of civil society, and civil society is antiblack.

60. Cedric J. Robinson, *Black Marxism* (Chapel Hill: University of North Carolina Press, 1983), 307.

61. I am indebted to Chris Chen for this useful formulation regarding the neutralizing force of liberal politics in literary studies.

CHAPTER EIGHT

1. Margaret Ronda, "Disenchanted Georgics: The Aesthetics of Labor in American Poetry" (PhD diss., University of California–Berkeley, 2009).

2. Eleni Sikelianos, "Life Pops from a Music Box Shaped Like a Gun: Dismemberments and Mendings in Niedecker's Figures," in *Radical Vernacular: Lorine Niedecker and the Poetics of Place*, ed. Elizabeth Willis (Iowa City: University of Iowa Press, 2008), 31. Indeed, formal choices are always also political and affective choices—and one way to understand the constructivist archival drive in the modernist long or serial poem (Williams, H. D., Olson, Oppen) is as this healing work of salvage.

3. Elizabeth Willis, "The Poetics of Affinity: Niedecker, Morris, and the Art of Work," *Radical Vernacular*, 223.

4. *Lorine Niedecker: Collected Works*, ed. Jenny Penberthy (Berkeley: University of California Press, 2002), 95, 165, 170, 137.

5. See Kirsty Robertson, "Rebellious Doilies and Subversive Stitches: Writing and Craftivist History," in *Extra/Ordinary: Craft and Contemporary Art*, ed. Maria Buszek (Durham, NC: Duke University Press, 2011), 184–203; and Anthea Black and Nicole Burisch, "Craft Hard Die Free: Radical Curatorial Strategies for Craftivism," in ibid., 204–21. These essays and others in the volume detail craftivism's history of protest, especially against nuclear arms in the 1980s and the World Trade Organization in the early 2000s.

6. Robertson, "Rebellious Doilies," 187.

7. Ann Cvetkovich, *Depression: A Public Feeling* (Durham, NC: Duke University Press, 2012), 168.

8. These activities are not without their detractors—often feminists themselves—who see the work of craftivism as a regressive return to homey comforts or as futile forms of protest. See Robertson, "Rebellious Doilies," 191.

9. Willis, "Poetics of Affinity," 229.

10. William Morris, "Art under Plutocracy," William Morris Internet Archive, https://www.marxists.org/archive/morris/works/index.htm.

11. Julie Carr, *Surface Tension: Ruptural Time and the Poetics of Desire in Late Victorian Poetry* (Champaign–Urbana, IL: Dalkey Archive, 2012), 147–88, 182–83.

12. Morris clearly articulates his vision for a postcapitalist society in which handcrafted objects circulate freely in his utopian novel *News from Nowhere*. In reality, his design company, The Firm, to Morris's consternation, produced finely made furnishings for the rich. See Fiona MacCarthy, *William Morris: A Life for Our Time* (New York: Knopf, 1995), 210.

13. Willis, "Poetics of Affinity," 226.

14. Elizabeth Robinson, "Music Becomes Story: Lyric and Narrative Patterning in the Work of Lorine Niedecker," in Willis, *Radical Vernacular*, 188–24.

15. Niedecker sent the calendar book to Zukofsky during the period of their most intense romantic interaction. See Jenny Penberthy, "Editor's Note," *Sulfur* 41 (Fall 1997), http://epc.buffalo.edu/authors/niedecker/calendar.html:

> Given that the poem was held by Zukofsky and given his dating on the back of the calendar—'Xmas 1934'—the poem was likely Niedecker's gift to the poet whom she had now known in person for a full calendar year. The gift looks forward confidently to another year of friendship just as it recalls the past year. A pocket calendar, an intimate mnemonics. But the poem is also a surrealist composition and an experiment in form. The calendar itself is under siege.

16. Penberthy, *Lorine Niedecker: Collected Works*, 41.

17. Rachel Blau DuPlessis, "Lorine Niedecker, the Anonymous: Gender, Class,

Genre and Resistances," in *Lorine Niedecker: Woman and Poet*, ed. Jenny Penberthy (Orono, ME: National Poetry Foundation, 1996), 137.

18. Robinson, "Music Becomes Story," 124.

19. William Shakespeare, *Romeo and Juliet*, II.2, http://shakespeare.mit.edu/romeo_juliet/full.html.

20. Perhaps it's too much of a stretch to read these delicate, ambiguous poems as responding to the rise of fascism, but I can't help thinking that a critique of boundaries, walls, and kinship ties comes to bear on world history as it was unfolding in the mid-1930s.

21. Penberthy, *Lorine Niedecker: Collected Works*, 58. Robinson reads this line as suggesting a letting go of resistance, rather than a soaring (or increase) of (political) resistance. I concur that it could be read either way ("Music Becomes Story," 122).

22. Lorine Niedecker, *"Between Your House and Mine": The Letters of Lorine Niedecker and Cid Corman, 1960–1970*, ed. Lisa Pater Faranda (Durham, NC: Duke University Press, 1986), 48.

23. Niedecker, *"Between Your House and Mine,"* 213. The words "grey" and "Rose" likely refer to Ruskin's wife Effie Gray and to the object of his pedophiliac obsession, Rose La Touche. If so, then I assume that Niedecker brings some measure of sardonic critique to the pleasures she lists here.

24. Niedecker, *"Between Your House and Mine,"* 51–52.

25. As Norton explains:

My Niedecker story starts with working at Inland Book Company in 1985, and finding a copy of Cid Corman's *ORIGIN* with her work in it. I still have it. Inland Book Company was like the SPD [Small Press Distribution] of the East Coast. It was in East Haven, CT, a bus ride and a world away from Yale. It was on an ugly stretch of road where the sycamores were all weirdly amputated. Nearby: a mattress factory and a cheese factory. I would wait for the bus back to Yale with workers from those factories. Most were developmentally disabled. Some smelled like cheese. Among the folk, like Niedecker. Then much later when I moved to Berkeley [to be the poetry editor at the University of California Press] I went down to SPD and bought the Jargon Society volume. Working and working to get the book [*Collected Works*] under contract, talking with Jenny Penberthy, leaving [the job] a little before it was published, getting it in the mail, being very HAPPY. Somewhere in there, I was so broke, I sold all my Jargon Society editions to Moe's. No regrets.
Private email, November 3, 2014.

26. As noted in *"Between Your House and Mine,"* in her later years Niedecker selected domestic and private life over a more overt politically or socially active life. As she wrote in a note to Bob Nero, rejecting his invitation to dinner, "I don't mourn the lone-ness of it [her life] for poetry. In fact [. . .] I have the presumption to feel that others writing should retire into themselves deeper than they do" (84–85). As an instance of her critique of private property, and there are many, we have the following

poem, titled "Foreclosure": "Tell em to take my bare walls down / my cement abutments / their parties thereof / and clause of claws // Leave me the land / Scratch out: the land // May prose and property both die out / and leave me peace." Significantly for this essay, it seems "poetry" (not prose) is more readily aligned with peace.

27. Private email: November 8, 2014. This handmade-work failure is documented in *Emergency Index*, vol. 2, ed. Yelena Gluzman and Sophia Cleary (New York: Ugly Duckling Presse, 2012).

28. Jill Magi, *SLOT* (New York: Ugly Duckling Presse, 2011), 33.

29. Damon is the author of *Post-literary 'America': From Bagel Shop Jazz to Micropoetries* (Iowa City: University of Iowa Press, 2011) and of *The Dark End of the Street: Margins in American Vanguard Poetry* (University of Minnesota Press, 1993) among other works. In these books she explores the poetry of marginalized subcultures and nontraditional or extraliterary spaces and communities.

30. Images of these and the other pieces have been published as a free PDF titled *Meshwards* by Dusie Press, http://www.dusie.org/Damon%20Meshwards.pdf.

31. Stephen Vincent, Buffalo Poetics listserv, February 23, 2003: https://listserv .buffalo.edu/cgi-bin/wa?HOME.

32. William Morris, *News from Nowhere*, William Morris Internet Archive, https://www.marxists.org/archive/morris/works/index.htm.

CHAPTER NINE

1. Berel Lang, *Holocaust Representation: Art within the Limits of History and Ethics* (Baltimore: Johns Hopkins University Press, 2000), 117.

2. For examples of inexpressibility *topoi*, see Ernst Curtius, *European Literature and the Latin Middle Ages*, trans. Willard R. Trask (New York: Pantheon Books, Bolingen Series 32, 1953), 159–62.

3. Hilda Schiff, ed., *Holocaust Poetry* (New York: St. Martin's Press, 1995), xix.

4. Lang, *Holocaust Representation*, 50.

5. See Hayden White, *Metahistory: The Historical Imagination in Nineteenth-Century Europe* (Baltimore: Johns Hopkins University Press, 1973).

6. Louis Zukofsky, "Sincerity and Objectification: With Special Reference to the Poetry of Charles Reznikoff," *Poetry: A Magazine of Verse* 37.5 (February 1931): 272.

7. "Sincerity and Objectification," 273–74.

8. Norman Finkelstein, *Not One of Them in Place: Modern Poetry and Jewish American Identity* (Albany: State University of New York Press, 2001), 205.

9. Charles Reznikoff, *Complete Poems*, ed. Seamus Cooney, 2 vols. (Santa Barbara: Black Sparrow Press, 1976/1977), II.

10. Lang, *Holocaust Representation*, 156.

11. See Milton Hindus, *Charles Reznikoff: A Critical Essay* (Santa Barbara: Black Sparrow Press, 1977), 10.

12. Lang, *Holocaust Representation*, 127.

13. Charles Reznikoff, *Holocaust* (Los Angeles: Black Sparrow Press, 1975), 7.

14. Charles Reznikoff, *Testimony: The United States 1885–1890 Recitative* (New

Directions and San Francisco Review, 1965); Charles Reznikoff, *Testimony Volume II: The United States [1885–1915]* (Santa Rosa: Black Sparrow Press, 1979).

15. Janet Sternberg and Alan Ziegler, "A Conversation with Charles Reznikoff," in *Charles Reznikoff: Man and Poet*, ed. Milton Hindus (Orono, ME: National Poetry Foundation, 1984), 127–36, 132.

16. Charles Reznikoff, *The Poems of Charles Reznikoff 1918–1975*, ed. Seamus Cooney (Boston: David R. Godine, 2005), 375 (emphasis added).

17. Charles Reznikoff, *Selected Letters of Charles Reznikoff: 1917–1976*, ed. Milton Hindus (Santa Barbara: Black Sparrow Press, 1997), 202.

18. L. S. Dembo, "An Interview with Charles Reznikoff," *Contemporary Literature* 10.2 (Spring 1969), 193.

19. Reznikoff, *Holocaust*, 111.

20. See Janet Sutherland, "Reznikoff and His Sources," in *Reznikoff: Man and Poet*, 297–307.

21. Sidra DeKoven Ezrahi, *By Words Alone: The Holocaust in Literature* (Chicago: University of Chicago Press, 1980), 37.

22. Sternberg and Ziegler, "A Conversation," 136.

23. On the term *archontic* see Jacques Derrida, *Archive Fever: A Freudian Impression*, trans. Eric Prenowitz (Chicago: University of Chicago Press, 1998), 1–34.

24. Linda Simon, "Reznikoff: The Poet as Witness," *Man and Poet*: 233–50, 246.

25. Reznikoff, *Holocaust*, 81.

26. Schiff, *Holocaust Poetry*, xxiii.

27. Raul Hilberg, *The Destruction of the European Jews* (New York: Holmes and Meier, 1985), 469.

28. Sutherland, *Sources*, 305.

29. See Laura Mulvey, "Visual Pleasure and Narrative Cinema," in *Visual and Other Pleasures* (Bloomington: Indiana University Press, 1973), 14–26.

30. Steve McCaffery, *Slightly Left of Thinking* (Tucson: Chax Press, 2008).

31. Robert Fitterman, *Holocaust Museum* (Denver: Counterpath, 2013), 103.

32. Charles Bernstein, "this picture intentionally left blank," *Jacket2*, http://jacket2.org/commentary/picture-intenionally-left-blank.

33. Friedrich Achtleitner, "the describability of the indescribable or attempting an afterword to *transcript*," in Heimrad Bäcker, *transcript* (Champaign–Urbana, IL: Dalkey Archive, 2010), 147.

34. See http://htmlgiant.com/reviews/conceptual-failure-as-several-kinds-of-success-in-robert-fittermans-holocaust-museum.

35. Alain Badiou, *The Century*, trans. Alberto Toscano (Cambridge: Polity Press, 2007), 54.

36. Ilse N. Bulhof and Laurens ten Kate, eds., *Flight of the Gods: Philosophical Perspective on Negative Theology* (Kampen, The Netherlands: Kok Agora, 2000), 7–8.

37. Heimrad Bäcker, *transcript*, trans. Patrick Greaney (Champaign, IL: Counterpath, 2010), 131.

38. Zukofsky, *Sincerity*, 284.

39. See Martin Heidegger, "The Origin of the Work of Art," in Martin Heidegger, *Basic Writings*, ed. David Farrell Krell (San Francisco: Harper, 1993), 199.

CODA

1. Rachel Blau DuPlessis and Peter Quartermain, eds., *The Objectivist Nexus: Essays in Cultural Poetics* (Tuscaloosa: University of Alabama Press, 1999), 312.

2. John Ciardi, "Foreword," in *Mid-century American Poets*, ed. John Ciardi (New York: Twayne, 1950), ix–xxx.

3. Maurice Valency, *In Praise of Love* (New York: Macmillan, 1958), 139.

4. Louis Zukofsky, *"A"* (Berkeley: University of California Press, 1978), 331.

5. Louis Zukofsky, *Prepositions + The Collected Critical Essays*, ed. Mark Scroggins (Hanover, NH: Wesleyan University Press, 2000), 189.

CONTRIBUTORS

RAE ARMANTROUT's most recent books—*Versed, Money Shot, Just Saying, Itself, Partly: New and Selected Poems,* and *Entanglements* (a chapbook selection of poems in conversation with physics)—were published by Wesleyan University Press. In 2010 her book *Versed* won the Pulitzer Prize in Poetry and a National Book Critics Circle Award. Her poems have appeared in many anthologies and journals: *Poetry, Lana Turner, The Nation, The New Yorker, Bomb, The Paris Review, Postmodern American Poetry: A Norton Anthology, The Open Door: 100 Poems, 100 Years of Poetry Magazine,* among others. Her books have appeared in Spanish, French, Italian, and German editions. She is recently retired from University of California–San Diego, where she was professor of poetry and poetics.

JULIE CARR's most recent books are *Think Tank* and *Objects from a Borrowed Confession. Someone Shot by Book* will be published by University of Michigan Press in 2018. She teaches at the University of Colorado in Boulder, lives in Denver, and cocurates Counterpath Gallery and Performance Space.

AMY DE'ATH is currently at work on her first academic book, *Unsociable Poetry: Antagonism and Abstraction in Contemporary Feminized Poetics.* Her criticism has appeared in *Women: A Cultural Review, The SAGE Handbook of Frankfurt School Critical Theory, Anguish Language* (Archive Books, 2015) and in a number of electronic journals. With Fred Wah, she is the editor of a poetics anthology, *Toward. Some. Air.* (Banff Centre Press, 2015). Her most recent poetry publication is *ON MY LOVE FOR gender abolition* (Capricious, 2016). She is a lecturer in contemporary literature and culture at King's College London.

JEFF DERKSEN's poetry books include *The Vestiges, Transnational Muscle Cars, Dwell, Until,* and *Down Time* and his critical books are *After Euphoria, Annihilated Time,* and *How High Is the City, How Deep Is Our Love.* With the research collective Urban Subjects he has coedited *Autogestion, or Henri Lefebvre in New Belgrade* and *The Militant Image Reader.* He works in the English Department of Simon Fraser University.

RACHEL BLAU DUPLESSIS, poet, critic, collagist, is the author of *Drafts* (written 1985 through 2012). Post-*Drafts* books include *Interstices* (2014), *Graphic Novella* (2015), *Days and Works* (2017), and the forthcoming *Numbers* (a collage poem). She has published numerous critical essays, most recently on modernist women writers, contemporary women's poetry, objectivist poetics, and Robert

Duncan's *H.D. Book*. Her critical books include *The Pink Guitar, Blue Studios*, and *Purple Passages*—a trilogy on gender, poetry, and poetics. She has edited the *Selected Letters of George Oppen* and *The Oppens Remembered*, coedited *The Objectivist Nexus*, and has written on Oppen, Zukofsky, and Niedecker.

GRAHAM FOUST is the author of seven books of poems, including *Time Down to Mind* (Flood Editions, 2015) and *Necessary Stranger* (Flood Editions, 2005). With Samuel Frederick, he has translated three volumes of poems by the late German poet Ernst Meister, including *Wallless Space* (Wave Books, 2014), which was short-listed for a National Translation award. He is director of undergraduate studies in the Department of English and Literary Arts at the University of Denver.

ALAN GOLDING teaches poetry and poetics at the University of Louisville and directs the Louisville Conference on Literature and Culture since 1900. He is the author of *From Outlaw to Classic: Canons in American Poetry* (University of Wisconsin Press, 1995) and of numerous essays on modernist and contemporary poetry and literary institutions. Current projects include *Writing into the Future: New American Poetries from The Dial to the Digital*, under contract with the University of Alabama Press, and *"Isn't the Avant-Garde Always Pedagogical,"* a book on experimental poetics and/as pedagogy. With Lynn Keller and Dee Morris, he coedits the University of Iowa Contemporary North American Poetry Series.

JEANNE HEUVING is the author of *The Transmutation of Love and Avant-Garde Poetics* from the Modern and Contemporary Poetics series (University of Alabama Press, 2016) and coeditor of *Inciting Poetics: Thinking and Writing Poetry*, forthcoming in 2019 from the University of New Mexico Press. Her cross-genre book *Incapacity* (Chiasmus, 2004) won a Small Press Traffic Book of the Year award. She is a professor in the School of Interdisciplinary Arts and Sciences at the University of Washington–Bothell and on the graduate faculty in English at the University of Washington–Seattle.

W. SCOTT HOWARD received his PhD in English and Critical Theory from the University of Washington. He teaches poetics and poetry in the Department of English & Literary Arts at the University of Denver, and is the founding editor of *Reconfigurations: A Journal for Poetics & Poetry / Literature & Culture*. His poetry collections include *ROPES* (with images by Ginger Knowlton) from Delete Press, 2014; and *SPINNAKERS* (The Lune, 2016). *Archive and Artifact: Susan Howe's Factual Telepathy* is forthcoming from Talisman House. His work has received support from the Modern Language Association, the Pew Charitable Trusts, the National Endowment for the Humanities, and the Beinecke Library, Yale University.

RUTH JENNISON is associate professor of modern and contemporary American poetry in the English Department at the University of Massachusetts–Amherst. She is the author of *The Zukofsky Era: Modernity, Margins, and the Avant-Garde* (Johns Hopkins, 2012) and articles and book chapters on twentieth- and twenty-first-century American poetics, Marxism, and the political economies of literary form. Her current book project, *Figurative Capital: American Poetry and the World System*, explores the relationship between poetry and uneven capitalist development. She is also coediting with Julian Murphet a volume of essays, poetics, and poems entitled *Out of Time: Communism and Poetics Now*.

DAVID LAU's books of poetry are *Virgil and the Mountain Cat* and *Still Dirty*. His essays and poems have appeared in *New Left Review*, *Boston Review*, *A Public Space*, and *Literary Hub*. A graduate of the Iowa Writers' Workshop and UCLA, he is coeditor of *Lana Turner*. He lives and teaches in Santa Cruz.

STEVE MCCAFFERY is the author of over forty books and chapbooks of poetry and criticism, and his work has been translated into a dozen or so languages. A founding member of the sound poetry ensemble Four Horsemen, the TRG (Toronto Research Group), and the College of Canadian 'Pataphysics, and long-time resident of Toronto, he is now David Gray Professor of Poetry and Letters at the State University of New York at Buffalo.

MARK MCMORRIS is most recently the author of *The Book of Landings*, a collection of poetry containing the second and third volumes of his trilogy *Auditions for Utopia*. A poet and critic, he has published articles on Louis Zukofsky's *Catullus* and *"A."* He is currently at work on a series of texts and drawings concerned with the exploration of walls. A professor of English at Georgetown University, he lives in Washington, DC.

CHRIS NEALON is chair of the English Department at Johns Hopkins University. He is the author of two books of criticism, *Foundlings: Lesbian and Gay Historical Emotion before Stonewall* (Duke, 2001) and *The Matter of Capital: Poetry and Crisis in "The American Century"* (Harvard, 2011), and three books of poetry: *The Joyous Age* (Black Square Editions, 2004), *Plummet* (Edge Books, 2009), and *Heteronomy* (Edge, 2014). He lives in Washington, DC.

JENNY PENBERTHY's most recent book is an edition of Kenneth Cox's essays, *The Art of Language* (Flood Editions, 2016). Her current projects are an edition of Lorine Niedecker's letters and a study of the London publisher Fulcrum Press. She is the editor of *Lorine Niedecker: Collected Works* (University of California Press, 2002).

BROC ROSSELL is a lecturer of critical and cultural studies at Emily Carr University of Art and Design in Vancouver, BC. He is most recently the author of the book-length poem *Festival* (Cleveland State University Press, 2015), among other chapbooks, essays, and poems; formerly the poetry editor at Brooklyn Arts Press, he publishes heterodox materials as The Elephants (www.theelephants.net).

ROBERT SHEPPARD is emeritus professor of poetry and poetics at Edge Hill University, and his most recent critical work is *The Meaning of Form in Contemporary Innovative Poetry* (Palgrave, 2016). His *History or Sleep: Selected Poems* is published by Shearsman (2016). Previous critical volumes include *The Poetry of Saying: British Poetry and Its Discontents 1950–2000* (Liverpool University Press, 2005) and *Iain Sinclair* (Tavistock House, 2007).

INDEX

Page numbers in italics refer to illustrations

CONTEMPORARY NORTH AMERICAN POETRY SERIES